The Politics of African-American Education

Based on the 1,800 largest school districts in the United States over a decade, *The Politics of African-American Education* documents the status of African-American education and the major role that partisanship plays. The book brings together the most comprehensive database on minority education to date that centers around three arguments. First, partisanship permeates African-American education; it affects who is elected to the school board, the racial composition of school administrators and teachers, and the access of African-American students to quality education. Second, African-American representation matters. The effectiveness of African-American representation, however, is enhanced in Democratic districts while representation in Republican districts has little influence. Third, political structures matter, but they are not determinative. Two different structures – election systems and the independent school district – create the rules of the game in US education politics and policy but do not limit others from using those rules to change the outcome.

Kenneth J. Meier is the Charles H. Gregory Chair in Liberal Arts and Distinguished Professor of Political Science at Texas A&M University. He is also a professor of Public Management at the Cardiff University School of Business (Wales). He was formerly the editor-in-chief of the *Journal of Public Administration Research and Theory* and the editor of the *American Journal of Political Science*. He is the founding editor of *Perspectives on Public Management and Governance*.

Amanda Rutherford is an assistant professor in the School of Public and Environmental Affairs at Indiana University. She is the book review editor for the *Journal of Public Administration Research and Theory* and is a member of the Rising Professionals Editorial Board for the *Journal of Student Financial Aid*. Rutherford's research interests include managerial values and decision making, performance management, representative bureaucracy, and education policy.

The Politics of African-American Education

Representation, Partisanship, and Educational Equity

KENNETH J. MEIER
Texas A&M University and Cardiff University

AMANDA RUTHERFORD
Indiana University

CAMBRIDGE
UNIVERSITY PRESS

CAMBRIDGE
UNIVERSITY PRESS

One Liberty Plaza, New York, NY 10006, USA

Cambridge University Press is part of the University of Cambridge.

It furthers the University's mission by disseminating knowledge in the pursuit of education, learning, and research at the highest international levels of excellence.

www.cambridge.org
Information on this title: www.cambridge.org/9781107512535

© Kenneth J. Meier and Amanda Rutherford 2017

First published 2017

Printed in the United States of America by Sheridan Books, Inc.

A catalogue record for this publication is available from the British Library.

Library of Congress Cataloging-in-Publication Data
Names: Meier, Kenneth J., 1950– author. | Rutherford, Amanda, author.
Title: The politics of African-American education : representation, partisanship, and educational equity / Kenneth J. Meier, Texas A&M, Amanda Rutherford, Indiana University.
Description: New York, NY : Cambridge University Press, 2016. | Includes bibliographical references and index.
Identifiers: LCCN 2016008817 | ISBN 9781107105263 (hardback) | ISBN 9781107512535 (paperback)
Subjects: LCSH: African Americans – Education. | African Americans – Education – Social aspects. | Education – Political aspects – United States. | Educational equalization – United States. | Academic achievement – United States. | Education and state – United States. | BISAC: POLITICAL SCIENCE / Government / General.
Classification: LCC LC2717.M45 2016 | DDC 371.829/96073–dc23
LC record available at https://lccn.loc.gov/2016008817

ISBN 978-1-107-10526-3 Hardback
ISBN 978-1-107-51253-5 Paperback

To Diane Jones Meier and Jeff Rutherford

Contents

Figures

Tables

Preface

The Politics of African-American Education: Representation, Partisanship, and Educational Equity was truly fifteen years in the making. In 2001 Val Martinez-Ebers suggested that the time had come to replicate the findings of the *Politics of Hispanic Education* and to gather new data for that purpose. This discussion led to the first national survey in 2002 and then two subsequent national surveys. The first paper using the new data for African Americans was presented at the 2003 annual meeting of the American Political Science Association. At that point the project bogged down because we discovered that African Americans were not only overrepresented on the nation's school boards, but they were even more overrepresented with at-large elections even in districts where they were a minority of the total population.

This anomalous empirical finding was not supported by any theory and was the first case of finding African Americans overrepresented in any US political institution (bear in mind this predates the Obama presidency). The project ground to a series of fits and starts that were particularly frustrating because Ken is a policy scholar not an elections person but could not go on to the policy questions without dealing with the electoral anomaly (work on Latino education as part of this project initially got off to a quicker start). Although there were several attempts to solve this problem, for the most part the project remained on the back burner with the hopes that more data would solve the problem.

A large number of graduate students and a few undergraduates devoted time to the project before we stepped back and simply asked: If electoral structures are biased against numerical minorities, how might a minority overcome such a bias? The answer, obvious in retrospect, is by forming coalitions with others and shifting the key political cleavage from race to some other dimension, in this case partisanship. With the electoral question solved, we proceed to the question that interested us the most (How did electoral structure affect the quality of the representation?) and submitted the first paper to a journal.

The editors and all the reviewers of that journal told us pretty directly that we were interested in the wrong question. The election issue was the most interesting and instructed us to deal solely with that. Because Ken was and is a journal editor, he knows that reviewers and editors are always right so we followed this advice. Once the initial article was published, we then turned to tracing out the policy consequences in African-American education again thinking that electoral structure was the key variable. As the analysis on this book progressed, we discovered that we were wrong. Partisanship not electoral structure is the defining factor in African-American education.

The findings of this book will be controversial given the long-standing myth in American politics that education policy is nonpartisan. This myth is widely endorsed by policy makers and also accepted among scholars. Even those scholars who specialize in the politics of education policy frequently see politics in terms of traditional social class distinctions or in the role of unions in urban education. Partisan politics is simply not considered in most discussions of education policy.

Although some might lament our infusion of partisanship into US education policy, neither scholars nor policy makers should hide from the political reality. Education policy, particularly on racial issues, divides the nation into Democrats and Republicans. These differences are so distinct both in terms of elections and in terms of actual policy outcomes that it is fair to claim that for black Americans there are two separate school systems in the United States – those with a Democratic voting majority and those with a Republican voting majority. The differences are so stark that statistical tests indicate that the two sets of school districts should be analyzed separately and not pooled.

This book stresses three basic themes. First, partisanship permeates African-American education; it affects who is elected to the school board, the school board members' ability to represent their black constituents, the racial composition of school administrators and teachers, and the access to African-American students to quality education. The impact on educational outcomes – graduation rates, test scores, and college preparation – shows that partisanship penetrates to the very core of the US education system. Even in such unexpected places as taking and passing advanced placement classes, this study finds partisan correlates despite extensive controls for other factors. The political reality is that an African-American child in a Democratic majority school district receives a significantly better education than an African-American child in a Republican majority school district.

Second, African-American representation matters. School board representation is important in generating bureaucratic representation in administrative roles. Black administrators are the key factor in generating black representation at the classroom level. African-American teachers greatly affect the quality of education received by African-American students. In all these cases, however, the effectiveness of African-American representation is enhanced in Democratic districts; at times, black representation in Republican districts has little discernable influence. As we like to note, African-American representatives get by with a little help from their friends; having political allies is paramount in majoritarian political systems.

Third, political structures matter, but they are not determinative. Two different structures – election rules and the independent school district – create the rules of the game in US education politics and policy. Both structures create biases that are intended to limit partisan politics. The independent school district sought to create a politics-administration dichotomy and limit the influence of politics on the education of children. The use of at-large nonpartisan elections attempted to transfer power to business and professions not associated with traditional political parties. Structures that create rules of the game, however, do not limit others from using those rules to change the outcome of the game. Indeed, this book demonstrates that at-large elections now benefit African Americans, particularly in districts with a Democratic majority. Similarly, the independent school districts in this study show a great deal of responsiveness to political forces on issues linked to African-American education.

As students of organizations, we approach the study of race and education from the perspective of organizations. This shapes our approach to the study by focusing it at the organizational level rather than at the student level. Substantial work on race and education uses student-level data, and that work is cited in various chapters. Using organizations as units of analysis can at times be more sensitive to institutionalized processes, and both politics and representation are shaped by institutional structures. The basic processes of representation in schools can occur in a wide variety of ways, and only some of them require direct contact between a student and a teacher within a classroom setting. We see our organizational-level work as a complement to existing studies at the individual level, providing some insights that are not possible with existing individual data sets.

A large number of individuals participated in this project or commented on research at various points. Financial support for the analysis was provided by the Spencer Foundation and the Carlos Cantu Hispanic Education and Opportunity Endowment. We would like to thank the army of graduate and undergraduate research assistants that have contributed their efforts including Seung-Ho An, Bettie Ray Butler, M. Apolonia Calderon, K. Jureé Capers, Kristen Carroll, Warren Eller, Alisa Hicklin Fryar, Fran Hill, Erik Gonzalez Juenke, Miner P. Marchbanks III, Soledad Artiz Prillaman, Rene Rocha, Meredith Walker, and Sadé Walker. We would like to thank seminar participants at Indiana University, Exeter University, the London School of Economics, Macalester College, the University of Houston, the University of North Carolina Charlotte, the University of North Texas, the University of Texas Austin, the University of Wisconsin Madison, and Texas A&M University for feedback on this project at various stages. Numerous colleagues provided comments and criticism but Kim Q. Hill, George Krause, David

A. M. Peterson and the anonymous reviewers for Cambridge University Press went well beyond expectations. Ken would especially like to thank Amanda. This is not just a joint product; the book would not have been written without her. Her tolerance for "just one more set of analyses" or "let's revise this section one more time" was truly amazing. We would also like to thank Robert Dreesen and the group at Cambridge University Press for both support and patience.

Representation, Partisanship, and Equality in Education

Racial inequities in access to quality education are one of the most persistent issues in American politics. African-American educational attainment lags behind all other groups in the United States and appears resistant to most policy levers. *The Politics of African-American Education: Representation, Partisanship, and Educational Equity* brings together the results of a major national study focused on the local politics of education. The study stresses four major themes.

First, racial disparities in education reflect, in part, political inequities. Although a wide range of factors influence the educational attainment of African Americans including income levels, housing patterns, employment opportunities, and myriad social factors, the correlation between African-American political power and access to quality education for African American students has persisted for more than two hundred years. Within the African-American community, consistent response to the lack of educational opportunities has been to mobilize politically through interest groups (such as the National Association for the Advancement of Colored People), protests, or politicians (by running for electoral office). The political side of educational equity will be the primary focus of this study rather than sociological or economic variables. We argue that while research sometimes overlooks this aspect of educational processes, it can be one of the most important in determining what opportunities are afforded to students.

Second, representation is an effective instrument for addressing African-American educational inequities. This study views political representation broadly to include African-American school board members, school administrators, and, most of all, school teachers. Representation in school politics occurs through a cascade effect with school board representation influencing administrative representation which, in turn, directly affects teacher representation. Increases in school board representation predict increases in administrative representation, and increases in administrative representation predict increases in teacher representation. Among these groups, African-American teachers are consistently associated with better educational outcomes for African-American students in policy outputs (gifted class assignments, special education assignments, suspensions, and expulsions) as well as in policy outcomes (test scores, graduation rates, and preparation for higher education).

Third, electoral and governance structures create biases in the political and bureaucratic systems that influence how representation and other factors affect African-American education. Electoral structures such as at-large elections are designed to bias electoral results to discriminate against numerical minorities. At-large elections also alter the relationship between constituents and the representative in ways that influence the policy positions that representatives take and their ability to enact policies. The independent school district, in turn, is designed to filter out the influence of electoral politics, particularly partisan politics, and substitute a neutral professional bureaucratic process. These theoretical biases play a major role in the current study, though much of what we thought we knew about these structures is inaccurate as reflected in the study's fourth theme.

Finally, partisanship permeates the local education process despite nonpartisan elections and other structural barriers. African Americans find willing coalition partners among white Democrats who share their views on race and education. This coalition shifts the political cleavage in elections from one of race to one of partisanship such that African Americans are much more successful in Democratic majority districts than in Republican ones, and this partisan advantage works best in at-large elections. The influence of Democratic partisanship does not stop at the voting booth. In Democratic majority jurisdictions, African-American school board members are significantly more successful in hiring African-American administrators and teachers. The partisanship influences are even felt at the classroom level. African-American teachers are always more strongly associated with positive outcomes for African-American students in school districts with a Democratic majority. The differences are frequently large, and in many cases we find no representational impacts of African-American teachers in Republican majority school districts.

Although this book is about African-American educational politics, the implications address broader questions related to representation and political structure. That political structures create biases is a common theme in political science (Knight 1992), and the study of such biases is prevalent in both US and comparative politics, particularly in regard to the design of electoral systems (see Chapter 3). The examination of school districts generates variation in electoral structures that does not exist at the federal level or, for the most part, at the state level in the United States.

Although the bulk of representational studies in terms of race or other factors linked to representation focus on legislative bodies, bureaucracies can also represent certain interests and have some clear advantages in the process (see

Chapters 5 and 6). The examination of school districts allows us to trace a single issue, educational equity, down to the implementation level in order to determine the full ramifications of representation. Many studies of representation stop at the legislative level and do not follow through to determine how legislative actions actually shape public policy as it works its way through the bureaucracy. Although representation as a process does not guarantee results, examining the full range of the policy process from legislation to top bureaucrats to street-level bureaucrats allows us to determine how much legislative representation actually matters in this policy area.

Why Study Education?

The study of partisanship and race in the context of K–12 education is important for several reasons. Education is an issue salient to both political parties and to the mass public. Nearly fifty million students are in the nation's primary and secondary school systems, and these numbers are likely to continue to grow over time (US Department of Education 2014). Yet, our educational systems have been consistently criticized as underperforming for the last three decades. Both federal and state governments have implemented a number of accountability systems intended to improve educational outputs and provide relief about the future ability of the United States to remain a dominant world power. The United States now spends more ($11,841) per pupil than most other countries on education (National Center for Education Statistics 2015). Yet, data continue to suggest that much work remains to be done. Critics of US education frequently cite the Program for International Student Assessment, which ranks the United States twenty-seventh in math, seventeenth in reading, and twentieth in science out of thirty-four countries (Program for International Student Assessment 2012).

The demographic characteristics of schools are also changing at rates faster than the general population. While the US population overall is expected to grow older, given the aging of non-Hispanic white baby boomers, the American fertility rate has also increased, in large part because of recent immigration into the country (Passel, Livingston, and Cohn 2012). This means the country's youth are more diverse than ever before, with nearly 50 percent of children five and younger identifying with a racial or ethnic minority group. Further, the rate of change among the many racial and ethnic groups in the nation's schools varies greatly. As seen in Figure 1.1, the proportion of Latino students is growing rapidly while the percentage of black students, as well as Asian/Pacific Islanders and Native American/Alaska Native groups, are much more stable.

Why Study African-American Education?

Demographic changes may also raise questions about why research should focus on black student outcomes as opposed to one of the other minority

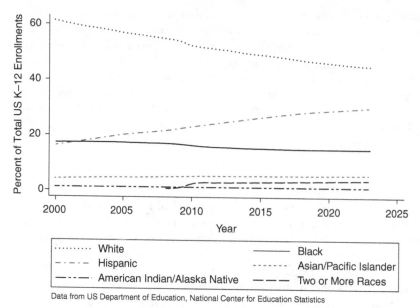

FIGURE 1.1. Share of student racial and ethnic groups in the United States, K–12 education, 2000–2025.

groups, especially given the trade-off in the growth of Latino students and the decline in the share of non-Hispanic white students. Although full studies of all minority groups in US education are worthwhile, a study of African-American students is especially needed.[1] Black students are persistently performing at lower levels than their peers, and solutions to this problem are few and far between. The problems of African-American education go well beyond the realm of education. Educational deficits in performance and attainment lead to larger gaps in long-term employment, health, housing, social capital, and contact with the criminal justice system.

A recent report by the National Center for Education Statistics (2014) highlights the persistent barriers facing black students in the classroom. For the 2011–2012 school year, the four-year adjusted cohort graduation rate was 67 percent for black students and 84 percent for white students; half of the African-American student population (compared to 11 percent of white students) in the country generally attends schools where graduation is not always the norm (Editorial Projects in Education 2008). On average, the performance of African-American high school seniors in math and reading is similar to that of a thirteen-year-old white student (Wiltz 2012). Unsurprisingly then, these

[1] The politics of Latino education differs substantially from that of African-American education in terms of access to representation on school boards, school administrative staffs, and teaching (see Leal, Martinez-Ebers, and Meier 2004).

students scored significantly lower than every other racial and ethnic group on standardized reading tests. African Americans scored the lowest of all student groups (defined as American Indian, Asian American, black, Mexican American, Puerto Rican, other Hispanic, and white) on all three portions (critical reading, mathematics, and writing) of the SAT and were also the lowest-scoring group for ACT composite scores (in which groups were defined as black, Native American, white, Latino, Native Hawaiian/Pacific Islander, two or more races, and did not respond) (Jaschik 2015a, 2015b). At the school level, more than 40 percent of blacks, compared to 6 percent of white students, attend high-poverty schools while 10 percent of black students and 33 percent of white students attend low-poverty schools (this categorization includes four levels of poverty, see Jordan 2014). Those students in high poverty schools (those where at least 75 percent of students are low income) are then more than twice as likely to be taught by uncertified or out-of-field teachers as compared to schools serving wealthier populations (Almy and Theokas 2010).

These facts highlight that the problematic racial education gap has yet to be closed in primary and secondary schools across the country. Those students who do graduate from high school face further challenges through an access gap in postsecondary educational settings as well as in the workforce. For example, black students continue to have both the lowest high school graduation and college enrollment rates; these students are often underprepared for college coursework because they have little to no exposure to advanced or gifted classes. Of the 60 percent of black freshmen in high school who persist and graduate (Aud et al. 2010), 55 percent enroll in a two- or four-year college immediately following high school. For a school with one hundred black students in the ninth grade class, sixty of these students will graduate high school. Only thirty-three of these sixty students will be college bound, largely to public or for-profit institutions (Aud et al. 2010). This means that only one in three black students who enroll in high school is likely to pursue postsecondary education, and many of these students will not make it to their college graduation. Translating educational opportunities into employment, blacks with less than or the equivalent of a high school degree experienced the highest rates of unemployment in 2008 (22 and 11 percent, respectively, for those with less than high school and those with a high school degree) (Bureau of Labor Statistics 2008). For those who have at least a bachelor's degree, unemployment rates for blacks (4 percent) were only second to those classified as American Indian/Alaska Natives (5 percent). Among working populations, blacks and Hispanics consistently have the lowest median annual earnings across all levels of education compared to their white and Asian counterparts. Though rates of change have varied over time, blacks have consistently had the lowest real median household income throughout the entire span (1968 to 2013) of Current Population Surveys (DeNavas-Walk, Proctor, and Smith 2013).

Although local political control is a well-enshrined feature of US education policy, that local control takes place within the political context created at the

TABLE I.I. *Party Platforms on K–12 Education*

	Democratic Party	Republican Party
2000	Have well-trained teachers in every classroom	Increased local control and more accountability to parents
	Turn around or shut down every failing school	Assist states in closing achievement gaps
	Ensure high school graduates have mastered certain basics	Expand school choice options and savings account plans
	Allow parents to choose the best school for their student	Ensure all children learn to read by reforming Head Start
	Ensure every eighth grader will be computer literate	Improve teacher training and recruiting (loan forgiveness and Troops-to-Teachers)
	All classrooms will have up-to-date technology	Support special education needs
	Eliminate the achievement gap	Return voluntary prayer to classrooms
2004	Smaller classroom and more individual attention	Continued reform through No Child Left Behind
	Place a great teacher in every classroom	Responsibility should focus on state and local level
	Raise teacher pay	State-specific plans for accountability
	Provide information to parents (parents are our most important teachers)	Every child should be able to read at the end of third grade
	Have strict discipline for drugs or violence in schools	Facility school choice and transparency
	Address the achievement gap, especially with Head Start access	Alternative pathways to teacher certification
	Develop high standards while encouraging school choice	Maintain discipline without fear of liability
2008	Set high standards and develop assessments	Continued accountability and periodic testing
	Recruit high-quality teachers	Recruit, reward, and train the best teachers
	Provide higher pay for effective teachers	Protect teachers from frivolous litigation
	Promote innovation and charter schools	Innovation in school (home school, single sex, varying schedules)
	Support special need populations, including English Language Learners	K–16 dual credit programs and public-private partnerships

	Democratic Party	Republican Party
2012	Invest in Head Start	More money is not the solution
	Raise Standards (using Common Core)	One-size-fits-all does not work; decentralization needed
	Expand school choice options	Expand school choice options
	Protect teachers from layoffs and reward great teachers	Merit pay for teachers and reform tenure system
	Address dropout crisis, especially for students of color	Stress parent involvement, Science, Technology, Engineering, and Mathematics, English First, and Abstinence Only

state and federal levels. Policies on accountability, quality, equity, efficiency, and especially funding are raised and addressed by state and local governments (see Chapter 2 for additional discussion). These policies may be more or less aligned with the interest of certain groups depending on who is in power. In the 2012 presidential election, for example, the Democratic and Republican Party platforms espoused several opinions about the direction of education. Both argued for equal access, with Democrats stating that education is the "surest path to middle class" that gives all students opportunities (Democratic National Convention 2012) and Republicans arguing educational opportunity and achievement "should be based on talent and motivation, not address, zip code, or economic status" (Republican National Convention 2012). Still, as displayed in Table 1.1, the two parties also diverged on a number of educational goals, perhaps most predominantly with Democrats advocating for higher levels of funding while Republicans argued that higher levels of funding did not constitute a feasible solution. Essentially, although both parties discuss closing the achievement gap and agree that schools are not performing to the level they should be, leaders of the parties have developed different means by which they hope to meet this goal.

Although schools are generally under the purview of local authority (i.e., school boards), national party platforms likely inform the views and opinions of elected leaders at lower levels of governance. School boards are generally elected in nonpartisan races where candidates do not explicitly run with a political party, but this does not mean that politics and ideology is removed from school boards altogether. Voters do not abandon their party-linked values simply because an election is designated as "nonpartisan." Similarly, the elites who contest school board elections are still quite likely to be connected with other officials and have ties to individuals in either the Democratic or Republican Party. In many cases, mayors, with clear party affiliations, may be part of the school board selection process and can have direct authority over education (Edelstein 2006). Given this, current theories of education for minority groups that do not consider partisanship (in this case, African

Americans) are underspecified and require revisions to adequately consider the role of politics.

Existing research on partisanship provides strong support for the notion that racial and ethnic groups tend to identify strongly with a single political party and are less likely to be even split among parties (Frey 2013; Pew Research Center 2012; but see Hajnal and Lee 2011). Since the New Deal era, the non-Hispanic white population has increasingly identified with the Republican Party while blacks have become nearly synonymous with the Democratic Party (Latinos also tend to identify as Democratic but not to the same extent as blacks, see Pew Research Center 2012). And while opinions on whether the American mass public is becoming more polarized were somewhat mixed in the past (DiMaggio, Evans, and Bryson 1996), most now agree that party elites and supporters have become dramatically more polarized in recent years (Druckman, Peterson, and Slothus 2013; Layman, Carsey, and Horowtiz 2006; Pew Research Center 2014) so that few elected representatives now self-identify as independent or bipartisan. Each party is more internally homogenous, which may have consequences for the representation of minority interests who may no longer be able to make appeals across parties (see Druckman et al. 2013). As politics shift so that the two dominant politics look less alike, representation for minority groups may only become more important. Without such representatives, the interest of minority groups may be overshadowed such that equitable outcomes are not achieved. Instead, minority groups may benefit from seeking to build coalitions with majority groups (see Chapter 3 for a more detailed discussion of why this case might exist for blacks and the Democratic Party).

Theoretical Mechanisms Linking Politics, Race, and Educational Opportunities

Politics is the determination of who gets what, when, and how (Lasswell 1950), and winners in political battles are those who can mobilize potential resources most effectively. The study uses a parsimonious theory to examine the politics of African-American education policy that encompasses three general concepts – resources, representation, and structure. The essential arguments are that the translation of resources into representation is affected by structural biases and representation is a major determinant of policy outcomes that benefit African-American students. The general theory will be applied to the ability of African Americans to get elected to school boards; to African-American representation among school administrators and teachers; and to the attainment of educational benefits for African-American students.

Resources

Political resources can be divided into those within the African-American community and those from the surrounding environment. The primary internal resource in politics for all groups is population and the ability to mobilize that population for political purposes such as elections. African-American representation levels and policy benefits should be positively correlated with African-American population. Traditionally, the urban politics literature focuses a great deal of attention on the ability to generate candidates for office, and that ability is linked to socioeconomic status (Parenti 1967; Wolfinger 1965). Although prior studies of African-American educational politics have found only modest relationships between African-American socioeconomic status and electoral outcomes (see Meier, Stewart, and England 1989), three measures will be included in the analysis – African-American median incomes, the percentage of African Americans with a college degree, and the percentage of African Americans who own homes. Higher levels of income, education, and home ownership are generally associated with greater voter turnout levels (Mossberger, Tolbert, and McNeal 2008; Wolfinger 1980); they are assets that are valuable in attaining positions within the education bureaucracy.

External resources in the community include factors that could be leveraged by the African-American community in political struggles. Potential *allies* are individuals and groups who share some common interests with the African-American community either in terms of educational equity goals or in terms of more general political outcomes. This study stresses the role of Democratic partisans as political allies consistent with a literature that argues that African Americans, particularly when they are a minority of the population, need to rely on coalitions with liberal whites to craft a governing majority (Browning, Marshall, and Tabb 1984). Democratic partisans can be interpreted as both individuals likely to support African-American educational goals and also as members of a set of institutions that have their own resources to mobilize voters to contest elections. Unions are a second potential ally of African Americans that have often been featured in the general education policy literature as influential (Katznelson 1981; Moe 2009). Although specific union data linked to school districts is difficult to obtain, surrogate measures are included in the models. Because resources are always relative and because the urban education literature has been greatly affected by social distance theory (Evans and Giles 1986), a measure of white social class (percentage of whites living in poverty) is included in all models.

The final environmental variable included in all models is a measure of the southern region. The meaning of the South in education politics covers a large collection of historical and contemporary variables that often resist further specification. Southern districts maintained *de jure* segregated school systems that were the locus of battles over desegregation and integration of schools. Southern states are also the location of a large number of historically black colleges and universities and, thus, can augment the political resources available to the African-American community. Although the current study was successful in generating election models that were precisely specified enough to render the South variable insignificant, it remained a factor in models of bureaucratic representation and policy actions.

Representation

There are three key positions of representation within a school district: school board member, school administrator, and school teacher. The school board provides the broadest type of influence; its members set overall policy for the schools within the district. The school board also has the important task of hiring a superintendent and providing for other professional personnel. The board in this process is able to determine, to some extent, who is managing the schools. If the school board includes members who represent minority group interests, then there is some likelihood that the board will hire school administrators who also represent minority interest (i.e., political principals seek like-minded agents; see, e.g., Waterman and Meier 1998).

School administrators implement policies approved by the school board but also have some leverage in day-to-day management of resources and personnel within schools. These individuals must approve student-tracking recommendations and disciplinary procedures on a student-by-student basis, and determine how to allocate resources to a number of school programs (Marzano, Waters, and McNulty 2005). These actions are likely to have some direct influence on student educational opportunities for majority and minority student groups. Similar to board members, however, the influence of school administrators on student outcomes (in this case, African-American students) can also occur indirectly through teacher hiring decisions. Just as the values and interests of the board determine who is hired to fulfill administrative roles, administrator values can shape the distribution of teachers. Where more black administrators are employed, the share of black teachers should also rise, all else being equal.

As much education literature has shown, teachers comprise the predominant in-school influence on student learning. While the school board and administrators set policies, they do not have the same degree of hands-on time with students in individual classrooms. Teachers determine how to react to student behaviors, make decisions about student promotions, and determine how much material students will be exposed to in a given day. Substantial literature has demonstrated that the link between teachers and student achievement is strong and persistent. Scholarship groups the effect of teachers into the categories of teaching ability, motivation, and school/classroom situation (Rowan, Chiang, and Miller 1997). The first factor, teaching ability, refers to a teacher's knowledge of a subject matter and training to teach using sound pedagogical tools. Motivation includes the teacher's attitudes and expectations for student achievement and some level of desire to achieve such expectations. The final factor includes teaching time, classroom size, and a host of other environmental characteristics over which the teacher has less control.

The second of these three umbrella categories is likely to be the most important in understanding the role of race and politics in education. A teacher's demographics, socioeconomic status, and other experiences are likely to inform his or her opinions and expectations of the students. Black teachers may be better suited to understand the needs of black students while also serving as positive role models (Dee 2004). In others words, black teachers may influence students in a passive manner in that a same-race teacher can instill confidence and generate higher aspirations among black students (Clewell and Villegas 1998). The presence of a same-race teacher may also dampen student fears that they will be perceived in a negative manner by teachers of different races (Steele 1997); this research corresponds to the general finding that teachers associate "whiteness" with intelligence (Morris 2005; Tyson 2003). Benefits may also be the result of active efforts by teachers, such as additional guidance and mentoring (Taylor 1999). In the same light, multiple studies have determined that teachers give same-race students more favorable assessments as well (Ouazad 2014).

While research has often discussed how student race influenced teachers' perceptions and actions, less work had been produced on the effect of teacher race and ethnicity on student outcomes. This changed with the work of Thomas Dee following experimental trials related to class size in Tennessee (Project STAR) in the late 1980s in which teachers and students were randomly assigned to classrooms. Dee (2004) found that assignment to same-race teachers was beneficial for both black and white students in terms of math and reading scores. These findings have been supported by more recent research as well (Clotfelter, Ladd, and Vigdor 2007; Pitts 2007). For example, using data from Florida, Egalite, Kisida, and Winters (2015) find that black and white student reading and math scores improve when assigned to same-race teachers; the authors show that benefits may be strongest for black and white students who were previously identified as low performing. In sum, where more black representation exists among teachers, black students should perform at higher levels. This may also be influenced by the presence of black board members and school administrators who are likely to advocate for black students in their own right but can also influence the recruitment and hiring of black teachers.

Educational Attainment

The public policy literature generally divides the results of policy into outputs and outcomes. Outputs are decisions and results that are generally under the control of the implementing agency whereas outcomes, often the variable that is really of interest, is determined by both policy and a wide variety of other factors. In employment policy, the number of workers trained is a policy output while the unemployment rate would be considered a policy outcome. Clearly a policy can influence policy outputs without affecting outcomes particularly if the outcomes are determined by a range of factors outside the control of the implementing agency.

As educational outputs, this study will examine a group of indicators that has become known by the term second generation education discrimination. We will examine the assignment of African-American students to gifted classes or to a set of special education classes comparing these assignments to the general student population in order to determine if African-American students are overrepresented or underrepresented in these classes. The application of discipline in terms of suspensions and expulsions will also be examined for evidence of racial disparities in the application of discipline.

Although racial disparities in the indicators of second-generation educational discrimination have been shown to be correlated with educational outcomes (see Chapter 5), this study will also examine a set of measures that tap into the performance of African-American students. Even though test scores are often the most prominent indicator of performance, the lack of a uniform national exam creates a series of measurement problems in comparing the racial gaps in performance across a large national sample of school districts. To surmount this problem, we present four quantitative case studies on individual states (California, Florida, Ohio, and Texas) and a pooled test of the ten states with the most school districts in our sample as the test score analysis. We also examine high school graduation rates in both the four state samples and the national data set and a set of college readiness indicators (SAT scores, course work taken, and advanced placement classes) for different states.

The National Survey of Schools

In the empirical chapters that follow, our examination of the role that politics plays throughout K–12 education is based on a national survey of school districts with more than five thousand students as of 1999. Surveys were conducted during the 2001–2002, 2003–2004, and 2008–2009 school years. Surveys were mailed to schools in the target population; up to three surveys were mailed to schools that did not initially respond. After the collection of mailed surveys, additional phone calls were made to any remaining districts to collect missing data. Of the 5,493 district years, 5,192 provided data on school board composition (for a response rate of 94.5 percent). The largest share of cases comes from California while Vermont has no cases (school districts in Vermont are typically smaller than five thousand students and would not be in the population of interest for this study). Some states have much larger black populations than others, but no state has a share of black teachers that is greater than or equal to the proportion of black students, on average. Those states that get the closest do so by the nature of small numbers.

Beyond this survey, control variables are collected from existing sources (see Table 1.2 for summaries by year). Data on resources and other demographic factors were collected from the 2000 Census of School Districts. Support for the Democratic Party was estimated using county-level election returns for the 2004 and 2008 presidential elections (see additional explanation in Chapter 3), and unionization data come from Bureau of Labor Statistics. The measures of racial disparities in education were taken from the Office for Civil Rights in the US Department of Education as well from the data archives of the various states.

TABLE 1.2. *Descriptive Profiles of Districts in Survey*

	2002 Mean	2004 Mean	2008 Mean
Percent Black School Board	9.80	9.62	9.14
Percent Black Administrators	10.12	10.26	10.34
Percent Black Teachers	6.92	6.82	6.47
Share Ward Elections	0.33	0.35	0.36
Share At-Large Elections	0.64	0.62	0.61
Percent Black Population	10.33	10.21	9.99
Percent Black Students	15.32	15.61	14.63
Black Education (College Percent)	15.89	15.87	15.82
Black Family Income (000s)	10.78	10.84	10.93
Black Home Ownership	47.48	47.59	47.89
Percent White Poverty	6.03	6.05	6.00
Located in South	0.38	0.37	0.37
Unionization	12.98	12.39	12.59
Percent District Democrat	47.60	47.63	47.17

A Road Map for the Book

This chapter served as the substantive and theoretical introduction to our study of African-American education politics. The study has both theoretical and substantive objectives. Theoretically, we seek to contribute to the general literature on representation and illustrate how structural biases and the presence of important political allies fundamentally influence representation whether that representation occurs in a legislature or in a bureaucracy. Substantively, we hope to present a comprehensive picture of the state of African-American education at the local level where students are actually taught. We do so by blending original data sets with existing data from federal agencies, state education agencies, election returns, and the US Census.

Chapter 2 provides the historical background that shapes current education politics for African Americans. The historical quest for equal access to quality education for African Americans has evolved from simply getting any education at all, to eliminating the "separate but equal" generation of inequality, to issues of second-generation educational discrimination, to the racial disparities in test scores, educational attainment, and preparation for future education. This chapter demonstrates how the contemporary politics of education are the continuation of political battles that date back at least two hundred years.

Chapter 3 examines the ability of African Americans to gain election to local school boards where many policy decisions are made. The chapter demonstrates how the traditional dispute over election structures (at-large vs. single-member districts [SMDs]) has been fundamentally transformed by partisanship. The key barrier to school board electoral success is no longer electoral structure but rather the partisan majority within the school district. Theoretically, the chapter shows how structural biases can be shifted by changing the nature of elections from one of race to one of partisanship or ideology. Substantively, the chapter demonstrates how one minority group has mobilized to achieve electoral equity and at times more than equity.

Chapter 4 investigates the ability of African-American school board members to increase the number of African-American administrators and teachers in the school district. Theoretically, the chapter tested the substantive representation effects of electoral structures and generally found that African Americans were better off with SMD elections. More dramatic than these structural influences were the partisan influences. The effectiveness of school board representation is always enhanced within a school district with a Democratic majority. Partisanship clearly matters more than electoral structure in the quality of representation that African Americans receive.

Chapter 5 turns the focus of education policy to students and the assignment of students to gifted classes or special education classes as well as the application of disciplinary actions (suspensions and expulsions). The structure of the independent school district greatly influenced these results. The different spheres of discretion meant that teacher representation was the strongest and most consistent factor in positive outcomes for African-American students. African-American administrators, particularly in districts with few African-American teachers, were often associated with greater racial disparities in discipline, a finding that reflects the role of school administrators in dispensing discipline. Partisanship even penetrated to this level in school districts by influencing the effectiveness of African-American teacher representation. The impact of African-American teachers was always larger in Democratic districts than in Republican ones; in some cases, African-American teachers had no association with positive outcomes for African-American students in Republican majority school districts.

Chapter 6 moves from decisions that affect African-American students to their educational attainment by looking at test scores, graduation rates, and preparation for higher education. The chapter employs several different data sets covering at times four individual states, ten large states together, and the national data set. The chapter underscores the importance of African-American teachers in the lives of African-American students with positive influences on test scores, graduation rates, and measures of college readiness (including the passing of advanced placement exams). Again the representation influence of African-American teachers was substantially larger in Democratic majority school districts than in Republican ones.

Chapter 7 summarizes the book's findings both in terms of its theoretical contribution to the study of political institutions, public policy, representation and race, and in terms of the substantive area of education policy. The chapter ends with a series of policy recommendations based on the findings of the book.

Two Myths

Separate but Equal and Nonpartisan Education

Underrepresented minority groups have become the majority of school-aged children in many public schools across the United States, and the last twenty years have seen a marked growth in scholarship on issues of race and education. While much of this research has referenced one or more policy changes at the federal or state level that have narrowed or exacerbated the gaps between minority and majority student achievement (e.g., Condron et al. 2013; Gaddis and Lauen 2014; Losen et al. 2015), there still remains a lack of recognition of the interplay between local politics and partisanship with issues of race and education. To be sure, the idea that politics plays a significant role in local education, while controversial, is certainly not new; a thread of literature deemed "the politics of education" has woven in and out of mainstream literature since the 1960s (Henig et al. 1999; Howell 2005; Portz, Stein, and Jones 1999; Rich 1996). Yet, as we will point out later in this chapter and throughout the remainder of the book, much of this research focuses on interest groups, unions, and internal board politics but often ignores the direct, explicit influence of partisan politics.

This chapter provides a brief overview of the development of African-American education in the United States over the past two hundred years. While a much deeper level of historical analysis may be found elsewhere (Kluger 2011; Spring 1994), the noteworthy events reviewed here will help to set the larger research of this book in context. This history is then overlaid with the development of school boards and the argument that local partisanship and political parties play a significant role in shaping school district policies that, subsequently, can determine the extent to which equal educational opportunities exist for majority and minority student groups.

Two considerations should be noted regarding the past and present states of access to education in the United States. First, racial tensions have not been unique to one portion of the United States. While these tensions were more pronounced and produced acute conflict in southern states, in no state has racial tension in education been entirely avoided. Further, racial inequities are not confined to the United States as a country. Different paths of race relations in countries around the world have produced situations in which populations have been divided into haves (social elites) and have-nots (minority groups of many kinds including recent immigrants). Second, despite the persistence of racial gaps in education in the United States, there has been and continues to be a widespread belief in and support for equal opportunity for education (see, e.g., Kiefer 2003). While this portion of the American Dream has yet to be real-ized, causing some to define equal education as a myth (Stiglitz 2013), the ideal of equal education will be important for future efforts in balancing the values of liberty (local, independent decision making) versus equity (equal opportuni-ties and common standards for all) or excellence (high standard performance) in local education governance structures (Wirt and Kirst 1997).

The Development of Schools – a Slow Start

The Boston English High School was the first public high school to open its doors in the country in 1821. Soon after this Bostonian innovation, policies requiring public education for school-aged children began to disperse quickly among the states (Labaree 1992). Yet this requirement only applied to Anglo-Americans (and often only to male students). Indeed, formal education for blacks was hard to come by and was hardly considered needed or wanted in many states. Long before the Boston English High School was estab-lished, northern and southern states alike (beginning with South Carolina in 1740) established compulsory illiteracy laws that deemed it illegal to teach blacks to read (Birnie 1927). These policies created a large barrier to black education even where individuals were willing to teach blacks; at the onset of the Civil War, less than 2 percent of black students were enrolled in any type of school (Snyder 1993). These rare schools were often located in northern states and were geographically isolated, resource poor, and without any integration with majority white institutions.

Following the Civil War, the scarcity of education for blacks slowly began to ease with the enactment of the Emancipation Proclamation (1863) and the Thirteenth Amendment (1865) as well as the creation of the Freedman's Bureau in the War Department and the Office of Education (later the Department of Education), which was created to help states establish effective systems of schools. The 1870 Census, however, determined that only 9.1 percent of African-American children attended school compared to 50 percent of their white counterparts (Collins and Margo 2006). Ten years later, following a Civil Rights Act that attempted to ban segregation in all public areas and that was subsequently declared unconstitutional by the Supreme Court, one-third of African-American students had enrolled in school (Weinberg 1977). Additional efforts were notable in the realm of postsecondary education as well. The first institutions for free blacks were established as early as 1837 (the Institute for Colored Youth, later Cheyney State University; the institution did not grant degrees, however, until 1932), and two federal laws helped to establish and strengthen historically black colleges and universities (HBCUs). Following the First Morrill Act of 1862, which provided land and funding for states to establish institutions aimed at lower- and middle-income (largely white) Americans, the Second Morrill Act of 1890 required states that maintained segregated higher education to provide at least one land-grant institution for African Americans. Importantly, the funding for these HBCUs had to be equal to that of the white counterpart land-grant institution (Redd 1998). Not all of these HBCUs granted the same type, level, and breadth of degrees as white institutions, but they did open pathways for increasing educational equity in later years. As such, the growth in K–12 and higher education for African Americans by the end of the nineteenth century was quite notable given the absence of education for these students just twenty years earlier. Daunting challenges related to a culture of racial divides and the concept of equal education, however, would persist for generations to come.

Despite state mandates that called for equal spending on black and white schools, allocations by unmonitored local officials often meant that white schools would receive several times more in funding per pupil compared to black schools (Walker 2005). Near equitable funding was only momentarily achieved in the South where black populations represented sizable voting blocs (Weinberg 1977). Unequal funding was solidified when the Supreme Court legitimized segregation through separate but equal facilities in *Plessy v. Ferguson* (1896). While this case may have received the most publicity, it was not the first to set a separate but equal precedent. As far back as 1850, the Massachusetts state court in *Roberts v. City of Boston* determined that the decision to refuse the admission of a black student to a white school was fully within the power of the local school committee. This decision was cited along with several others in *Plessy*, and it serves as a reminder that separate but equal was perceived to be acceptable in regions that were thought to be the most tolerant toward equality for blacks.

While separate but equal in *Plessy* might have been seen as a victory for some given the dilapidated condition of many black schools, some states responded to the ruling not by providing better facilities but by closing black schools altogether (Tindall 1952). For example, in *Cumming v. Board of Education of Richmond County, State of Georgia* (1899), the Supreme Court allowed the local school board to close the public black schools while maintaining two public white schools. This opinion was based on the concept that there was no clear evidence that the school closure decision was based on discrimination and that the local authorities had discretion over the distribution of funds for public education. If schools for blacks did not exist, state and local officials would not have to make the facilities equal. For years to come, many states would legally require segregation in schools as well as in many other facilities such that the concept of "separate" was certainly implemented while "equal" was not.

The Urban Education Reforms

Parallel in time to the changes in access to education for African Americans but developing separately, the Progressive Era spawned a series of reforms that targeted the perceived ill-effects of the patronage orientation of nineteenth-century politics. The movement is credited with influencing the adoption of civil service systems, the creation of city manager government, and other policies and procedures to limit the influence of political parties (Hays 1964; Wiebe 1967). The success of the progressives in education equaled and perhaps exceeded their success in city, state, and national governments (Reese 2002).

The spoils system in nineteenth-century urban education operated much as it did in other areas of government. Partisan elections dominated by political machines contested for control of school systems and the right to use patronage in appointing school administrators and teachers. In such a system, teachers were hired based on political loyalty rather than competence in the classroom. The progressive reforms severed schools from city government, creating the independent school district as the predominant governing structure for K–12 education (Tyack 1974). Adding to this isolation from city politics, a variety of barriers to partisan political mobilization were created. Elections were made nonpartisan and contested at times different from the normal electoral cycle for partisan positions. At-large elections replaced ward or single-member district (SMD) elections that were perceived as facilitating the ability of partisans and their immigrant supporters in gaining electoral advantage. At-large elections were sold as a way to attract the interests of better educated, civic-minded citizens with broader views of the public good and were intended to bring such civic leaders into the governance of public education (Wiebe 1962).

The independent school district also fully adopted the politics administration dichotomy, regarded at the time as the ideal way to govern a political system (Goodnow 1906; Wilson 1887). The school board (the political branch) was restricted to policy questions and had its administrative role limited to hiring a professional manager, the superintendent, to implement policies following the "best practices" of the day. Those best practices included provisions for hiring and retention of teachers and other employees based on merit and the adoption of the best scientific approaches to educating students. Such a structure was designed to limit as much as possible any influence of partisan politics on the education of America's children.

These reforms without question changed the politics of education in the United States. Structures were redesigned to increase the influence and access of business and professional elites and limit the influence of political parties and immigrant groups (Tyack 1974; Wiebe 1962). The reforms did not eliminate politics from education, however, but merely advantaged some forms of politics and disadvantaged others. At-large elections are majoritarian institutions and clearly intended to limit the influence of any minority in a community by restricting its access to policy positions. At the same time, these reforms created a myth that education policy was nonpartisan in nature.

The Progressive Era reform structures were not ostensively designed to disadvantage African Americans; Jim Crow laws and a variety of other policies and implementation strategies were able to do that independently. Owing to the majoritarian nature of at-large election systems, however, minority groups including African Americans would face additional barriers to policy influence when seeking to create more equal educational opportunities. Before those political struggles could start, however, black Americans first had to gain access to any form of education. Groups like the National Association for the Advancement of Colored People (NAACP), an organization founded in 1909 with the goal of eliminating racial barriers and injustices through legal action (NAACP 2009), would soon come into play not only in the policy sphere of education but throughout many other policy circles to advance access and equality for blacks.

Building Black Political Momentum

At the turn of the twentieth century, illiteracy rates for blacks in the South hovered around 50 percent, nearly 40 percentage points higher than whites (Margo 1990). Schools were still largely decentralized, although national sentiment was growing increasingly negative toward so-called out-of-control political machines that needed to be held accountable to the public. Education for the (white) masses became politically popular, and some great advances were experienced. Between 1890 and 1918, school attendance increased by 711 percent and standardized testing was introduced for the first time (Tyack 1974).

Although school districts were beginning to take on higher levels of centralization during the Progressive Era, the quality of education within and across states varied widely. Generally, while white education was severely limited in some portions of the United States, black students were much worse off (Anderson 1988). Where schools for blacks existed, physical conditions were poor and learning materials nonexistent. Even where materials might be available, some states placed limits on what these schools were able to read to again secure the prevention of any revolt against white supremacy. Overcrowding was common, and many black students did not continue past an elementary education before leaving school altogether, limiting chances of experiencing higher education and undercutting black economic mobility (although the first known black student graduated from Middlebury College in Vermont in 1823 and the first black Rhodes Scholar was named in 1907). Despite these firsts, the status of black education remained relatively flat throughout World War I and the Great Depression, which further emphasized funding differences between black and white schools.

Racial and ethnic minority groups continued to gain social and political capital, and the push to reverse separate but equal policies and to invalidate segregation in education gained steam. In 1931, *Alvarez v. Board of Trustees of the Lemon Grove School District* was the first case to successfully push back on the constitutionality of desegregation. The court ruled that the Lemon Grove school district could not place Mexican Americans in separate "Americanization" schools. In 1946, the US district court also decided that educating students of Mexican descent in separate facilities was unconstitutional in *Mendez v. Westminster School District*. Pressure for black equality, while experiencing less action at the K–12 level, was achieving some success in the realm of postsecondary education. In *Murray v. Pearson* (1936), the University of Maryland was required to admit African-American students or establish a separate but equal facility; the university elected to admit black students, increasing access and also allowing room for interaction among black and white students. Following suit, the Naval Academy opened its doors to the first African-American men, and the first blacks graduated from an army flight school in Alabama in 1943 (Taylor 1999). These cases helped to set an important precedent for later rulings that would further invalidate *Plessy v. Ferguson*.

In the midst of the evolution of court cases calling into question the validity of segregation in education, advocacy groups also began to build momentum around cases that could have some chance of countering separate but equal. Although the NCAAP was not originally intended to focus solely on education, the organization made a conscious decision to make strides in this area during the early 1930s. Strategies of NAACP leaders included making separate educational facilities economically costly and inefficient as well as pointing to clear violations of "equal" education (e.g., *Sweatt v. Painter* [1950] and *McLaurin v. Oklahoma State Regents* [1950]). Cases were won related to segregation by exclusion (*Missouri ex rel. Gaines v. Canada* [1938]) and disparities in teacher pay for whites and blacks (*Alston v. School Board of City of Norfolk* [1940]). While these victories were meaningful, many black groups lacked unity in their positions on education, which, at times, created some barriers in fighting against segregation in schools. While many supported the views of Booker T. Washington, who discussed the need for blacks to fulfill vocational positions that were indispensable for national economic development, others followed W. E. B. DuBois in his call for leadership of the upper classes (the "talented tenth") and education according to ability in a manner that mirrored white standards (Johnson and Watson 2004).

Dissembling Separate but Equal

As late as 1948, the United States still had more than seventy-five thousand one-room schools, and dropouts were quite common after the fifth grade (Williams and Laurits 1954). Accumulated together, however, the events of the 1930s and

1940s set the stage for a larger upheaval of Jim Crow norms throughout the southern states and present in many areas north of the Mason-Dixon line. By 1950, the NAACP was committed to the strategies of Thurgood Marshall and opted to take action against the equal portion of the separate but equal guideline in *Plessy v. Ferguson*. Should the equal clause be proven faulty, the separate clause would also be considerably weakened (Guinier 2004). *Brown v. Board of Education* was initially filed in 1951, came before the Supreme Court in October of 1952, and became an umbrella for five cases:

- *Brown v. Board of Education* (1951), where African-American parents attempted but failed to enroll their children in schools in their neighborhoods in Topeka, Kansas.
- *Belton v. Gebhart* (1952) and *Bulah v. Gebhart* (1952), claiming unequal education for black and white students in Delaware. The two cases were merged in the process of appeals.
- *Bolling v. Sharpe* (1954), in which black parents sought to have black students admitted to a new school that had multiple empty classrooms in the District of Columbia.
- *Briggs v. Elliot* (1952), where, in Clarendon County of South Carolina, African-American parents asked for busing for their black students as part of equalizing what provisions were available for white students.
- *Davis v. County School Board* (1952), where 450 black students in Farmville, Virginia, protested the poor conditions of their schools and sought assistance from the NAACP.

The bundling of these cases into *Brown v. Board of Education* illustrated that segregation was a national point of conflict (a success for the efforts of the NAACP). After multiple rounds of hearings, the Supreme Court declared racial segregation to be against the Fourteenth Amendment Equal Protection Clause in 1954. Separate but equal was overturned and caused ripples of reactions throughout the country. Despite the order to end segregation "with all deliberate speed," the lack of tangible guidelines and oversight from the Supreme Court for how to end segregation provided a loophole for resistance. District courts were also hesitant to ensure compliance by many jurisdictions to desegregation requirements. Additionally, the actions of the courts were counter to Congress in the fight over a balance of powers. One hundred and one members of Congress (all from southern states) wrote the Declaration of Constitutional Principles, also known as the Southern Manifesto, accusing the Supreme Court justices of abusing their power and claiming that their decision would be reversed through the Tenth Amendment (US Congress 1956). Although the president did not join with the legislative branch in supporting this Manifesto, he also did not provide meaningful support (e.g., executive action) for the court orders. At the state level, legislatures declared the Court's decision null and void while others passed laws that prohibited individuals from pursuing desegregation. Senator Harry Byrd of Virginia, for instance, instituted "massive resistance" encouraging white policy makers in the state to prevent school integration, even at the cost of closing entire school districts (Smith 2002). Reactions among the black population in many states also did not help further the implementation of *Brown*. Parents were often reluctant to force their children into hostile environments, and those that took action were subject to much intimidation (Meier, Stewart, and England 1989).

In the years that followed the *Brown* decision, federal troops were called into several local jurisdictions to intervene in white protests and riots against desegregation in schools, perhaps most famously in Little Rock, Arkansas. The implementation of *Brown* was so fragmented that by 1960, nearly one hundred years after the end of the Civil War, at least five southern states had less than 1 percent of black students attending school with their white peers (Dye 1969). Only after the implementation of the 1964 Civil Rights Act and the ensuing creation of the civil rights divisions of the Department of Justice and the Department of Health, Education, and Welfare – agencies permitted to discontinue federal funds from parties practicing discrimination – did schools have a greater incentive to foster the integration of black and white students (Rosenburg 2008). These offices increased enforcement and were more willing to sue those districts that did not comply. Civil rights policies were further complemented by at least two notable events. First, the Elementary and Secondary Education Act (ESEA) provided support for low-income students (programs included Title 1 financial assistance to districts with large shares of low-income students and bilingual education). The ESEA was largely intended to address educational inequalities that existed for several types of students, including but not limited to African Americans. Second, the Equality of Educational Opportunity Study, commonly known as the Coleman Report, stated that African-American students benefitted from education in integrated schools (Coleman et al. 1966). This policy provided much momentum for the busing of students to further the implementation of integration efforts despite continued racial tensions in many parts of the country. Whereas 99 percent of black students in the South attended all-black schools in 1964, only 20 percent of black students were in all-black southern schools in 1971 (Orfield and Yun 1999).

From First- to Second-Generation Discrimination

Issues of race continued to be battled in the courtroom (e.g., *Green v. County School Board of New Kent County* [1968] and *Alexander v. Holmes County Board of Education* [1969]), where additional delays in desegregation efforts were no longer being tolerated. Civil rights movements were brought from the streets to living rooms across the country by television sets, and school integration rates successfully increased. By 1976, the percent of black students attending school with whites increased to 45.1 percent (Orfield and Lee 2005). The South became home to the most desegregated schools, and some of the focus on desegregation was then placed on large urban cities in northern states. As overt segregation between schools declined – often forcefully – such that white and black students were educated together, however, a number of "second-generation" discrimination issues developed. Initially, these mechanisms included overt segregation within schools such as separate classrooms or separate lunch rooms for black and white students. Once these clear discriminatory practices were addressed, inequalities shifted to include the tracking and sorting of students as well as practices used to discipline students (Meier et al. 1989). These types of second-generation discrimination are subtler and often harder to recognize at the surface level but can cause major challenges to the promise of equal education for all groups within schools.

Academic tracking or grouping can be defined as "the process whereby students are divided into categories so that they can be assigned in groups to various kinds of classes" (Oakes 1985). Grouping dates back to at least the mid-1800s in the United States; the concept gained popularity in the 1920s but then faded until the 1950s when attention to the space race amplified interest in specialized training (though it was used in many classrooms with mixed results throughout the interim period) (Findley and Bryan 1971). Through tracking and grouping, students are classified as slow, average, or accelerated learners and are then placed on corresponding tracks of learning. Students are assigned to classes each year, and decisions of which classes students should be assigned to are largely influenced by past performance (Oakes 1985). As a result of this effort to produce better learning environments, sorting structures have often lessened variance among student ability within classrooms while allowing ability differences across classrooms to grow. Classes that are more homogeneous are often seen as easier to teach. Students are exposed to the same type of curriculum, with the highest-ability classrooms learning more material at a faster pace as compared to lower-ability classrooms. Beyond the regular tracking of ability, some students may be placed in special education classes that can isolate them from regular interaction with other students. These classes exist to suit the needs of students "considered unable to profit from regular instruction" (Heller, Holtzman, and Messick 1982). While some of these classes are tailored to students with specific disabilities diagnosed by medical professionals, other classes take shape based on the decisions of administrators and teachers within the school.

Following years of cases to integrate schools, the NAACP and other organizations shifted some attention to fighting to achieve equity in academic tracking within classrooms in the 1960s. Federal courts were generally slow to actively tackle the issue of tracking, though the issue has surfaced in many circuit courts. One of the early successes for addressing racial segregation in tracking policies occurred in *Hobson v. Hansen* (1967). The plaintiffs argued that one of the policies that prohibited low-income and black students from equal education was the system of homogenous ability groups that was determined, to a large extent, on status as opposed to ability.

The effect of *Hobson* on breaking tracking norms was limited as it showed only that tracking produced discriminatory effects but did not necessarily have any discriminatory intent. As such, tracking continued and was often most prevalent among districts under court-ordered desegregation plans, where some schools began to systematically place black students in lower tracks, at times to such an extent that the former Department of Health, Education, and Welfare threatened to withdraw federal funding (Eitle 2002; Smith 2004). Additional cases, especially those under purview of the Fifth Circuit Court, did prohibit grouping and tracking in previously segregated schools until a unitary system was achieved and tracking would not be influenced by prior segregation norms (see *McNeal v. Tate County School District* [1975]; *United States v. Gadsden County School District* [1978]; and *United States v. Tunica County School District* [1970]). Some of the gains made by these cases would not last long, however. By the mid-1980s, when many assumed segregation and discrimination was an issue of the past, additional rulings sided with schools in supporting the notion that socioeconomic status was a legitimate reason for tracking (*Quarles v. Oxford Municipal Separate School District* [1989]; *Georgia State Conference of Branches of NAACP v. Georgia* [1985]; *Montgomery v. Starkville Municipal Separate School District* [1987]). These rulings were problematic in that discrimination, although no longer as overt, was certainly not an issue of the past; and districts now had license to separate minority and majority students along academic tracks that would have longer-term effects on student discipline, graduation, college readiness, and the school-to-prison pipeline.

A second major type of second-generation discrimination that emerged in the wake of forced school integration was inequitable disciplinary procedures, including corporal punishment, in- and out-of-school suspension, and expulsions, for different student groups. School discipline has traditionally been seen as helping to secure a safe school environment and creating an environment suitable for learning (Duke 1989), and teachers were expected to act as a substitute for the parent during school hours (interestingly, conversations about what forms of punishment were acceptable began as far back as 1890 in reference to physical punishments such as strikes across the knuckles or raps on the head with pointers) (Middleton 2012).

By the mid-1970s, questions began to arise about the discretion held by teachers and school administrators of when and how often to use various levels of disciplines on minority student groups. Unlike more mixed literature on academic grouping, research on disciplinary decisions consistently agrees that minority students are far more likely to receive punishment than their peers (Skiba, Peterson, and Williams 1997; Thorton and Trent 1988). Although the reason for this overrepresentation is not always clear, it regularly appeared to be more common following school desegregation (Larkin 1979; Thorton and Trent 1988), especially in categories of suspensions and expulsions. For instance, during the 1972–1973 school year, 11.8 percent of black students were suspended compared to 6.1 percent of Latinos, 6.0 percent of whites, 5.6 percent of American Indians, and 2.4 percent of Asian/Pacific Islanders (this disproportion has only continued to increase over time) (Losen and Martinez 2013). Eyler, Cook, and Ward (1983) showed that black students are two to five times more likely to be suspended than white students and note that black student suspensions also last much longer than those for whites. They found the most powerful individual-level predictors of suspensions to be low grade-point averages, low tests scores, and whether a student was male or black. Statistics related to school discipline only worsened with the rise of zero tolerance policies in the 1980s and 1990s (Stone 1993).

Even when disparities in discipline were noted, however, court responses were ambivalent. Cases such as *Dixon v. Alabama State Board of Education*, 5th Cir. (1961) and *Woods v. Wright* (1964) helped to establish due process rights for black students but did not fully articulate whether discipline was discriminatory. In *Hawkins v. Coleman* (1974), racism was proven to exist within the school in question; the court ordered the district to take corrective action but refused to interfere with administrative discretion, essentially removing threats of enforcement from the district. Cases such as *Tasby v. Estes* (1978) also established that statistical evidence was not sufficient proof of discrimination, especially as related to intent (see also *Coleman v. Franklin Parish School Board* [1983] and *Parker by Parker v. Trinity High School* [1993]). Because no consistent precedent was strongly established through these cases, discussion of disciplinary norms and equity would continue to be debated by school administrators, teachers, parents, and minority rights organizations.

The court cases and other policy actions in this area generally ignored that racial disparities in grouping and tracking were correlated with racial disparities in discipline and both were correlated with educational attainment (see Meier et al. 1989). These intercorrelations indicated that discriminatory patterns were likely institutionalized in the rules and procedures of public education (Feagin and Feagin 1978) and would occur without any conscious effort on the part of teachers and administrators. This meant that efforts to challenge such practices essentially had to change accepted educational procedures and the court requirements to demonstrate intent created substantial barriers to eliminating any racial disparities.

Gaps Going Nowhere Fast

Issues of discrimination, while perhaps less salient than during the civil rights movements of the 1960s, have continued to be an undercurrent through much education policy making at the federal and state level in the United States. Many districts continued to struggle with school integration at the close of the 1970s. Citing the goals of the Fourteenth Amendment, Congress passed the predecessor of the Individuals with Disabilities Education Act in the Education for All Handicapped Children Act in 1975 in order to provide more amenable service to students with disabilities. This policy was an important step in recognizing the importance of equity in schools, even though the focus on this specific policy was not necessarily based on race or ethnicity. In that regard, national attention related to racial educational equity increased in salience alongside the widely publicized document titled *A Nation at Risk* in 1983. The report – claiming that the state of education had eroded in the United States – helped to strengthen the implementation of a system of standards-based education and shifted the national conversation from one based solely on quality to one that recognized the need for both quality and equity.

As some policies appeared to push educational equity forward, progress was not made without pushback. A series of Supreme Court cases in the early 1990s affirmed an interest in limited federal supervision of desegregation in favor of local authority. These decisions signaled that local desegregation plans were not intended to be permanent but were only to allow for corrective action. In *Freeman v. Pitts* (1992), for example, the Court ruled that a district could be released from judicial oversight before the district was declared to be free of discriminatory practices (see also *Board of Ed. of Oklahoma City Public Schools v. Dowell* [1991] and *Missouri v. Jenkins* [1995]). The decision by the Court to back off of oversight mechanisms in many ways allowed for the continuation of second-generation discrimination practices but also created room for resegregation in many districts.[1]

Despite the continued presence of segregation in schools, at least one policy of the 1990s changed some of the incentives for schools to prioritize the success of black (as well as other minority and economically disadvantaged) students. In reauthorizing the ESEA through the 1994 Improving America's Schools Act, Title I programming changed from permitting less challenging standards for disadvantaged students to requiring that all students meet the same standards developed by a given state (Manna 2008). Title I became the largest single federal funding stream for K–12 education, and the policy received widespread support from both Republicans and Democrats.

This policy change was, overall, insignificant in substantially altering norms and practices at the local level to increase the likelihood of equal educational opportunities for black students. Yet, it did provide for the expansion of performance and accountability data that began to illustrate the significant gaps that existed between white and black students across the country in test results, dropout rates, and graduation. The broader availability of these data was one of many forces that contributed to policies aimed at decreasing these gaps in the widely discussed No Child Left Behind Act (NCLB) of 2001. The passage of NCLB brought the goal of closing the achievement gap among student groups

---

[1] Without the ability to impose remedies that operate across school districts, the degree of school segregation will reflect the degree of residential segregation.

(in grades, test results, dropout rates, college-going rates, and more) to the forefront of education policy and school accountability mechanisms. NCLB required that all groups of students were to show adequate yearly progress in achievement test scores and mandated that at least 95 percent of each population take state exams at the appropriate times (thus diminishing the ability of schools to systematically dismiss or excuse students from taking standardized tests in order to thwart resulting progress reports) (Bohte and Meier 2000; Yell, Katsiyannas, and Shiner 2006). Equity reentered the national discussion on education, and states began to focus on the development of data analytics that could assess the progress of students by race and socioeconomic status. That scores were now disaggregated by various groups again brought a higher level of national awareness to racial gaps in schools and spurred much research and popular discussion of whether and how certain interventions might lessen such gaps. NCLB intended for all students (regardless of race, income, disability, or language) to be proficient in reading and math by 2014; as mentioned in the following text, this goal has yet to be achieved.

Progress or Lull?

Currently, great debate continues regarding second-generation discrimination inequities as well as the persistence of the achievement gap that exists along racial lines. While scholars and education practitioners alike often agree that systemic changes are needed to address these issues, opinions are mixed in identifying which solutions will and will not be effective for producing such changes effectively.

First, second-generation discrimination continues to survive in schools across the country. In terms of academic grouping and tracking, recent suits have been filed by the Office for Civil Rights (*Ridley, C. et al., v. State of Georgia et al. (Dublin City School District)* [2004]; *United States & Coleman v. Midland Independent School District* [1998]; *United States v. Yonkers Board of Education* [1997]). Debate also continues on the topic of how to track student progress while avoiding discrimination. For example, the Obama administration has allowed for ESEA waivers that allow for schools to combine student groups into super subgroups. While this allowance may aid in data reporting and can allow large schools to show progress, it can also cloud information regarding how underrepresented groups are actually performing and whether the achievement gap is changing (Center on Education Policy 2012). Instead, more attention has arguably been focused on questions of school discipline. Although not always defined as a form of discrimination, much attention continues to focus on what disciplinary mechanisms should and should not be used in schools as well as how disciplinary offenses should be defined. Skiba et al. (2002), for example, found that white students were more likely to be disciplined for narrow offenses such as smoking, vandalism, and obscene language while black students were more likely to be disciplined for broader, subjective offenses like excessive noise, disrespect, and loitering. Many have linked these types of offenses to lower likelihoods of school success and completion and to larger school-to-prison pipelines, which hinder not only black educational access but also larger social and economic prospects (Christle, Jolivette, and Nelson 2005; Losen et al. 2015).

One notable example of the discipline debate stems from the Los Angeles Unified School District (LAUSD), home to the nation's largest school police force. In 2011, when black students represented 10 percent of the LAUSD student population, black students received 15 percent of tickets issued by the police force (20 percent in 2010). White students, by contrast, received 3 percent of citations but formed 9 percent of the student population. Both the sheer volume of citations (twenty-eight per day on average) and the disproportions present in citations generated much conversation about whether juvenile court was an appropriate place to send students for some types of minor infractions (not wearing a helmet, jaywalking, etc.) (Ferriss 2012).

Additional scrutiny was given to discipline in schools following the deaths of Michael Brown[2] and Eric Garner[3] in 2014. Discussions in popular media have pointed to zero tolerance policies, or policies that mandate preset consequences for rule violations; the use of police forces in schools; and the implicit bias in individual attitudes as contributing to two unsettling statistics: that 95 percent of suspensions are for nonviolent behaviors and that black students are currently suspended and expelled at a rate that is three times that of white students (Smith-Evans and Skiba 2014). Zero tolerance rules have been especially criticized as being overly harsh for offenses that are too broad in scope, enough so that the US Departments of Education and Justice released a guide on school discipline in 2014. Aiming to "prevent, severely reduce, and ultimately eliminate expulsions and suspension in early childhood settings, and more broadly, to improve school climates and discipline across the educational system," the *Guiding Principles* recommends that schools clearly define offenses (e.g., "acting in a threatening manner") to ensure fairness and to foster growth in the socioemotional and behavioral health of students (Blad 2014, 2). The *Guiding Principles* also encourage schools to analyze data and assess progress of their practices while enhancing staff training and developing family and community partnerships. The previously mentioned LAUSD became the largest school system to ban suspensions solely for willful defiance in 2013 (shortly before the *Guiding Principles* document was released). The decision was not made without pushback; school board members were divided on the issue, with some members not wanting to give students a "free pass" (Blad 2014).

---

[2] Michael Brown was shot in August 2014 by a white police officer in Ferguson, Missouri. The circumstances of the shooting were disputed and involved widely publicized protests.

[3] Eric Garner passed away following an encounter with a police officer on July 17, 2014 in New York City. The unclear events and cause of death were linked to a number of demonstrations centered on black-white racial tensions.

Beyond the narrower discussions of second-generation discrimination tactics, local, state, and federal policy makers continue to struggle with narrowing the black-white achievement gap (Gregory, Skiba, and Noguera 2010; Jencks and Phillips 2011; Ladson-Billings 2006; Norman et al. 2001). While the raw achievement statistics for blacks across a number of indicators has improved to a degree in recent years, and many schools have attempted to take action to lessen gaps through expanding early childhood programs, reducing class sizes, and hiring high-quality teachers, the black-white gap is stubbornly persistent. Perhaps most notable among court actions was a joint decision on two cases in 2007 – *Parents Involved in Community School v. Seattle School District No. 1* and *Meredith v. Jefferson County Board of Education* – in which the relation of overt discrimination to student assignment and tracking again surfaced. In a contentious 5-4 split (with two separate opinions from the majority), the Court ruled that public schools cannot maintain integration by using race as a factor to assign students to schools. All opinions rendered in the case drew from interpretations of the intent of *Brown*, yet each came to a different conclusion about how race can be used in decision making by schools. The case also included an amicus curiae from 553 researchers across forty-two states and the District of Columbia that concluded "(1) racially integrated schools provide significant benefits to students and communities, (2) racially isolated schools have harmful educational implications for students, and (3) race-conscious policies are necessary to maintain racial integration in school" (Brief for 533 Social Scientists, 2006, 2). The brief warned of the negative consequences in what became the majority opinion. The decision not only directed policy in the two regions represented in the case, but it affected a number of other districts that operated under similar procedures. Consequently, some argue that, in many areas, schools are now more segregated than they were in the mid-1960s (Frankenberg, Lee, and Orfield 2003).

In terms of legislative initiatives beyond the court, President Barack Obama introduced the Race to the Top (RTT) initiative as part of the American Recovery and Reinvestment Act in 2009. RTT consisted of $4.35 billion for states that were awarded through a competitive grant process. In order to receive this funding, states were asked to implement performance-based assessments for teachers, adopt Common Core standards, lessen restrictions on charter school programs, successfully turn around underperforming schools, and find systematic approaches to using data in decision-making processes (US Department of Education 2009). Only four states (Alaska, North Dakota, Texas, and Vermont) did not apply for this funding. At the same time, critics of RTT are not small in number, and many groups take issue with the philosophies behind national standardized tests (over local, decentralized control) or charter school programs (that sometimes take away local power). Following RTT, President Obama also announced a system for state waivers from NCLB policies if certain other contingencies were in place (college-ready assessments, teacher evaluations, etc.). This policy was intended to address constraints in

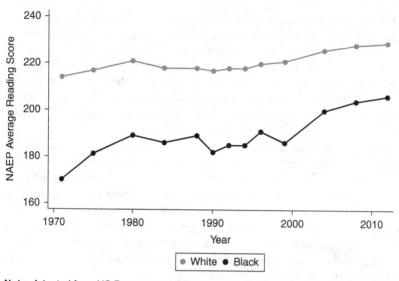

Note: Adapted from US Department of Education (2009).
Black includes African American. Race categories exclude Hispanic origin.

FIGURE 2.1. Trend in NAEP average reading scores for white and black nine-year-old students.

NCLB that arguably do not allow for innovation and reform (US Department of Education 2013).

Whether NCLB, RTT, or other reforms have worked is not clear. In the most recent reports from the National Assessment of Educational Progress (NAEP), reading and math gaps have declined since the 1970s, but changes in gaps have become harder to achieve in more recent years (gaps in math scores continue to be larger than gaps in reading scores). Figures 2.1, 2.2, and 2.3 display historical trends for the black-white reading gap for nine-, thirteen-, and seventeen-year-olds, respectively. While the current gaps are significantly smaller than those in the 1970s and have largely continued to decline over time, the rate of this decline has greatly slowed. Gaps for mathematics, displayed in Figures 2.4, 2.5, and 2.6, are arguably worse; while black-white math scores have improved over time, the black-white gap has not significantly narrowed for any of these three ages since the early 1990s.

The consequences of these gaps will only grow in importance as the demographics of the school populations continue to change. While the black student population is not shifting drastically, growth in Latino and Asian populations means that public schools are becoming majority-minority very quickly (though private school enrollment still tends to be overwhelmingly white, see Krogstad and Fry 2014). Additional issues such as gaps by income or gender as well as teacher layoffs in cities with large deficits compound existing continuations of first- and second-generation discrimination. Minority students,

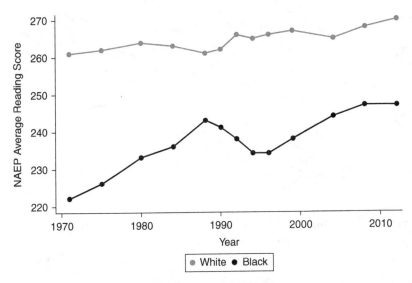

Note: Adapted from US Department of Education (2009).
Black includes African American. Race categories exclude Hispanic origin.

FIGURE 2.2. Trend in NAEP average reading scores for white and black thirteen-year-old students.

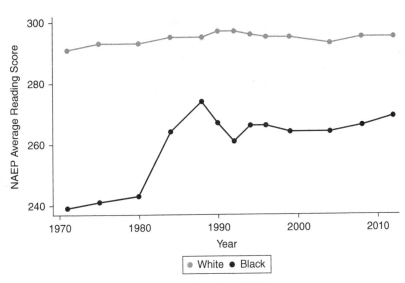

Note: Adapted from US Department of Education (2009).
Black includes African American. Race categories exclude Hispanic origin.

FIGURE 2.3. Trend in NAEP average reading scores for white and black seventeen-year-old students.

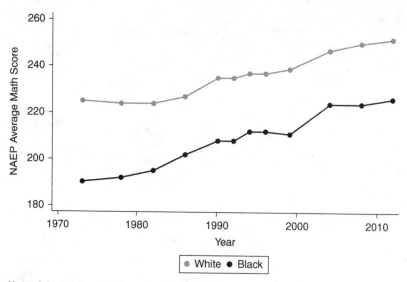

Note: Adapted from US Department of Education (2009).
Black includes African American. Race categories exclude Hispanic origin.

FIGURE 2.4. Trend in NAEP average math scores for white and black nine-year-old students.

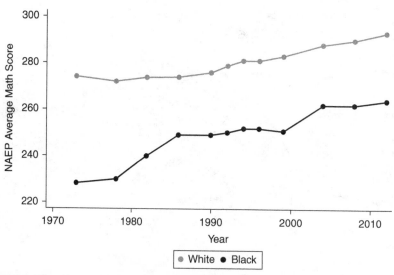

Note: Adapted from US Department of Education (2009).
Black includes African American. Race categories exclude Hispanic origin.

FIGURE 2.5. Trend in NAEP average math scores for white and black thirteen-year-old students.

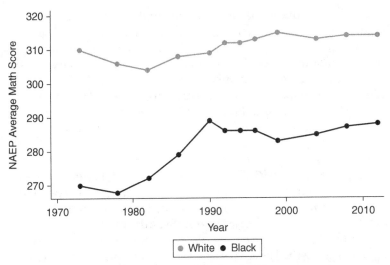

FIGURE 2.6. Trend in NAEP average math scores for white and black seventeen-year-old students.

for example, are highly concentrated in the lowest-achieving schools in many parts of the country; in California, black students are six times more likely than their white peers to attend the worst-performing third of schools in the state (Education Trust West 2010).

Yet demographic shifts, commonly cited as one of the most prominent factors to consider in K–12 policy related to equity and accountability, are not the only factors that should be given attention in understanding the mechanisms at play in education that produce gaps among racial and ethnic groups. In addition to historical events, family characteristics, and school infrastructure, greater attention should be given to the politics that drive decisions in education, from federal and state policy makers to the ideology of local communities. As outlined in the following text, this factor has been largely ignored but can have a significant effect on educational opportunities afforded to students.

The (Discounted) Role of (Local) Partisanship in Equal Educational Opportunities

The Progressive Era reforms provided a window to see how politics is not separate from education. Yet, after these reforms took place, politics was again largely removed from the discussion of educational processes, outputs, and outcomes. While discussion of the politics of education can be found at the perimeter of some educational research, much of this literature has not been

linked with studies of educational equity, first- and second-generation discrimination, or achievement gaps. This is especially the case in assessing the
role of local party politics. In fact, education is often viewed as a nonpartisan
territory – leaders of both Democratic and Republican parties encourage K–12
education improvement and success (albeit through sometimes differing pathways, see Chapter 1), and local school boards are largely elected in nonpartisan
races. As we noted earlier, a look at the history and development of local school
governance reveals that the assessment of schools as nonpartisan is grossly
misguided.

By the early 1800s, in the midst of steady growth by US states and territories and long before the Civil War, school committees began to develop
into bodies that were separate from the rest of a town's jurisdiction. These
governing bodies became formalized in 1826 in Massachusetts and quickly
spread throughout the country. These separate boards were generally funded
by local taxes and were formed as more schools were established to accom-
modate population growth. These boards were given primary authority over
the management of local public education, and this governance structure set a
precedent for local control that has continued to the present. This governance
structure created a decentralized system that lasted until the turn of the century
when Progressive Era efforts to remove corruption and politics from the local
and state governance of schools transformed boards from large groups of individuals in power under a system of patronage to a small group of individuals
who were appointed by the mayor. Centralization efforts have continued since
the early 1900s; in 1932, 127,520 local boards existed, while approximately
fourteen thousand boards are present today (Berry and West 2010; Scribner
and Layton 1995).

In assessing local school decisions and dynamics, the issue of political
ideology was introduced as least as far back as the discussion of competing
local values by Berube and Gittell (1969). Iannaccone (1975, 43), for example, described the micropolitics of education as concerned with "the interaction and political ideologies of social systems of teachers, administrators
and pupils with school buildings." The niche of existing education politics
research is centered on understanding the competing values in the community
that influence decision-making processes and, thus, policy outcomes. Mitchell
(1990, 166) argues that "both the context and the form of schooling is determined through the conflicts and coalitions found at the core of local, state,
and national political systems." In discussing the tensions between the values
of liberty and equality that surround education, Petersen and Fusarelli (2005,
x) contend that "board members are supposed to be trustees – that is, public
officials acting on behalf of all district residents. In practice, they are much
more like delegates advancing their personal agenda or the agenda of supporting political groups."

In the twenty-first century, these sentiments continue. School board members
who once oversaw all aspects of local public education must now "compete

with political actors scattered throughout the federal, state, and local governments as well as organized interest in the private sphere" (Howell 2005, 5). The public, however, largely continues to perceive school governance as a local issue; in a recent Phi Delta Kappa/Gallup poll (Bushaw and Calderon 2014), responses to "Who should have the greatest influence in deciding what is taught in public schools?" included 56 percent for the local school board, 28 percent for the state government, and 15 percent for the federal government (1 percent of respondents were unsure or did not answer). Many continue to find that education policy is not free of politics. Despite the fact that Progressive Era reforms were intended to remove politics from school governance, Finn (2003) notes that "[t]he inventors of school boards thought their reforms would keep education out of politics. In fact, it's immersed public schools in politics." Finn describes three types of individuals on school boards – aspiring politicians, former school employees who want to settle the score, and advocates of various causes. Finn and Keegan (2004, 1) also comment that "the romantic notion that local school boards are elected by local citizens has been replaced with the reality that these elections are essentially rigged. They are held at odd times, when practically nobody votes except those with a special reason to do so." This sentiment is further supported by a recent study of the American Association of School Administrators that found that 90 percent of school superintendents in large urban districts reported that interest groups actively placed pressure on board policies and operations (Opfer 2005).

Today's school board elections can substantially vary in structure, timing, and saliency. Board members may be elected as at-large members, in which the entire district votes for candidates, or through SMDs (or wards), where the district is split into smaller territories (see Chapter 3). Elections for various board positions may be staggered, and the timing of elections may coincide with state and national November elections or may be held separately. Importantly, many school board elections are ignored by voters (many local school board races experience voter turnout below 10 percent), which can lead to cases of long-serving incumbents who serve specific interest groups or positions for those using the school board as a credential that will boost the candidate in future, larger, and more contentious positions. Yet, the races can still be steeped with political content. Candidates, while running in a nonpartisan race, may gain the endorsement of the mayor or other elected officials linked to parties (Flannery 2013). Some races can become part of large campaigns; in 2011, for example, more than $2 million was spent on just three contested races in Colorado, North Carolina, and Virginia (Stover 2012). While research commenting on the political nature of local school governance exists, almost none of these studies consider the role of political parties and partisanship. Instead, much of this literature concentrates on the role of interest groups, especially teachers' unions (e.g., Anzia 2011). This book is intended to fill this gap by illustrating how (in)equities in educational opportunities for black students can be directly and strongly linked to partisanship.

Linking Research on Educational Equity and Party Politics

How can partisanship and race be justifiably linked in this research? We argue that politics is divided down racial lines. Brown-Dean et al. (2015) make this argument clear: political parties are now more sharply divided by race than any other issue, and this division is more pronounced than any other time in recent history. In the 2014 congressional elections, whites steadily voted for Republicans (62 percent) while only 10 percent of black voters did not provide support for Democrats (both Latinos and Asian Americans now vote majority Democrat as well). These racial divides (more than 50 percent for blacks vs. white) were much more pronounced than those for education (<5 percent), income (<20 percent), age (<15 percent), or gender (<10 percent) (see Brown-Dean et al. 2015, 18). While Brown-Dean et al. (2015, 12) take a different stance on the power of parties at the local level, arguing that parties "lack incentives to invest significant resources on turnout for local elections," they contend that "as overall turnout declines in local elections, the electorate may become less representative of the racial diversity of the community as a whole."

Even where research recognizes that partisanship and politics is part and parcel of local education systems, parsing out how and when the effects of partisanship are meaningful for student equity can be quite challenging. Currently, a wide variety of educational issues clearly have a partisan dimension. This includes the general preference by Republicans to oppose federal, more centralized reform efforts in favor of local control.[4] The dispute over Common Core standards has been painted as a federal initiative and has become a rallying point for Republican candidates. While both parties tend to support innovative school choice initiatives that allow students to leave failing schools, the support is stronger and more consistent for Republicans (those on the left have often been hostile to school vouchers). The link between a school board election and ideology or political party is not always transparent, and the larger effect of partisanship through the school system can get even murkier. An increasing number of scholars and popular news outlets alike recognize the role that business, interest groups, and partisan endorsements can play in the values and subsequent decisions of school board members (Reckhow et al. 2015).

A full recognition of the role of partisanship in public education in the United States also requires an understanding of the multiple dimensions of what partisanship is. Although political parties have a structure and a formal organization, at their base they are a collection of individuals who share a common set of values. There is no obvious reason why the partisan differences in values would not come out in discussions of education policy. Public education, after all, can be framed as a symbol of big government because schools are the largest public employer in the country. Educational systems frequently challenge

---

[4] The federal versus local distinction has been muddied somewhat by teachers' unions' opposition to standardized testing and the link of this testing to federal law.

beliefs and values when they teach evolution or sex education or address questions of race, federalism, and democratic rights (Berkman and Plutzer 2010 provide a good example of this discussion). It makes no sense to continue to ignore the partisan dimensions of US public education. The remainder of this book will bring light to how scholars may examine the effect of partisanship throughout the system of school districts, starting with the election of school board members and ending with student achievement and equity indicators.

Conclusion: Two Myths of Race and Education

This chapter examined two myths of race and education policy. The myth of separate but equal held sway over US education policy for more than one hundred years before it was finally rejected. Segregated education while always separate was never really equal. The myth of nonpartisan education policy that has persisted an equally long period of time, however, still dominates the scholarly and practical thinking in the United States. The empirical analysis in this book will demonstrate that partisanship has become a major driving force in educational equity that permeates the entire process of education from elections all the way down to the classroom and student performance. At times this relationship is direct; at other times it operates through a variety of other variables, but it is omnipresent.

3

The Politics of African-American School Board Representation

Partisanship, Structure, and Resources

Representation is a central concept in the study of politics (Eulau and Karps 1977; Mansbridge 1999; Pitkin 1967). With the increase in descriptive representation of women and racial minorities in legislative bodies worldwide, scholarly effort has focused on how electoral structures affect this descriptive representation (Baldez 2006; Canon 1999; Cox 1997; Epstein and O'Halloran 1999; Krook 2006; Lublin and Voss 2000; Norris 2004; Schwindt-Bayer and Mishler 2005; Shotts 2003a, 2003b).[1] Similar to the comparative literature, US scholarship concludes that the electoral success of minorities can be linked to electoral structures (Behr 2004; Canon 1999; Engstrom and McDonald 1982, 1986, 1997; Lublin 1997; Sass and Mehay 2003; Shah, Marschall, and Ruhil 2013, among others). One issue involving the relationship between electoral systems and African-American representation in the United States remains in doubt. At-large elections, long thought to limit the election of minorities to office, may have declined in influence, but the issue remains contested (see Leal, Martinez-Ebers, and Meier 2004; Trounstine and Valdini 2008; Welch 1990).

This chapter investigates how electoral structure influences African-American representation with study of the 1,800 largest school districts in the United States for the years 2001, 2004, and 2008. The logic of median voter models as applied to minority politics requires that the racial minority in question also be a numerical minority. If African Americans are a voting majority in a school district, then they should attain a majority of the seats on the board regardless of whether the system uses at-large elections or single-member districts (SMDs). As a result, the initial analysis in this chapter will focus on only those school districts where African Americans are less than 50 percent of the total population. In these cases, our findings linking electoral systems to

[1] Portions of this chapter were previously published as Meier and Rutherford (2014). This chapter has been augmented by substantial additional analysis.

38

descriptive representation show that African Americans actually do better in at-large systems. While this minority group may have been disadvantaged by at-large districts thirty years ago, they have overcome these hurdles and now appear to be better off under this type of electoral structure in the case of school board elections. Because this finding is neither predicted by theory nor precedented in the empirical literature, we consider several possible explanations and find that how electoral structures influence partisan incentives explains the apparent advantage of at-large elections for African Americans. These findings indicate that electoral structures designed to produce certain results (majoritarian outcomes) generate a set of rules that can actually be used in practice to increase the representation of racial minorities under specific conditions.

Voting Rights Litigation

While African Americans gained the legal right to vote in 1870 under the Fifteenth Amendment, several states actively sought to undermine access to voting for minority groups through literacy tests, poll taxes, grandfather clauses, and restricted voter registration methods. Prior to the passing of the Voting Rights Act (VRA) in 1965, for example, only 5.1 percent of blacks were registered to vote in Mississippi (Davidson and Grofman 1994). Through the support from national figures such as Lyndon Johnson as well as grassroots efforts and various marches by civil rights groups, the VRA was seen as a meaningful policy that would protect minority access to the polls (Arnwine and Johnson-Blanco 2013). This protection was offered most prominently through Sections 2 and 5. Section 2 prohibited voting laws that were discriminatory in intent or in practice and also allowed for federal observers at polling sites. Section 5 provided additional protection by requiring jurisdictions determined to have a history of discrimination (defined by a formula in Section 4(b)) to gain preclearance for any change in voting laws. Preclearance states originally included Alabama, Georgia, Louisiana, Mississippi, South Carolina, Virginia, and forty counties in North Carolina and was extended in 1975 to include Alaska, Arizona, and Texas.

In areas of the country that used literacy tests, poll taxes, grandfather clauses, restricted voter registration, or open intimidation and violence, the use of electoral structures such as at-large elections appear on their face to be more racially neutral. At the same time, the biases of at-large elections as a majoritarian institution were well known in both the North and the South. At-large elections were part of the progressive reforms of city government (and urban school districts) and designed to limit the voting influence of white ethnics (Davidson and Korbel 1981). The extensive experience with such systems would have been apparent to political jurisdictions that were now prohibited from using more overt methods of racial discrimination in voting.

A host of voting rights litigation against existing voting laws followed the passage of the VRA. Many of these cases challenged at-large elections on the grounds that at-large structures were linked to discrimination through vote dilution (Davidson and Grofman 1994). Dilution occurs when a voting structure minimizes or eliminates the voting power of a group; the system would allow the white majority to minimize the votes of African Americans in the presence of racially polarized voting. Although Section 5 preclearance requirements were largely not applied following the passage of the VRA, the 1969 decision in *Allen v. State Bd. of Elections*, involving complaints regarding elections in Virginia and Mississippi, made preclearance a prominent issue. Section 5, as interpreted by *Allen*, essentially generated greater oversight of election procedures in covered jurisdictions, allowing the court to monitor for vote dilution while forcing compliance when and if needed (Davidson and Grofman 1994). This decision was followed by an attempt to determine which factors would provide substantial evidence of vote dilution (and thus unconstitutional discrimination) in *White v. Regester* (1973) and *Zimmer v. McKeithen* (1973). The *Zimmer* criteria included no minority slating, unresponsive legislators, tenuous justifications for preferring at-large systems, and the existence of past discrimination, but still remained relatively vague in clarifying when and how evidence would be determinative of vote dilution.

Many additional suits followed *Allen* and *Zimmer* in which plaintiffs, bearing the burden for proving vote dilution, called for at-large systems in covered jurisdictions to change to SMD systems. In *Mobile v. Bolden* (1980), however, the court stepped back in the progression of VRA litigation. *Bolden* specified that discriminatory effects must be accompanied by discriminatory intent. Plaintiffs would have to prove both that an electoral structure generated racially discriminatory effects and that the structure was intended to produce such an effect.

Six years later the Court defined a three-pronged test for determining dilution – the minority group must be large in number and geographically concentrated to the extent that they would constitute a majority in a SMD; must be politically cohesive; and must prove the majority group votes as a bloc against minority group interests – in *Thornburg v. Gingles* (Blackman and Luschei 1999).

The courts and the Justice Department continued to have significant influence in the interpretation, implementation, and enforcement of the VRA. Since the passage of the policy, there have been more than six hundred successful cases of Section 2 litigation affecting more than nine hundred jurisdictions (Lee 2006). For many of these successful cases, the model remedy is to transition from an at-large system to a SMD system. For example, between 1970 and 1989, forty-two of the forty-eight cities in Alabama with populations of six thousand or more changed from at-large to SMD structures (Arnwine and Johnson-Blanco 2013). SMD structures are largely accepted as providing greater minority access to polls following cases such as *Baker v. Carr* (1962) and *Reynolds v. Sims* (1964) that codified the idea of "one person, one vote" for jurisdictions across the country.

The first step in any analysis of the politics of education, specifically how politics plays a role in the generation of educational inequities, is to examine the electoral process. School board members play a crucial role in both financial and policy decisions that are likely to affect students. To the extent that African Americans are fairly represented on school boards, it is likely that African-American policy preferences will be reflected in policy debates and political decisions. Given this initial starting point and the recent cases litigated under the VRA, it is important to determine whether disparities in African-American representation are still evident in at-large districts compared to SMD elections. Because the median voting logic predicts that at-large elections detrimentally affect minority populations, we will focus primarily on jurisdictions where African Americans are a minority population in determining whether and how electoral structures affect descriptive representation.

Electoral Systems and African-American Representation

Extensive literature holds that electoral systems create a set of rules that can advantage some groups and disadvantage others (Davidson and Korbel 1981; Hays 1964; Norris 2004; Tyack 1974). Electoral structures worldwide come in a large variety of forms. Within the United States, however, two systems dominate. At-large elections are majoritarian systems that elect all representatives by the entire jurisdiction; ward, or SMD, elections divide the jurisdiction into smaller electoral units where candidates run for a single seat in smaller electoral units. At-large elections permit a simple majority of voters to control all seats in an election;[2] SMDs allow for the possibility that a numerical minority in the entire jurisdiction might be able to win an election in one of the individual wards.

The relative merit of at-large versus ward elections has generated a lively debate on the descriptive representation of African Americans in the United States. Because Congress relies on SMDs as do the overwhelming majority of positions for state legislatures, the analyses have focused on local governments – city councils and school boards.[3] A large number of studies on both city councils and school boards concludes that blacks are more likely to be elected in SMDs than in at-large elections (Davidson and Grofman 1994; Davidson and Korbel 1981; Engstrom and McDonald 1981; Karnig and Welch 1982; Lublin 1999;

---

[2] An at-large electoral system could be designed to be less majoritarian by allowing individuals to cast fewer votes than seats or by allowing individuals to cast all their votes for a single candidate. Such systems are relatively rare in the United States.

[3] Studies at the national or state level are also limited by the extensive racial gerrymander whereby minorities are clustered into a few districts to create majority-minority districts. As a result, Grose, Mangum, and Martin (2007, 452) conclude that African Americans can get elected to Congress only in districts with at least 40 percent African-American population. School boards are distinctly different in access. Our data in 2008 contain 540 African-American board members in at-large systems with less than 40 percent black population. In addition, 293 African Americans serve on boards with less than 10 percent black population regardless of the electoral system.

Marschall, Shah, and Ruhil 2010; Moncrief and Thompson 1992; Polinard et al. 1994; Robinson and England 1981; Stewart, England, and Meier 1989; Trounstine and Valdini 2008). In some cases, these studies are able to document a change in representation within a jurisdiction after the electoral system changed (Davidson and Korbel 1981; Polinard et al. 1994).[4]

Based on the logic of the median voter, wards/SMDs should produce more descriptive representation for racial minorities if electorates are polarized along racial lines (i.e., that race is a significant electoral cleavage)[5] and if the SMDs are drawn in such a way that they are not microcosms of the overall jurisdiction, either as a result of residential segregation or perhaps because they are gerrymandered to facilitate racial representation. In such circumstances, blacks (and other numerical minorities) are likely to achieve greater descriptive representation in SMD systems than in at-large systems because they can run in smaller, more homogeneous districts with larger black populations.

Other studies question the detrimental impact of at-large elections on descriptive representation, either disputing the negative impact on minorities in general or suggesting that the impact has disappeared over time. MacManus (1978) concluded that electoral arrangements do not directly impose any significant burden on the election of blacks (but see Davidson 1979; MacManus 1979). Other studies that find no impact of electoral structure include Cole's (1974) examination of sixteen New Jersey cities, Arrington and Watts's (1991) study of North Carolina school boards, and Fraga and Elis's (2009) examination of Latino representation in school districts in California.

A second set of studies has suggested the ill-effects of at-large elections have declined either because most of the at-large systems in jurisdictions with large minority populations have been changed (as the result of lawsuits or pressure from the Justice Department) or because black candidates have adapted their candidacies to the realities of at-large elections (see Sass and Mehay 2003; Welch 1990). The studies concluding that at-large elections no longer matter for descriptive representation, however, are not definitive. Because populations have continued to shift and the vigor of the Justice Department in challenging electoral systems has waned (Leal et al. 2004; Trounstine and Valdini 2008), there are now more jurisdictions with sizable black populations that rely on at-large elections.[6] The recent Supreme Court decision (*Shelby County, Ala. v. Holder* 2013; Childress 2013) and the recent litigation under the California VRA (Merl 2013) also suggest this issue is not settled.

---

[4] Marschall, Ruhil, and Shah (2010) note that representation has increased much more on councils than on school boards.

[5] This study will not address the extent of racial polarization. There is an extensive literature in public opinion that shows strong correlation between race and attitudes on a wide variety of public policy issues.

[6] There are 154 school districts in this study with at least 15 percent black population and an at-large election system suggesting that at-large systems still coexist with significant African-American populations.

The literature has also ignored one fundamental element of US elections – the role of partisanship. Although the overwhelming majority of local elections, particularly school board elections (87 percent) are nonpartisan, political parties are likely to have an interest in who wins these elections (either as a tryout for recruiting candidates to run for partisan offices or because local governments implement policies enacted by state and federal law). Individual partisans are also likely to participate in local elections and are likely to vote consistent with their partisan ideology. More active partisans are likely to help recruit candidates for local office, assist in campaigning, or contribute funds. In short, there is no reason to expect that party identifiers will check their partisanship at the door simply because a local election is defined as nonpartisan (Browning, Marshall, and Tabb 1984, 44).

The Political and Racial Context of School Districts

The primary responsibility for elementary and secondary education in the United States is vested in local school districts. More than any other political institution, local education was dramatically transformed by the Progressive Era movement and the creation of the independent school district with its separate taxing authority (see Chapter 2). Schools were removed from the jurisdiction of local governments, and the reforms for school districts included nonpartisan elections with candidates running at-large rather than within smaller SMDs (or wards) during elections that were not coincident with other state or national elections. Patronage appointments were replaced by professional administrators and teachers with hiring based on a merit system; executive authority was vested in a professionally trained superintendent. The objective of these changes was clearly to disadvantage political parties with their ties to recent immigrants and advantage the interests of middle-class and upper-class business and professional interests (Davidson and Korbel 1981; Hays 1964; Tyack 1974). Although framed as a way to eliminate politics from education, the reforms in reality simply transformed the political environment from one favoring urban political machines to one favoring the interests of the reform coalition. The low turnout of nonpartisan elections held in the spring has meant an electorate dominated by those with a direct interest in schools, primarily parents and teachers. This electoral condition generated one factor not anticipated by the reformers in large urban areas – the increased activity and influence of teachers' unions in recruiting and electing school board members (Katznelson 1981).

Contemporary school district politics in the United States also often has a racial dimension (Henig et al. 1999; Orr 1999; Portz, Stein, and Jones 1999; Rich 1996). Access to education was central to the civil rights movement, and the legal and political efforts to desegregate schools lasted for several decades (Bullock and Lamb 1984) and continue to the present day (Orfield and Lee 2005). The elimination of *de jure* segregation then shifted to other issues with racial elements including equal funding (Evans, Murray, and Schwab 1997), greater choice among schools for minorities and others (Witte 2000), disparities in school discipline (Skiba et al. 2002), assignments to special education classes (Eitle 2002), and, with the requirement to publish test scores by race under the federal No Child Left Behind law, the racial gap in test scores (Jencks and Phillips 1998; Thernstrom and Thernstrom 2003). Although not every issue in education politics has a racial element, a substantial number explicitly or inexplicitly link to racial disparities.

Modeling African-American Representation

The median voter model is a relatively model of the political process. Similarly, the literature on race and representation in the United States specifies a relatively parsimonious theoretical model whereby minority representation is a function of minority resources, electoral structure, and allies (see Chapter 1). All factors relate to the ability of minority groups to mobilize political resources within the constraints of electoral structures (for a full discussion see Browning et al. 1984; Meier, Stewart, and England 1989). The primary electoral resource is the size of the group's population, and population size is always the most significant factor in all empirical assessments of minority representation. In addition to population size, the urban politics literature, built primarily on studies of white ethnics, argues that viable electoral candidates require a middle-class status that permits sufficient time for participation in politics (Karnig 1976; Wolfinger 1965). Middle-class status also provides a base for raising campaign funds. Although this argument has intuitive appeal, most empirical studies of African-American representation find that African-American levels of income, education, and other resources have little impact on the level of representation. Our model will include measures of African-American education, income, and home ownership as well as a measure of white poverty designed to tap the relative economic status of blacks versus whites.

The role of electoral structure, the central concern of this chapter, is incorporated using an interaction between structure and population (see Engstrom and McDonald 1981). The theory implies that structure affects the efficiency of the process of translating population into votes. Comparing the various structure coefficients as they interact with population provides an estimate of how well the group is represented relative to its population under different electoral structures.[7]

---

[7] The advantage that ward elections have over at-large elections should be contingent on the degree of residential segregation. If there is no residential segregation, all of the smaller wards are racially the same as the entire jurisdiction, and African Americans will be a minority in all of them. Unfortunately, incorporating residential segregation correctly requires an interaction with ward election systems. Given that the specification already includes the ward variable and its interaction with population, adding this second interaction generates massive collinearity and

Finally, Browning et al. (1984) in their comparative case studies of San Francisco–area local governments recognized that when racial minorities are a numerical minority, they need to be part of an electoral (and governing) coalition. Lacking a population majority, a racial minority needs to rely on the votes or the support of white liberals who share the minorities' views on various election issues. The clear evidence from case studies, however, is difficult to translate to large-N studies because "white liberals" is usually measured by demographic surrogates such as education (see Marschall et al. 2010). This study will introduce two new measures of allies – a school district–level measure of Democratic partisanship and the relative influence of unions. Democratic partisanship as reflected in voting behavior is a reasonable indicator of political preferences. Given that African-American support for the Democratic Party often exceeds 90 percent, it is only a modest leap to conclude that voting patterns are a good indicator of shared political values. Unions provide both allies and also some organizational capacity with experience in contesting elections.[8] Unions can generate substantial labor and in-kind contributions that are valuable in local elections that are less likely to be completely media driven.

Data and Measurement

The data for this analysis were drawn from three sources. Basic demographic and socioeconomic information were collected from the 2000 US Census school district files; school districts are not conterminous with cities or other jurisdictions and require the use of special census files. Data on the partisan distribution of school districts were constructed using data on elections returns for 2004 and 2008 presidential elections (see following text). The data pertaining to school board representation for 2001, 2004, and 2008 came from original surveys of all school districts with student populations of more than five thousand as of 1999. This cut-off point covers a clear majority – approximately 75 percent – of all primary and secondary school enrollment. Of the 5,493 district years, 5,192 (a 94.5 percent response rate) provided data on school board composition. Because the theoretical logic concerns numerical minorities, we eliminate all school districts that have an African-American majority (leaving 4,980 total district years); and because some census data are coded as missing,[9] the actual number of cases in the analysis is a bit less.

makes the regression estimates unreliable. We provide some evidence on the role of residential segregation later in the chapter by splitting the sample.

[8] One other resource is the black church that has been the basis of organization and mobilization in African-American community (McDaniel 2008). Unfortunately, data on black church members in general does not exist; the Glenmary Research Center, the primary source of church membership data, does not include black churches in their decennial census.

[9] In a jurisdiction with a small minority population, e.g., there may not be a sufficient number of black families to get an estimate of black home ownership.

The original surveys of school districts collected information on the electoral structure of the school districts as well as the racial representation on the school board. Representation is measured as the percentage of African Americans on the school board, the most common method of measuring racial representation in the literature.[10] The measure of African-American population is from the 2000 Census files and is the percentage of the population that is African American within the school district.[11]

School boards have two predominant electoral structures. Approximately 59 percent use pure at-large systems with all representatives elected at-large. Another 29 percent use pure SMD systems with all members elected from such districts. A modest number of districts are dependent school districts, and board members are appointed by the chief elected official for the jurisdiction that contains the school district rather than elected (3 percent).[12] The remaining districts (9 percent) mix these three systems. To avoid losing all the mixed electoral system cases, the ward variable and the appointed variable were measured as the proportion of members that were selected by ward or by appointment and thus ranges from zero to one (by analogy, the at-large variable is measured similarly).

Four measures of the relative resources of the African-American community are included – the percentage of African Americans over the age of twenty-five with a college degree, the percentage of African-American families that own a home, the per capita income for African Americans, and the percentage of whites living in poverty. The first three variables capture the absolute level of black socioeconomic resources. The latter measure is often included in these models as a measure of social distance based on the argument that white voters may be more willing to accept a middle-class black candidate over a lower-class white candidate (Evans and Giles 1986; Rocha and Hawes 2009).

---

[10] A modest number of studies treat school board and city council membership as a count variable (Marschall et al. 2010; Trounstine and Valdini 2008) with a control for board size (the range is 5 to 19). The percentage measure of representation strikes us as having greater face validity because the concern with proportionality compares population to representation rather than simply the presence of representation. A total of 796 district-years in this analysis have two or more African-American representatives, and the difference between 14 percent and 28 percent or 42 percent representation could have substantive benefits.

[11] We use the 2000 Census for all demographic variables rather than interpolating the years between the decennial census. These demographic variables change only slowly for African Americans given their relatively stable population. The only demographic variable (see following text) with a consistent substantive effects is the percentage of black population, and the correlation between these figures for 2000 and 2010 is .9792. Interpolation of census figures would not influence the reported results.

[12] This 3 percent includes those districts that are taken over by state governments or other units. A small set of large urban districts in major cities have been taken over and run (usually temporarily) by another unit of government. In such cases, boards are usually dismissed and appointed individuals take their place. Less visible are those districts where state government takes them over as the result of financial or performance problems and seeks to improve district performance (McDermott 2011; Rutherford 2014).

Creating a measure of potential allies or coalition partners has focused on a measure of liberal whites. Such a measure is difficult to estimate because we do not have public opinion data on subnational jurisdictions as small as cities and school districts. We use the percentage of Democratic voters as our first surrogate. The Democratic percentage variable was calculated by taking presidential election returns for 2004 and 2008 at the county level (the closest level of aggregation to school districts) and regressing these percentages on a set of demographic variables including race, income, and education. The coefficients from these regressions were then used to adjust the Democratic percentages for the county where the school district is located to a school district Democratic percentage.[13] As an example, Harris County Texas (Houston) has a Democratic percentage of 47.8 but contains several school districts that range from 36.3 percent Democratic (Channelview Independent School District) to 61.4 percent (North Forest Independent School District).[14] The measure of Democratic partisanship should be viewed as more than just a measure of liberal whites; the Democratic Party is also a political institution and is unlikely to be a passive actor in the electoral process.

Using national elections for the president to estimate overall partisanship of a school district is the best available approximation for two reasons. First, all jurisdictions vote at the same time for the same candidates, allowing for better comparisons across school districts. Using elections for congressional or state legislative elections would need to overcome issues of competition, timing, and turnout. Many of those races are uncontested or virtually uncontested given that no funds are spent to support the election of one of the party's candidates. Senate and gubernatorial elections occur at different times of the year and, in the case of gubernatorial elections, runoff systems can vary substantially (e.g., in a state like Louisiana, the two final candidates might both be from the same party). Because turnout is generally much lower in these elections, accurately estimating partisanship at the school district level becomes difficult. Second, using public opinion data based on national public opinion polls and some spatial aggregation techniques (see Warshaw and Rodden 2012), we have a measure of ideology for the school districts with 20,000+ students. The correlation between this ideology measure and our partisan measure for these large districts is 0.8. We interpret this as a strong indicator of validity of our partisanship measure.

A second potential set of allies for African Americans are unions, especially teachers' unions that have played a strong role in school board elections

---

[13] As an illustration, the county regressions show that a 1 percentage point increase in black population is associated with a .39 percentage point increase in Democratic vote. If a school district had 10 percentage points more black population than the county that the school district was located in, we adjusted the district Democratic percentage upward by 3.9 percentage points.

[14] The North Forrest Independent School District was taken over by the State of Texas in 2013 and merged with the Houston Independent School District.

(Katznelson 1981; Moe 2009). The ideal measure would be the percentage of the teaching force in each district that is a member of either the American Federation of Teachers (AFT) or the National Education Association. Neither organization is willing to provide membership numbers at the school district level; the AFT does not even provide figures at the state level. As a result, we opted for using the percentage of the workforce that was unionized in that state. This assumes that the presence of unions within a state are either correlated with the level of teacher unionization, and thus that teachers are more likely to be unionized, or simply that unions per se might be a potential source of allies for African Americans.[15] The union measure also taps elements of organizational structure in the community that the Democrat measure might not. Unions aggressively contest elections and can generate volunteers as well as in-kind contributions; such resources are especially valuable in low turnout elections such as those for school boards (Bascia 1994).

The data set contains measures of each of the variables for three different years. Panel data sets such as this one can be affected by both serial correlation and unit heterogeneity (Durbin and Watson 1951; Levin, Lin, and Chu 2002). We deal with the serial correlation problem by including a set of dummy variables for the individual years. To adjust for unit heteroscedasticity, we cluster the standard errors by district (Wooldridge 2003).

At-Large Elections and Black Representation

Table 3.1 relates African-American population to African-American representation on the school boards in four regressions. Column 1 uses a single independent variable, black population. Because the intercept of this equation is essentially zero, the slope coefficient can be interpreted as a representation ratio. An increase of 1 percentage point in black population is associated with a 1.048 percentage point increase in black representation.[16] There are two surprises here: the representation coefficient is not less than one, and it is significantly albeit modestly greater than one. African Americans receive slightly more representation than would be expected based on population alone. School boards are anomalous institutions in American politics in this regard; black representation ratios are consistently less than one in all other

---

[15] We also tried the per capita contributions of education interest groups to political candidates (http://www.opensecrets.org/) and a per capita measure of education interest groups provided by David Lowery from the comparative state interest group data set (Lowery and Gray 1993). Neither variable was related to school board election outcomes. We also tried a measure of public-sector unionism, but this measure was unrelated to election outcomes.

[16] This relationship is generally linear and does appear to fit the cube law linking population or votes to legislative seats. The outliers do bend the regression line a bit so that both a cubic and a fourth order polynomial have all significant terms (although add little explanation). The fourth order polynomial is a rough step function with a positive linear term, a negative squared term, a positive cubic term, and a negative fourth order term.

TABLE 3.1. *Impact of Electoral Structure on the Quantity of Black Representation: School Board Seats*

Independent Variable	Dependent Variable: Percent Blacks on School Board			
	Model 1	Model 2	Model 3	Model 4
Intercept	0.140	−0.132	0.103	−4.761*
	(0.215)	(0.254)	(0.564)	(1.038)
Black Population Percentage	1.048*	1.142*	1.143*	1.126*
	(0.023)	(0.046)	(0.048)	(0.049)
Ward Elections		0.394	0.484	0.878*
		(0.380)	(0.417)	(0.428)
Ward X Population Percentage		−0.179*	−0.178*	−0.158*
		(0.055)	(0.056)	(0.055)
Appointed System		2.214	2.199+	2.409+
		(1.248)	(1.330)	(1.355)
Appointed X Black Population		0.016	0.014	0.010
		(0.067)	(0.069)	(0.069)
Black Education (College Percent)			0.011	0.001
			(0.010)	(0.010)
Black Family Income (000s)			0.003	−0.004
			(0.010)	(0.005)
Black Home Ownership			−0.020*	−0.009
			(0.006)	(0.006)
White Poverty Percentage			0.072	0.138*
			(0.046)	(0.049)
Unionization				0.085*
				(0.040)
District Democrat Percent				0.064*
				(0.019)
2004	0.059	0.070	0.071	0.083
	(0.181)	(0.183)	(0.186)	(0.187)
2008	0.403+	0.406	0.420	0.460+
	(0.258)	(0.262)	(0.266)	(0.268)
R^2	.61	.62	.62	.62
F	673.15	389.74	262.17	224.91
Standard Error	8.83	8.75	8.81	8.77
N	4980	4952	4879	4836

Districts where blacks are less than 50 percent of total population; errors clustered by Local Education Agency ID (LEAID); standard errors in parenthesis.

* $p < .05$; + $p < .10$

legislative bodies.[17] We will return to this puzzle of black overrepresentation after examining the role of structure and other factors as determinants.

The classic way to examine electoral structure is to create a set of interaction terms as recommended by Engstrom and McDonald (1981). They proposed an equation that included black population, a dummy variable for ward electoral systems, and the interaction between the dummy variable and black population. This estimation presents a direct test of whether representation in ward systems is significantly different statistically from that in at-large systems. We follow that recommendation with two slight adjustments. First, some school boards are appointed rather than elected, so we include another set of coefficients for appointive systems.[18] Second, other school board selection processes are mixed with some members elected at-large and some by ward (and in some cases some members are appointed). Rather than omitting the mixed systems, we substitute the proportion of members elected by ward (or appointed for that variable) in the interaction. This substitution means that our interpretation will compare pure ward with pure at-large systems but use the full range of cases for more efficient estimates.

The second column of Table 3.1 contains this interactive regression, and the third column then adds four resources variables that the literature suggests can affect black electoral success – black education levels (percent with college degrees), black median family income, black home ownership, and percentage of whites living in poverty. These demographic factors that translate into economic resources have only a modest relationship with representation (the joint f-test = 2.96, p. = .02, shows these predictors add to the empirical model but do not reveal many significant relationships), suggesting that black representation on school boards is almost exclusively a function of black population and electoral structure (Marschall and Ruhil 2006; Marschall et al. 2010; Rocha 2007, but see following text).

Using the results in column 3, in a pure at-large system, the ward election variable, the appointive variable, and their interactions will be equal to zero. The relationship between black population and black representation in an at-large system reduces to the following:

Representation = .103 + 1.143 Population

Because the intercept (.103) is not significant, this equation indicates that blacks in at-large systems are overrepresented by approximately 14 percent, a percentage that is statistically different from equal representation (that is a

[17] Meier et al. (1989, 63) report a representation coefficient of 1.002 for their 1986 data so equal representation on school boards is not a recent phenomenon, but see the underrepresentation reported by Marschall et al. (2010).

[18] Appointed systems are generally found in dependent school districts that are so named because they are subunits of another unit of government such as a county or a city. Districts that are taken over by the state or another unit would also fall into this category during the takeover period.

slope of 1.0). For a pure ward system, the appointive variables are equal to zero and the second set of coefficients (the ward set) can be added to the initial at-large coefficients as follows:

Representation = .103 + .484 + (1.143 – .178) Population
Representation = .587 + .965 Population

Because the ward intercept term (.484) is not significant, one concludes there is no difference in intercepts in the two electoral systems. The slope interaction, however, is statistically significant; blacks receive less representation in ward-based systems than they do in at-large systems. A 1 percentage point increase in black population is associated with only a .965 percentage point increase in black representation in ward systems. Although this representation coefficient is not statistically different from 1.0 suggesting blacks are equitably represented by ward elections, it is significantly different from the at-large slope and thus blacks are significantly worse off than they would be with at-large elections. As an illustration with 40 percent of the population, black representation is predicted to be 45.8 percent in an at-large system but only 39.2 percent in a ward system. The differences are statistically significant and show the opposite effect that electoral systems have on Latino representation (Leal et al. 2004).

For appointive systems, both the slope and the intercept differ in interesting ways. Because the ward variables are equal to zero in an appointive system, the representation relationship in these districts becomes:

Representation = .103 + 2.200 + (1.143 – .014) Population
Representation = 2.303 + 1.129 Population

Any interpretation of this equation, however, needs to be qualified simply because the slope change is not statistically significant and the intercept coefficient only significant at the 0.10 level, in part due to the small number of these systems for this set of districts. The basic conclusion is that appointed systems are little different from at-large elections in terms of descriptive representation. Because board members are appointed by the mayor or another electoral official, descriptive representation is often a way to make symbolic gestures to various communities. Whether such representation has any substantive impact is open to question.[19]

The final regression equation in Table 3.1 introduces partisanship and unions to the model. Although only 13 percent of these school board elections are partisan and elections are generally not held at the same time as

[19] The other structural element is board size, which Marschall et al. (2010) find is important for whether blacks get any representation (as opposed to proportional representation) on a board. They find size matters for city councils but not school boards. In this data set, board size does matter but the impact of it is small (0.38 percent increase in representation if board size goes from five to nine; 96.5 percent of school boards have five, seven, or nine members). Including total size in the equations in Tables 3.1 and 3.2 does not change the findings about structure or any other variables (not shown).

partisan elections, there are reasons why one might expect that black representation might be affected by the partisan distribution in the district. Browning
et al. (1984) contend that racial minorities need to form coalitions with liberal
whites to govern, and the Democratic Party would be the logical place to seek
liberal whites. Education issues at times split on partisan lines, and the general
expectation is that African Americans might perceive more commonality with
the Democratic Party on such issues given their strong ties to the party. The
regression shows that partisanship matters; all other things being equal, a district with 50 percent Democrats would have an additional 3.2 percent black
school board members. Unions also matter. A 10 percentage point increase
in the unionized workforce (this is a significant jump given the range is from
2.9 percent in North Carolina to 23.2 percent in New York), however, would
add less than 1 percent to representation. Adding these variables has a major
impact on the intercept, which suggests that the influence of these variables will
occur primarily in districts with smaller black populations. Their addition also
brings white poverty into statistical significance.

Table 3.1 presents the puzzle of African-American representation in stark
terms. African-American politicians have somehow overcome the logical limitations of at-large elections to the extent that they have not just neutralized
the impact but to the point where black electoral fortunes are better in at-large
elections. This finding is clearly a puzzle in the literature given that there are
no formal or even anecdotal discussions of why at-large elections could overrepresent African Americans when they are a minority of the population.

We considered five explanations for this phenomena and found each of
them wanting. First, because school board elections are characterized by low
voter turnout (Wirt and Kirst 1997), we considered whether African Americans
might be relatively more likely to vote in school board elections because they
are more likely to have children in the schools. To assess this hypothesis, we
control for the racial distribution of the school enrollment. While the inclusion
of this variable is significant, it does not affect the relationship between structure and representation (see Table A3.1).

Second, we probed whether the differences might be a function of the different age distributions of African Americans and others. Younger populations
are disadvantaged because those under the age of eighteen cannot vote. When
we controlled for the racial percentages of the voting age population in the
models in Table 3.1, the results did not affect the relationship between structure and population (see Table A3.2).

Third, African-American politicians have several decades of experience in
running for and winning urban elections. This experience could translate into
greater levels of skill that might provide an advantage in running in at-large
elections. Although we have no measure of candidate skill, we do have a prior
measure from 1992 of successful black candidates. When we control for prior
successful black candidates, however, the impact of at-large elections remains
undiminished (see Table A3.3).

Fourth, one might think that these results are an anomaly generated by demographic trends. Many whites left urban school systems as the result of desegregation or other migration reasons and thus created school districts with de facto black majorities (Clotfelter 2004; Schneider 2008; Wilson 1985). More recently, large numbers of Latinos have moved into these urban districts. Might the results reflect black majorities or black pluralities exploiting the electoral system in regard to Latinos? We assessed this possibility even though the analysis deleted all school districts with an African-American population majority. Controlling for Latino population, however, had no impact on the basic findings (see Table A3.4).[20]

Fifth, many recent immigrants to these school districts, particularly in urban areas, are not citizens. As such, noncitizens generally cannot vote in elections (there are some exceptions, see Kini 2005, but they are not common). As the number of noncitizens increases, the relative weight of the vote of citizens, including African-American citizens, increases. Controlling for the percentage of noncitizens, however, had no impact on the findings presented (see Table A3.5).

Having eliminated these five explanations, how else might African Americans overcome the biases of at-large elections, and who might have the incentive to create a system that permits them to overcome these biases? Electoral structures are simply a set of rules with biases, and there is no logical reason why any one group would not seek to use the existing rules to the group's advantage. The logical way to overcome the biases is to put together a slate of candidates to run as a bloc or to put together a majority coalition behind a candidate in an at-large election.[21] If this coalition fairly or overrepresented blacks among its candidates and if the coalition supporting the candidates was a majority, at-large elections would generate results very much like those for Table 3.1.[22] Who might have an incentive to put together such a slate of candidates or such a coalition? One possibility is a group, like the Democratic Party, that needs African-American votes or sees compatibility with African-American political interests. When might the Democratic Party have the incentive and capacity to put together coalitions and slates of candidates for school board elections (particularly given that most of these elections are on their face nonpartisan)? Democrats would have this incentive and capacity if they are a majority in

---

[20] Black overrepresentation comes at the expense of white representation not at the expense of Latinos. Although Latino population is unrelated to black representation, Latino representation has a slight negative relationship with African-American representation. The percentage of Latinos on the school board is significant when entered into the final model in Table 3.1, but the coefficient is only -.0275 indicating that 10 percent Latino representation reduced black representation by .275 percent all other things being equal.

[21] On the use of nonpartisan slating groups to block the election of minority representation see Fraga (1988).

[22] This is complicated a bit given that not all at-large members are elected at the same time; school boards generally have staggered terms.

the school district and if they need African-American votes to win elections other than school board elections. Supporting African-American candidates for school board elections could be one way for a party to demonstrate a credible commitment to push African-American issues in other policy jurisdictions. Based on this logic, the implication is that if the Democratic Party can win school board elections, it would also have the incentive to put together a coalition at the school district level to build stronger ties between the party and African-American voters. When Democrats constitute a voting majority in the school district, the inherent biases of at-large elections should overrepresent Democrats and hence African Americans who are part of the Democratic majority.

We can test this logic with a measure of Democratic vote at the school district level and run regressions that divide the districts into those with a Democratic majority and those with a Republican majority (Table 3.2).[23] Again we combined the regressions to generate a single regression for ward and at-large districts in jurisdictions with potential Democratic majorities and those without as follows:

Democratic districts

At-large   Representation = −2.330 + 1.208 Population
Ward   Representation = −1.663 + 1.057 Population

Republican districts

At-large   Representation = −2.957 + .928 Population
Ward   Representation = −2.553 + .883 Population

These results show a pattern that is consistent with the Democratic Party acting to create coalitions for the school board in districts where the party is a majority. In Democratic school districts, African Americans gain 121 percent of the representation that their population merits (with a modest threshold) in at-large elections but only 106 percent of the representation in ward systems.[24] In Republican school districts, structure has no significant impact on representation. African Americans are slightly underrepresented in both at-large and ward systems with Republican majorities, but the level of underrepresentation is not statistically different from zero (or from 1.0). The coefficients, however, are statistically different from those for the Democratic districts. The other interesting finding is that the independent impact of partisanship only adds to the prediction in districts that have a Republican majority, but this is to be expected given

---

[23] This appears to be the optimal point to split the sample as other splits do not present results as clearly as those presented here. The split still contains error because there are questions of mobilization and the measure of partisanship is based on national vote totals that could be affected by the candidates running for the presidency. The partisan variable should be considered just an indicator of some underlying dimension that reflects the propensity of the population to vote Democratic.

[24] The at-large coefficient is significantly different from 1.0; the ward coefficient is not.

TABLE 3.2. *Partisan Fortunes and the Impact of Structure on Representation: School Boards*

Dependent Variable: Percent Blacks on School Board		
Independent Variable	<50% Dem	>50% Dem
	Model 1	Model 2
Intercept	−2.970	−2.330
	(1.794)	(2.572)
Black Population Percentage	0.928*	1.208*
	(0.072)	(0.063)
Ward Elections	0.417	0.667
	(0.553)	(0.591)
Ward X Population Percentage	−0.045	−0.151+
	(0.071)	(0.079)
Appointed System	3.042	1.463
	(2.655)	(1.542)
Appointed X Black Population	0.172	−0.050
	(0.149)	(0.075)
Black Education (College Percent)	−0.011	0.013
	(0.013)	(0.014)
Black Family Income (000s)	−0.004	−0.007
	(0.009)	(0.005)
Black Home Ownership	−0.004	−0.014+
	(0.009)	(0.008)
White Poverty Percentage	0.092	0.218*
	(0.063)	(0.082)
Unionization	0.045	0.043
	(0.060)	(0.058)
South	−0.404	−0.072
	(0.783)	(0.970)
District Democrat Percent	0.079*	0.018
	(0.038)	(0.038)
2004	0.047	0.022
	(0.232)	(0.305)
2008	0.290	0.540
	(0.322)	(0.452)
R^2	.53	.68
F	92.22	128.03
Standard Error	8.376	9.019
N	2672	2152

Districts where blacks are less than 50 percent of total population; errors clustered by LEAID; standard errors in parenthesis.

* $p < .05$; + $p < .10$

that the sample split absorbs the party impact for the Democratic majority districts. Partisanship and party incentives, therefore, appear to predict results that are consistent with the existing empirical patterns.[25] To make sure the findings occur as the result of party rather than region given the Republican domination of the South, we also add a control for southern districts.[26] We classified a district as southern if it was located in a state that operated a *de jure* segregated school system in 1954 when the Supreme Court declared such systems unconstitutional for the first time.[27] The coefficient for South is not statistically significant and its inclusion has no impact on the relationship for the party variable.

The nature of comparison in the preceding text stresses the marginal effect of electoral structure. The other way to combine the coefficients is to contrast how changes in party affect the coefficients for the various structures. For at-large elections, a Democratic majority increases the impact of the

[25] To systematically demonstrate the role of political parties would require a survey of party officials (school board officials are generally hesitant to discuss political influence given the norm of the independent school district). Lacking that information, we conducted eight semistructured interviews with school board members, Democratic Party officials, and journalists covering school board elections. In half the districts, respondents mentioned the role of parties and partisanship in the elections; in two districts, party officials stated that they actively participated in recruiting candidates to run for the school board and considered this activity part of their overall political strategy. In other districts, the respondents stated that the Democratic Party did not take an active role but that the coalitions that recruited and supported school board candidates (teachers' associations, unions, advocacy groups, black churches, the NAACP, etc.) were very similar to the coalitions supporting Democratic candidates. Much of the influence of partisanship is informal and focuses on the recruitment and support of African-American candidates by individuals who identify with the Democratic Party.

[26] A modest number of empirical studies investigate the regional aspects of representation in the United States. The scholarship in this area yields inconsistent findings and usually does not examine substantive representation. Rocha's (2007) work on school boards finds regional effects for African Americans and Latinos. Sass and Mehay (1995), in a study of 2,500 US cities with varying populations, found that African Americans fared worse in terms of representation in southern cities with at-large elections in 1981 than any other region while district elections had a substantial positive effect. Bullock and MacManus (1993) found that southern cities (populations 25,000+) that used at-large election by post or that had pure at-large systems decreased representation for African-American city council members, but other at-large forms had no impact. Sass and Pitman (2000) examine African-American representation on city councils in southern US cities from 1970 to 1996 and found that a transition from at-large elections to district elections had a large impact on black representation, but that effect nearly disappeared by 1991. Welch (1990) also finds that in southern cities with at least 10 percent black population at-large systems were more equitable than those in the North (on mayors see Marschall and Ruhil 2006).

[27] This creates a larger number of southern states than does the eleven states of the old Confederacy rule. The grouping also includes border states such as Kansas, Kentucky, Missouri, and Oklahoma, as well as states such as Maryland and Delaware. If region is to represent the unique political and educational history of the South, the classification needs to include states that had policies consistent with that political history. Using the traditional definition of South produced identical results (not shown).

population-representation slope from .928 to 1.208, a gain of approximately 28 percentage points. For ward elections, a Democratic majority increases the size of the population-representation slope from .883 to 1.057 or approximately 17 percentage points. This indicates that a Democratic majority is an advantage regardless of the electoral system, but with at-large elections African Americans can use the bias of a majoritarian system to further increase the size of their electoral benefits.

One final issue remains to be addressed – the role of residential segregation as it influences the structure-representation relationship. The efficiency of ward elections at generating minority representation requires that populations in the small electoral units not be a microcosm of the entire jurisdiction, that is, it requires some degree of residential segregation.[28] If there is no residential segregation, then a minority candidate has no better chance of winning in a smaller electoral district than in an at-large election. There should be an interaction between residential segregation and electoral structure. An African-American–white residential segregation measure was calculated for each school district using block-level data from the 2000 Census; using block-level data generates greater variation because it is quite possible for a block to be composed of a single race. This measure is essentially a Blau similarity index that indicates the probably that the next person one meets at random will be of the same race. Because this is a measure of integration, we reverse coded it to measure segregation.

The optimal way to estimate the impact of residential segregation is to include it in the final model in Table 3.1 and also to interact it with ward elections (because segregation theoretically will only affect results in ward systems). Unfortunately, interacting residential segregation with ward elections and also interacting population with ward elections generates massive collinearity and precludes reliable estimation. Consistent with the discussion linking representation to partisanship, we will partition the sample and run regressions for those school districts using pure ward election systems and those using pure at-large systems for both Democratic majority and Republican majority districts. By including the measure of segregation in these regressions, we can determine if, as predicted, the degree of residential segregation improves electoral fortunes in ward-based elections.

Table 3.3 presents these four regressions, and Figure 3.1 illustrates the coefficient estimates of population and partisanship. The residential segregation variable ranges from 0.02 (almost completely integrated) to 0.95 (virtually completely segregated). The regression coefficient can be interpreted as the increase in black representation for a completely segregated district (compared to one that is fully integrated), all other things being equal. The table shows, as predicted, that residential segregation has no impact on representation in at-large systems. The ward system equations show that the degree of segregation matters but only in a jurisdiction with a Republican majority; residential segregation does not matter

---

[28] We thank K. Juree Capers for providing these data to us.

TABLE 3.3. *Partisan Fortunes and the Impact of Structure on Representation: School Boards, Split Models*

	Dependent Variable: Percent Blacks on School Board			
Independent Variable	Democrat Majority		Republican Majority	
	Ward	At-Large	Ward	At-Large
Intercept	−7.222	−2.483	−4.095	−4.802*
	(6.458)	(2.884)	(2.297)	(1.982)
Black Population Percentage	1.131*	1.195*	0.773*	0.961*
	(0.062)	(0.074)	(0.068)	(0.076)
Black-White Segregation	2.682	1.805	6.016*	−1.559
	(3.163)	(1.638)	(2.832)	(1.856)
Black Education (College Percent)	0.022	0.027	−0.006	−0.001
	(0.033)	(0.018)	(0.047)	(0.016)
Black Family Income (000s)	−0.030	−0.012	0.010	−0.051
	(0.060)	(0.006)	(0.078)	(0.051)
Black Home Ownership	−0.019	−0.005	−0.013	0.003
	(0.020)	(0.010)	(0.017)	(0.012)
White Poverty Percentage	0.150	0.297*	0.035	0.126
	(0.130)	(0.109)	(0.080)	(0.097)
Unionization	0.250+	0.054	−0.113	0.129*
	(0.140)	(0.077)	(0.118)	(0.065)
District Democrat Percent	0.029	−0.008	0.129*	0.085+
	(0.104)	(0.047)	(0.059)	(0.046)
2004	1.078	−0.051	−1.214*	0.846+
	(0.823)	(0.410)	(0.447)	(0.382)
2008	2.743*	0.033	−0.311	0.423
	(0.875)	(0.587)	(0.551)	(0.475)
R^2	.76	.60	.59	.39
F	65.60	57.09	85.11	31.45
Standard Error	8.76	9.22	8.36	8.30
N	408	1472	977	1331

Districts where blacks are less than 50 percent of total population; errors clustered by LEAID; standard errors in parenthesis.
* $p < .05$; + $p < .10$

in jurisdictions with Democratic majorities. The maximum impact of segregation in Republican majority areas with ward elections is approximately a 6 percentage point increase in black representation, all other things being equal.

Residential segregation likely contributes to racial polarization in election results. Segregation tends to be correlated with negative racial attitudes (Sigleman and Welch 1993, but see also Oliver and Mendelberg 2000), which should in turn correlate with racially polarized voting. The absence of a relationship in Democratic majority jurisdictions as a result likely occurs because

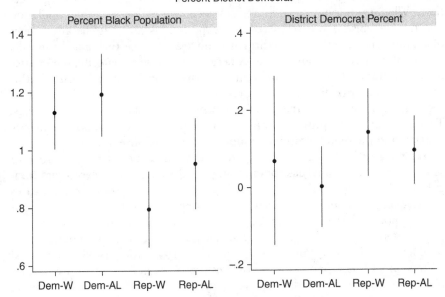

FIGURE 3.1. Effect of structure and partisanship on board representation.

the votes of liberal whites limit the degree of polarization and thus the clustering in racially homogeneous units becomes less necessary to elect African-American representatives.

The results of Table 3.3 reinforce the earlier findings in regard to the importance of partisanship. Democratic majorities facilitate coalitions that include African Americans; this process is able to overcome the bias in at-large elections and advantage African Americans in those systems relative to ward elections (Table 3.2). Democratic majorities also are associated with a reduced impact for segregation presumably because even in ward systems with Democratic majorities the parties perform the same coalitional functions with liberal whites supporting black candidates (Table 3.3). A comparison of the population coefficients in both Tables 3.2 and 3.3 indicate that when there are majoritarian election systems (at-large elections), a Democratic majority is associated with higher levels of African-American representation.[29]

African-American Majority Districts

Theoretical literature on voting and electoral structure is based on a median voter model. Under this model, voters who are a minority of the population

[29] The level of explanation in each of these circumstances varies a great deal. African-American representation is best predicted in ward systems with Democratic majorities and least well predicted in at-large systems with Republican majorities.

can be disadvantaged by majoritarian electoral structures such as at-large elections. When traditional racial minorities become a majority of the population and the franchise is not restricted, the expectations are that the advantages of majoritarian electoral structures will now advantage the racial minority. In school districts with an African-American population majority, the politics of representation looks very different from the portrait painted earlier in this chapter. In majority districts, African Americans hold 71 percent of board representation compared to the 9 percent they hold in black minority districts. This large jump in representation indicates that examining the black majority districts and the representational politics is a worthwhile exercise.

Table 3.4 presents analyses that parallel those in Table 3.1 for this group of school districts. The analysis contains only 102 black majority case-years compared to the nearly five thousand minority cases.[30] At the same time, these cases are frequently the most analyzed cases simply because they provide insight into the policy changes that can occur as the result of representational change (for cities see Marschall and Ruhil 2007; Trounstine 2010; on school districts see Henig et al. 1999; Portz, Stein, and Jones 1999; Rich 1996). The initial regression with just population illustrates that African Americans are quickly overrepresented in school districts where they are a majority of the population. At 50 percent of the population, this equation predicts African Americans will hold 63 percent of the school board seats, and this predicted representation level will gradually increase to 99 percent at 100 percent of the population. Equally interesting in this equation is the high standard error (20.1) and low level of prediction. Black population is only able to explain 17 percent of the variation in this truncated sample.

The second column adds the structural interactions. These structural interactions are not significant but show that the base relationship for at-large elections is not estimated with a great deal of precision (the joint f-test for all four variables is 1.0 with p = .42). In effect with the small number of cases, individual school districts that are outliers can significantly move these individual coefficients but not produce statistically significant changes. The appointed systems intercepts cancel each other out and the representation coefficient is approximately 1.0. Although comparisons of the population coefficient between Tables 3.4 and 3.2 need to be done cautiously because they focus on two different populations, the efficiency of the translation of population into seats drops below 1.0. This relationship is consistent with the idea that in African-American majority districts, there is some preference for having non-African-American representatives on the school board. Again this is speculative because we have far too few cases to generate statistically significant results and using sensitivity analysis does not necessarily show a structural break between black minority and black majority districts when estimated with the full sample.

---

[30] Because most districts are minority black, analysis ... looks on all cases together (Table A3.6 in the Appendix) looks more similar to Table 3.1 than Table 3.4.

TABLE 3.4. *Impact of Electoral Structure on the Quantity of Black Representation: School Board Seats, Majority Districts*

Independent Variable	Dependent Variable: Percent Blacks on School Board			
	Model 1	Model 2	Model 3	Model 4
Intercept	20.580	24.255	−24.448	−25.358
	(13.686)	(19.719)	(23.238)	(28.790)
Black Population Percentage	0.830*	0.847*	0.971*	0.981*
	(0.188)	(0.264)	(0.200)	(0.240)
Ward Elections		13.181	38.095	37.961
		(28.788)	(32.231)	(33.056)
Ward X Population Percentage		−0.296	−0.620	−0.612
		(0.410)	(0.439)	(0.440)
Appointed System		−23.677	−7.471	−5.917
		(33.889)	(32.364)	(31.065)
Appointed X Black Population		0.192	−0.088	−0.101
		(0.498)	(0.486)	(0.464)
Black Education (College Percent)			1.836	1.791
			(1.337)	(1.335)
Black Family Income (000s)			0.761	1.063
			(1.643)	(1.889)
Black Home Ownership			0.092	0.066
			(0.135)	(0.166)
White Poverty Percentage			1.388	1.353
			(0.962)	(1.019)
Unionization				1.353
				(0.760)
District Democrat Percent				0.020
				(0.333)
2004	−3.852	−4.013	−3.642	−3.828
	(3.777)	(3.889)	(4.026)	(4.271)
2008	−1.945	−2.466	−2.609	−3.258
	(5.253)	(5.228)	(5.505)	(5.800)
R^2	.17	.21	.28	.29
F	7.82	5.75	6.49	5.86
Standard Error	22.052	21.975	21.34	21.67
N	103	103	103	103

Districts where blacks are more than 50 percent of total population; errors clustered by LEAID; standard errors in parenthesis.

* $p < .05$; + $p < .10$

Columns 3 and 4 add the basic resources variables (first the demographics and then the political allies' variables). Essentially these regressions show that only the size of the black population appears to matter in terms of statistical significance. The size of the population coefficient remains in the .7 to .75

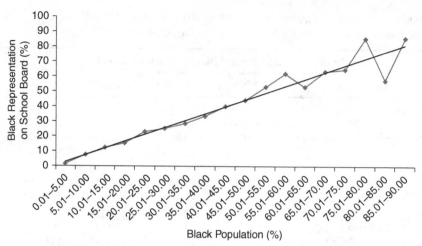

FIGURE 3.2. Average black representation by population interval.

range (it is not significantly different from 1.0 in any of the regressions) and indicates that numbers alone dominate election results in these majority black jurisdictions. The four resources variables in Model 3 (black college graduates, black family income, black home ownership, and whites below poverty) jointly add some explained variation to the model even though the individual coefficients are not significant (joint f-test = 2.51, p. = .059). The allies' measures (Democrats and union members) are neither individually nor jointly significant. A conservative conclusion is that only population matters.

Even with the full set of controls, the standard error of this model is large and the level of explained variation is small. One interpretation of the predicted majorities on the school board and the low level of predictive power is that majority population numbers create a resource that permits African-American politicians a great deal of discretion in governing a school district in terms of the politics. In many cases, keeping representatives from other groups on the board might serve as a signal that the school district is interested in retaining the participation of these groups in the education system. Because many black majority districts face severe financial constraints, the logic of coalitions shifts from one of winning elections to one of retaining support for the educational system.

A good way to illustrate the change in behavior among African-American majority school districts is by graphing the percentage of the population by the percentage of seats using a set of intervals. Figure 3.2, for example, presents a graph at 5 percentage intervals (0–5, 5.01–10, etc.). The graph shows that when African Americans are 50 percent of the population there is a steeper jump in the representation level. This is followed by a leveling off of the slope of the line such that increases in population do not return equal increments in representation. This pattern generally holds until the African-American population increases to approximately 85 percent of the total (there are also very few cases in categories in which the black population is greater than 60 percent in this data set). Although in-depth cases studies on the politics of black majority school districts would be best able to determine if African Americans seek to retain some nonblack representation in jurisdictions where they have a majority of the population, the figure is consistent with that hypothesis.

Have Things Changed?

The findings in this chapter differ substantially from the literature on both school districts and city councils, and there are two explanations for this difference. First, that the larger sample size and the better measures of allies in this study generate a better view of the politics of urban education. Second, the politics of education has changed, and race and the related questions of electoral structure no longer hold the central position that they once did. We can take a preliminary look at these two explanations by taking advantage of some existing historical data. In 1989 with largest study of school districts in the United States to date, Meier et al. (1989) examined 174 school districts with enrollments of at least fifteen thousand and at least 1 percent black population. We have been able to match 140 of these districts with 2008 data from our study. Many of the other cases dropped out of the comparison either because they are consolidated with other districts (or lost their unique identity in other ways) or were among the few that did not respond to the 2008 survey.

Table 3.5 presents parallel models for the subsample of districts in 1986 and 2008. These models only include the population and the structural interactions because the earlier study used a different set of control variables that do not match well with the current set.[31] Given how dominant population is in the models and given our interest is in the structural interactions, these simpler regressions should provide the insight we desire in regard to change. The striking finding is that these models are essentially similar over time. A joint f-test for whether the difference in coefficients was not zero (comparing 1986 and 2008) was statistically insignificant. The African-American population has gotten slightly more efficient at translating numbers into representation but not significantly so. Within the smaller sample of school districts, structure does not matter, and this lack of impact has not changed over time. Given the findings in Table 3.3 and the lack of differences found in Table 3.5, it is quite likely that the earlier insignificant results were simply a result of having too few cases to probe the impact of the structural variation.[32]

---

[31] Meier et al. (1989) used a different specification that did not include the intercept terms. The specification they used was introduced by Engstrom and McDonald (1981) and was considered the standard at the time.

[32] A second way to examine the dynamics of this relationship is to use the 2001–2008 panel and lag the dependent variable. When this is done, it illustrates how highly path dependent

TABLE 3.5. *Impact of Electoral Structures, 1986 and 2008 Comparison*

Dependent Variable: Percent Blacks on School Board		
Independent Variable	1986	2008
	Slope	Slope
Intercept	−0.479	−0.732
	(1.368)	(2.199)
Black Population Percentage	1.033*	1.178*
	(0.068)	(0.171)
Ward Elections	−0.967	6.012
	(2.922)	(3.645)
Ward X Population Percentage	−0.025	−0.256
	(0.134)	(0.239)
Appointed System	3.144	11.448+
	(3.365)	(5.111)
Appointed X Black Population	−0.132	−0.317
	(0.122)	(0.216)
R^2	.68	.63
F	90.56	40.25
Standard Error	9.412	11.446
N	140	140

Standard errors in parenthesis.
* $p < .05$; + $p < .10$

Conclusions

This analysis explores enduring puzzles regarding black representation in education policy – the extent of descriptive representation in different electoral systems and whether the negative impact of at-large elections has declined. We find that, on average, African-American school board members have overcome the limitations of at-large elections. In assessing exactly how African Americans have done this, a new theoretical idea was postulated. The findings indicate that one possible way to overcome such bias is through putting together a majority coalition to back African-American candidates in at-large electoral systems. Such slates and coalitions are more likely in areas with Democratic voting dominance. In districts with a Democratic majority, African-American representation in at-large elections is 18 percentage points higher than it is in ward elections. In Republican districts, structure matters very little; however, the representation levels are lower than in Democratic districts, all other things

the process is. The only two variables that are significant are representation in the prior year and level of black population. The bias of structure is all incorporated in the 2001 value of representation.

being equal. Our findings thus indicate that partisanship can be a salient factor in securing representation for African Americans in systems where they were traditionally underrepresented.

Our findings are consistent with the seminal work of Browning et al. (1984) who examined the incorporation of minorities in ten Northern California cities. While our study confirms the importance of a Democratic majority, by itself a Democratic majority is not sufficient for an African American to win electoral office. Fourteen percent of school districts with 10 percent black population and a Democratic majority in our study have no African Americans on the school board.[33] Neither is a Democratic majority a necessary condition given that African Americans attain 92 percent of the representation that their population entitles them to in at-large elections in Republican jurisdictions (see Table 3.2).

The combination of partisanship and at-large elections in the US context might be considered parallel to the comparative elections findings in regard to gender. That literature finds that "district magnitude," the number of candidates elected from an electoral district, is positively associated with more women representatives (Kenworthy and Malami 1999; Kunovich and Paxton 2005; Norris 1985; Paxton 1997; Reynolds 1999; Rule 1987). The district magnitude results are greatly influenced by systems that have a single nationwide electoral district and operate under proportional representation systems. In such systems, parties run a slate of candidates. The evidence for US school districts is consistent with the logic in these comparative systems except that the slating is not done using formal rules (i.e., established party lists) but rather done informally or as an ad hoc coalition.

One open question is whether the findings here are an anomaly and African Americans on school boards are unique. Using the logic of the incentives created by electoral systems in terms of getting elected and forming governing coalitions, however, suggests that other cases can be identified and studied. City councils are an obvious case. Electoral systems are not immutable. As with any set of procedural rules, political parties and likely other political institutions have an incentive to create informal processes that overcome the biases of the formal electoral system. Election systems establish rules of the game and incentives; they do not necessarily determine winners.

The findings in this chapter for at-large elections are unusual and, therefore, it is important to specify the precise factors that make African Americans a unique case. African-American voting patterns are the most cohesive of any racial or ethnic group in the United States and regularly register 90 percent+ support for the Democratic Party. This overlap has two implications. First, it creates an incentive for Democratic Party officials and candidates to reach out to African Americans and include them as part of the electoral coalition. The relative advantage of making an electoral appeal to a group that is likely

---

[33] The same figure for Republican majority districts with 10 percent black population is 29 percent.

to generate a 90 percent return rate as opposed to a group with a 65 percent return rate (Latinos) should be fairly obvious. Second, it means that African-American voters are more likely to see common policy interests with Democrats than with Republicans; a perception that is backed by an extensive history of relationships. These common interests mean that African Americans have supported white Democrats in many elections and would likely support white Democrats over black Republican candidates. This suggests that the relative efficiency and effectiveness of African Americans overcoming the bias of at-large elections given a Democratic majority is greater than it is for other minority groups. This does not mean that such results cannot occur in other cases, only that they will not occur on average as they do for African Americans.

Given the current controversy over the VRA and whether or not it should be continued, the implications of this study for the VRA need to be specified precisely. This study does not find that electoral structures do not matter. It finds that one minority group, African Americans, can overcome the biases of at-large elections in specific circumstances – in areas with a Democratic voting majority. Given the unique political history of African Americans in the United States, the findings here cannot necessarily be generalized to Latinos, Native Americans, Asian Americans, or other racial or ethnic minorities. Additional research is required to determine the impact, if any, of electoral structure on the political representation of these racial and ethnic minorities. The study also documents the average case; in many situations African Americans are significantly underrepresented on school boards, and structure along with local conditions could well be a factor in this pattern.

This assessment should be considered the first step in a new series of studies on the impact of electoral structure on minority representation owing to three events that are likely to affect the electoral process. First, the Supreme Court in *Shelby County, Ala. v. Holder* (2013) has weakened the VRA and this has encouraged some local jurisdictions to change to majoritarian electoral structures (Childress 2013). The effectiveness of the VRA has always in part been a function of the ability of the federal government to apply pressures to local governments during those periods when the national administration supported the objectives of the act (see Smith, Kedrowski, and Ellis 2004). The *Shelby* case means that even during supportive administrations, federal civil rights officials now lack an important instrument to use in order to prevent electoral discrimination. The result will be a greater reliance on the political pressures at the local level as examined in this chapter rather than on the orientation of the president or the Department of Justice.

Second, similar to other areas, there is an effort by states to move into the void created by the federal government. The California VRA has resulted in many California jurisdictions switching from at-large elections to ward systems, and some states such as Washington are considering similar laws. This pattern of state action is not uncommon in other policy areas such as environmental policy or antitrust policy where aggressive state governments have pushed policies beyond what the federal government was willing to do. Much of federal environmental policy in recent decades has been a response to pro-environmental actions taken by California and other states (e.g., Glicksman and Levy 2008).

Third, the Military Overseas Voting and Empowerment Act requires states and communities to facilitate absentee voting by members of the US military. To reduce the costs of compliance with this law, some states such as Michigan have moved all local elections to November concurrent with other elections and other states such as New Jersey now allow that scheduling. If November elections increase voting turnout (i.e., there is not significant roll off) for school board elections, this could complicate the relationships between population numbers and electoral structure. The impact of the November elections would depend on the relative changes in turnout across the racial groups, and at the present time this has not been definitively studied. These three factors as well as the unique situation of African Americans and the Democratic Party suggest that examinations of the impact of electoral structure on representation will continue to be relevant to determining the electoral fortunes of various racial and ethnic groups.

This chapter has demonstrated that African-American representation, particularly the ability to translate population into elected officials, is affected by the selection structure of the school district (at-large vs. SMD) and the partisanship of the electorate. The question remains, does representation matter? Does it affect the education of African-American students? To this issue, we now turn in the next three chapters.

Appendix

TABLE A3.1. *The Percent of Black Students and the Impact of Electoral Structure on the Quantity of Black Representation: School Board Seats*

Dependent Variable: Percent Blacks on School Board	
Independent Variable	Slope
Intercept	−4.442*
	(1.036)
Black Population Percentage	0.747*
	(0.077)
Ward Elections	0.637
	(0.426)
Ward X Population Percentage	−0.130*
	(0.054)
Appointed System	1.956
	(1.327)
Appointed X Black Population	0.054
	(0.069)
Black Education (College Percent)	−0.006
	(0.009)
Black Family Income (000s)	0.0004
	(0.005)
Black Home Ownership	−0.003
	(0.006)
White Poverty Percentage	0.175*
	(0.050)
Unionization	0.072+
	(0.039)
Percent Black Students	0.240*
	(0.035)
District Democrat Percent	0.046*
	(0.018)
2004	−0.016
	(0.192)
2008	0.219
	(0.271)
R^2	.64
F	251.47
Standard Error	8.58
N	4752

Districts where blacks are less than 50 percent of total population; errors clustered by LEAID; standard errors in parenthesis.

* $p < .05$; + $p < .10$

TABLE A3.2. *Black Voting Age Population and the Impact of Electoral Structure on the Quantity of Black Representation: School Board Seats*

Dependent Variable: Percent Blacks on School Board	
Independent Variable	Slope
Intercept	-4.594^*
	(1.026)
Black Population Percentage	0.490^*
	(0.115)
Ward Elections	0.623
	(0.417)
Ward X Population Percentage	-0.119^*
	(0.052)
Appointed System	2.113
	(1.345)
Appointed X Black Population	0.056
	(0.069)
Black Education (College Percent)	-0.013
	(0.009)
Black Family Income (000s)	-0.004
	(0.007)
Black Home Ownership	-0.008
	(0.006)
White Poverty Percentage	0.184^*
	(0.049)
Unionization	0.082^*
	(0.038)
Black Voting Age Population	0.616^*
	(0.105)
District Democrat Percent	0.056^*
	(0.018)
2004	0.072
	(0.189)
2008	$0.453+$
	(0.269)
R^2	$.64$
F	218.01
Standard Error	8.61
N	4836

Districts where blacks are less than 50 percent of total population; errors clustered by LEAID; standard errors in parenthesis.

* $p < .05$; $+$ $p < .10$

TABLE A3.3. *1992 Black Representation and the Impact of Electoral Structure on the Quantity of Black Representation: School Board Seats*

Dependent Variable: Percent Blacks on School Board	
Independent Variable	Slope
Intercept	−4.821*
	(1.088)
Black Population Percentage	0.975*
	(0.059)
Ward Elections	0.999*
	(0.456)
Ward X Population Percentage	−0.156*
	(0.056)
Appointed System	2.605+
	(1.445)
Appointed X Black Population	0.006
	(0.073)
Black Education (College Percent)	0.005
	(0.012)
Black Family Income (000s)	−0.006
	(0.005)
Black Home Ownership	−0.008
	(0.007)
White Poverty Percentage	0.132*
	(0.049)
Unionization	0.078+
	(0.042)
1992 Black Representation	0.189*
	(0.034)
District Democrat Percent	0.065*
	(0.020)
2004	0.136
	(0.199)
2008	0.472
	(0.293)
R^2	.64
F	216.32
Standard Error	8.74
N	4276

Districts where blacks are less than 50 percent of total population; errors clustered by LEAID; standard errors in parenthesis.

* $p < .05$; + $p < .10$

TABLE A3.4. *Latino Population and the Impact of Electoral Structure on the Quantity of Black Representation: School Board Seats*

Dependent Variable: Percent Blacks on School Board	
Independent Variable	Slope
Intercept	−4.721*
	(1.030)
Black Population Percentage	1.126*
	(0.049)*
Ward Elections	0.874*
	(0.430)
Ward X Population Percentage	−0.159
	(0.055)
Appointed System	2.417+
	(1.353)
Appointed X Black Population	0.009
	(0.069)
Black Education (College Percent)	0.0002
	(0.010)
Black Family Income (000s)	−0.003
	(0.006)
Black Home Ownership	−0.009
	(0.006)
White Poverty Percentage	0.140*
	(0.050)
Unionization	0.084*
	(0.041)
Latino Population	−0.004
	(0.010)
District Democrat Percent	0.065*
	(0.019)
2004	0.082
	(0.187)
2008	0.460+
	(0.268)
R^2	.62
F	209.22
Standard Error	8.769
N	4836

Districts where blacks are less than 50 percent of total population; errors clustered by LEAID; standard errors in parenthesis.

* $p < .05$; + $p < .10$

TABLE A3.5. *Noncitizens and the Impact of Electoral Structure on the Quantity of Black Representation: School Board Seats*

Dependent Variable: Percent Blacks on School Board	
Independent Variable	Slope
Intercept	−4.564*
	(1.041)
Black Population Percentage	1.127*
	(0.049)
Ward Elections	0.866*
	(0.428)
Ward X Population Percentage	−0.161*
	(0.055)
Appointed System	2.496+
	(1.347)
Appointed X Black Population	0.004
	(0.069)
Black Education (College Percent)	−0.001
	(0.010)
Black Family Income (000s)	−0.001
	(0.005)
Black Home Ownership	−0.012+
	(0.007)
White Poverty Percentage	0.136*
	(0.048)
Unionization	0.085*
	(0.040)
Percent Noncitizens	−0.037
	(0.027)
District Democrat Percent	0.068*
	(0.019)
2004	0.087
	(0.187)
2008	0.463+
	(0.268)
R^2	.62
F	209.65
Standard Error	8.77
N	4836

Districts where blacks are less than 50 percent of total population; errors clustered by LEAID; standard errors in parenthesis.

* $p < .05$; + $p < .10$

TABLE A3.6. *Impact of Electoral Structure on the Quantity of Black Representation: School Board Seats, All Districts*

	Dependent Variable: Percent Blacks on School Board			
Independent Variable	Slope	Slope	Slope	Slope
Intercept	0.038	−0.150	−0.010	−5.143*
	(0.225)	(0.260)	(0.549)	(1.080)
Black Population Percentage	1.074*	1.158*	1.161*	1.136*
	(0.021)	(0.039)	(0.041)	(0.042)
Ward Elections		0.102	0.236	0.693
		(0.406)	(0.447)	(0.453)
Ward X Population Percentage		−0.151*	−0.151*	−0.130+
		(0.050)	(0.051)	(0.051)
Appointed System		4.273*	4.350*	4.575*
		(1.545)	(1.605)	(1.654)
Appointed X Black Population		−0.137+	−0.143+	−0.141+
		(0.080)	(0.081)	(0.084)
Black Education (College Percent)			0.014	0.002
			(0.010)	(0.010)
Black Family Income (000s)			0.006	−0.003
			(0.012)	(0.006)
Black Home Ownership			−0.019*	−0.007
			(0.007)	(0.007)
White Poverty Percentage			0.063	0.129*
			(0.049)	(0.051)
Unionization				0.095*
				(0.042)
District Democrat Percent				0.068*
				(0.019)
2004	0.352	−0.018	−0.020	−0.005
	(0.275)	(0.194)	(0.197)	(0.199)
2008	0.352	0.345	0.356	0.394
	0.275	(0.275)	(0.279)	(0.281)
R²	.70	.70	.70	.70
F	841.71	399.07	273.60	244.78
Standard Error	9.296	9.229	9.288	9.242
N	5055	5055	4982	4937

Errors clustered by LEAID; standard errors in parenthesis.

* $p < .05$; + $p < .10$

4

Race and Street-Level Bureaucrats

With a Little Help from My Friends

Policies are rarely self-implementing, and education policies are no exception. The decentralized structure of American education allows for both extensive discretion by school districts as well as discretion within individual schools. School are archetypical street-level bureaucracies with vast discretion vested in teachers with only modest oversight even in the current era of high stakes testing (Davis 2011; May and Winter 2000; but see Boser and Hanna 2014 for a differing view). School boards can be conceptualized as political principals who, by necessity, must delegate to agents to carry out their policy objectives. One of the most proposed hypotheses about principal-agent relationships, the ally hypothesis, holds that principals should select agents who share their values in order to maximize the objectives that the principal seeks.[1] Given the importance of race in education policy, African-American school board members are quite likely to believe that African-American administrators and teachers will share their values and that increasing the number of black teachers and administrators can generate positive gains for black students (see Chapters 5 and 6).

The reform structures of the Progressive Era with its effort to separate policy from administration and the creation of a professional superintendent means that school boards cannot directly hire teachers and can rarely hire administrators. They do hire the superintendent, however, so a board priority focused on the racial diversity of faculty and staff is something that a superintendent can ignore only by assuming some risk. The organizational structure of school districts creates a chain of principal-agent relationships whereby the

---

[1] Knott and Miller (2008) are highly critical of the ally hypothesis and proposed that under certain circumstances principals must make a credible commitment to an agent who does not share goals to protect themselves from their own failings.

superintendent hires administrative personnel and the administrative personnel hire teachers.[2]

This chapter will examine the racial representation of the administrative and teaching faculty of our national sample of school districts with two objectives in mind. From a substantive perspective, we seek to show how school board representation and partisanship directly affect the composition of the district's administrative and teaching staff. From a theoretical perspective, we seek to build on Chapter 3 and the impact of structure and partisanship on representation by examining whether or not there are downstream consequences of partisanship on the various ways to select school board members.

The Links among Structure, Politics, and Representation

Electoral structures create the rules of the game for contesting elections and, as a result, affect who gets elected. Much work both in US and comparative politics has linked the descriptive representation of women and minorities to various electoral structures (Baldez 2006; Canon 1999; Engstrom and McDonald 1982, 1997; Epstein and O'Halloran 1999; Leal, Martinez-Ebers, and Meier 2004; Meier and Rutherford 2014; Norris 2004; Sass and Mehay 2003; Shah, Marschall, and Ruhil 2013; Shotts 2003a, 2003b; Trounstine and Valdini 2008, among others). Chapter 3 shows how electoral structure along with partisan values generated African-American school board representation in numbers far greater than expected. With the increase in descriptive representation of women and racial minorities in legislative bodies worldwide, scholarly effort has shifted to examine how descriptive representation leads to substantive representation; but we still know much less about how electoral structures per se affect postelection substantive representation (versus the level of representation). Electoral systems are linked to descriptive representation, but they are not tied directly to how effective descriptive representatives are if they are elected by different systems. This chapter contends that descriptive representation interacts with electoral structure and partisanship, among many political factors, to affect substantive representation. We argue that, theoretically, proponents of single-member (SMD) and at-large districts use the same logical models to argue for greater substantive representation but assign different weights to variables in the model. Our empirical analysis provides a critical test of the theoretical arguments.

This chapter begins by setting the question of African-American representation in context. After defining the key concepts of descriptive and substantive representation, we will clarify the argument about how various structures

---

[2] The exact nature of this process varies from district to district. In some cases, there is a separate personnel office that is doing the hiring, in other cases individual principals have the authority to hire. We know of cases in smaller school districts where the superintendent sits in on the interviews of all teachers.

should affect substantive representation. Electoral structures create a context, but this context combines with other factors – primarily partisanship in this case – to influence substantive representation. We add to the theoretical discussion a focus on policy allies and link this to partisanship because the political landscape of a school district, traditionally viewed as nonpartisan, should be related to the ability of minority representatives to gain policy benefits for their constituents. We investigate how electoral structure influences representation for African Americans in our national study of the 1,800 largest school districts in the United States. Although the direct impact of electoral structures on substantive representation is modest, the role of structure is greatly affected by partisanship, which both interacts with structure to affect representation and has a major influence in its own right. This is an especially important finding in the context of school districts, where school board members are largely selected in "nonpartisan" elections.

Descriptive versus Substantive Representation

Much of the literature on US electoral structures concerns *descriptive representation*, or whether the proportion of minority representatives elected approximates the minority population proportion (see Chapter 3). The number of minority officials in office, however, does not indicate how well they represent the interests of the minority community. Pitkin (1967), among others, defines descriptive representation as representatives that mirror the physical traits of their constituents and *substantive representation* as representatives acting on behalf of their constituents (see also Davidson and Korbel 1981, 1004). Eulau and Karps (1977) identify four components of responsiveness that constitute the nature of substantive representation – policy, service, allocation, and symbolic responsiveness. Policy responsiveness occurs when the representative aligns policies with the interest of the represented. Service responsiveness involves the ability of the representative to obtain particular individual or group benefits for the represented. Allocation responsiveness refers to the representative's ability to secure policy benefits for the represented through pork barrel exchanges. Finally, symbolic responsiveness refers to public gestures that develop a sense of trust and support between the representative and the represented.

All of these components can be considered substantive representation, that is, representing the interests of the representative's constituents. For this study we operationally define substantive representation as the ability of an African-American school board representative to both attain allocation responsiveness (the ability to hire additional black employees, for similar operational definitions of representation see, among others, Eisinger 1980; Karnig 1980; Kerr and Mladenka 1994; Mladenka 1989; Sass and Mehay 2003) and policy responsiveness (the ability to generate policy benefits for black constituents). These two forms of representation are not independent of each other; black school board members can set general policies that create opportunities for black students by expanding quality academic opportunities or limiting the application of discipline. Much of the representational impact of school board members, however, is likely to be indirect by hiring black administrators and teachers who then engage in representation activities. Some other indirect influence of black legislators can also result simply from raising issues, speaking on policies, or oversight of the bureaucracy (Grose 2011; Minta 2011; Tate 2014; for similar work on Latinos see Casellas 2011; Rouse 2013).

African-American administrators play two distinct roles in the policy responsiveness of representation. First, they have an indirect role through their strong association with hiring African-American teachers. Second, they can adopt policies that can be applied either schoolwide or districtwide in terms of grouping, tracking, discipline, or other factors (see Pitts 2005; Roch, Pitts, and Navarro 2010) that can positively affect students.

Much literature documents a variety of ways that black teachers can benefit black students (Grissom and Redding 2015; Grissom, Kern, and Rodriguez 2015). First, African-American teachers are associated with positive academic grouping outcomes – fewer black students assigned to special education, vocational, and other low status groups and more black students assigned to gifted and talented classes (Foster 1997; Meier, Stewart, and England 1989; Ogbu 1994). Black teachers are also associated with more equitable disciplinary actions in regard to black students (Meier et al. 1989). Second, although much literature contends that African-American teachers are better at teaching African-American students (Clewell and Villegas 1998; Denbo 2002; King 1993), the empirical results were fairly mixed until the Tennessee STAR experiment. The STAR experiment randomly assigned students to classes ostensibly to examine the impact of class size on student performance. Dee (2004, 2005) took advantage of this random assignment design to study the impact of African-American teachers on African-American students and concluded that African-American students learned significantly more from same-race teachers than they did from white teachers. Third, African-American teachers and administrators might not take any specific actions but simply serve as role models to African-American students (King 1993, 121; see also Egalite, Kisida, and Winters 2015). Dee (2001, 5) notes "for under privileged black students, the presence of a black teacher may encourage them to update their prior beliefs about their educational possibilities." Whether through role models or different teaching techniques, however, higher minority student educational performance is consistently associated with the presence of minority teachers (Meier et al. 2001).

Electoral Systems and African-American Representation

Electoral systems can take many forms. As noted in Chapter 3, in the United States most elections are either at-large elections whereby all representatives are elected by the entire jurisdiction or ward/SMD elections where candidates run for a single seat in smaller electoral units. The logic supporting ward/SMDs as producing more descriptive representation for minorities assumes that electorates are polarized along racial lines (i.e., that race is a significant electoral cleavage) and that the SMDs are drawn in such a way that they are not microcosms of the overall jurisdiction (either as a result of residential segregation or perhaps because they are gerrymandered to facilitate racial representation). In such circumstances, blacks (and other numerical minorities) are likely to achieve greater descriptive representation in SMD systems than in at-large systems because they can run in smaller, more homogeneous districts with larger black (or other numerical minority) populations. The empirical literature, while not always in agreement, generally illustrated the detrimental impact of at-large elections (see Meier and Rutherford 2014; Shah et al. 2013 and the work cited therein). The results of Chapter 3 directly challenge these results and suggest that partisan context greatly affects the link between structure and representation.

Although descriptive representation is important for understanding representation, an equally pressing issue is how electoral structure (at-large vs. SMDs) can affect black *substantive* representation. Is a black representative elected at-large more or less effective in representing the interests of the black community than a representative elected from a SMD? Several scholars (Guinier 1991; Sass and Mehay 2003; Swain 1993) argue for the advantages of at-large elections by stressing that at-large elections facilitate the creation of multiracial governing coalitions. Guinier (1991, 1111) suggests "constituents within isolated single-member districts have little influence over the behavior of representatives from other single-member districts." The argument is that the system of at-large elections is more beneficial because African-American officeholders can augment their influence by building coalitions with other non-African-American elected officials who represent the same electoral constituency (and thus face the same electoral incentives). This argument parallels an earlier argument by Browning, Marshall, and Tabb (1984) that minorities need to form coalitions with liberal whites to gain policy benefits (but see Marschall, Shah, and Ruhil 2010). With help from their friends (allies), minorities can achieve their representational goals.

The idea of coalition building between African-American representatives and nonblack officials in at-large systems, however, may have an Achilles heel. In at-large systems black representatives may need to downplay issues important to the minority community in an attempt to appeal to the median voter and win elections (Epstein and O'Halloran 1999; Meier et al. 2005). This can be problematic because it implies that the representative will sacrifice responsiveness to the black community by adopting issue positions at the median voter for all constituents rather than issue positions at the median voter for black constituents.

Others argue that the structure of ward elections is the most beneficial system for minority representatives to act substantively (see Leal et al. 2004; Lublin 1999). A ward electoral system permits candidates to win by securing a majority of the votes cast within a much smaller area with more racial homo-geneity than that of an at-large system. This system is more advantageous for black representatives, the argument suggests, because it is easier for them to acquire seats *and* then advocate policies that represent the interest of the black community. Lublin (1999), in his critique of Cameron, Epstein, and O'Halloran (1996), contends that SMDs are vital to blacks being elected into office and that these districts bolster the quality of candidates elected.

The empirical evidence on structure and substantive representation has been modest. In the most direct study linking descriptive representation and electoral structure to substantive representation, Sass and Mehay (2003) ana-lyze whether or not black city council members have greater policy influence in jurisdictions that use at-large elections rather than ward election systems. They test this proposition by estimating the hiring of municipal police officers. The results show that cities with an at-large electoral system hire a "substan-tially greater proportion of black police officers" (Sass and Mehay 2003, 334).[3] These findings suggest one of two possibilities. The first possibility is that black representatives elected in an at-large system have a significant amount of influ-ence over policy decisions. The other possibility suggests that perhaps white representatives are responsive to the interests of the black community when elected at-large.

In contrast, two other studies have found that representatives elected through SMDs generate more benefits for minority constituents. Although a series of studies of urban school districts have linked minority hiring to representation systems (Leal et al. 2004; Meier and Stewart 1991; Meier et al. 1989; Robinson, England, and Meier 1985), none of these studies examines whether at-large or ward representatives are more effective. They simply relate the descriptive legislative representation to bureaucratic representation rather than distinguish among the effectiveness of representatives elected in various systems. One previ-ous school board study examines this question. Meier et al. (2005) examined 1,009 Texas school districts to find that minority school board members elected in an at-large system were less effective in securing allocative benefits than rep-resentatives elected from SMDs. That study is limited, however, by its focus on a single state, its cross-sectional analysis, and its focus only on minority hir-ing as an outcome. A recent study of Maori representation in New Zealand is also relevant (Crisp, Demirkaya, and Millian 2014). They find Maoris elected from Maori reserved seats are stronger advocates of Maori interests than those elected from nonreserved seats. A reserved position has some similarities to a SMD that is majority-minority. There remains, however, substantial uncer-tainty in how different electoral systems have affected representation and, more importantly, none of the studies addressed policy representation.

---

[3] Sass and Mehay specify electoral structure with a dummy variable rather than as an interaction. This specification means that electoral structure should have the same impact on representation whether the group has zero representation or 20, 35, or 60 percent representation.

A Theory of Political Structure and Substantive Representation

The literature on substantive minority representation has offered a variety of viewpoints that, at times, provide conflicting implications. By empirically analyzing black substantive outcomes in the educational sphere, we shed light on a portion of the debate regarding how and when representation matters. The impact of the two systems we study, at-large and SMDs, can be clarified through formal logic to illustrate how electoral structure is linked to representational effectiveness. This section gives a brief overview of the two systems considered here and generates a set of testable hypotheses, each of which we examine with our school district data. The basic logic is that structure by itself is unlikely to be crucial, rather structure interacts with other contextual factors to fully determine how descriptive representation is translated into substantive representation.

First, we must consider why a black candidate elected in an at-large system might be less (or more) effective at pursuing black interests than one elected from a SMD. Following Meier et al. (2005), we begin with the following assumptions:

Assumption 1. Rational voters will vote for candidates most likely to represent their interests.

Assumption 2. Rational candidates will seek to satisfy constituency interests (either strictly for reelection or to pursue policy goals).

Assumption 3. Race is an important political issue (i.e., political preferences differ based on race), but blacks do not compose a majority of the electorate.

For example, consider a district where the large majority of voters are white so that the median voter is also highly likely to be white. These voters will tend to elect someone who represents their interests (assumption 1) which, if the electorate is polarized by race, likely do not include issues most central to black voters (assumption 3). In order for a black candidate to successfully win an election, he or she must craft a campaign targeted at the nonminority median voter (assumption 2). In some cases, this may lead to the downplaying or outright rejection of positions supported by black voters. Once in office, if the black candidate shifts his or her focus from the expressed campaign positions to those that match more closely with black constituents, he or she can alienate the median voter and risks losing office in the next election (Downs 1957).

The problems associated with moving to the median voter position in an at-large system mean that minority candidates should fare better *descriptively* in SMD systems that are likely to have one or more districts with a black majority. In terms of substantive representation, however, Guinier (1991), Sass and Mehay (2003), and Swain (1993) argue that having minority candidates run and win in at-large elections improves eventual policy outcomes by increasing the likelihood that black elected officials will find coalition partners with white elected officials because they represent similar constituencies.

To illustrate precisely the differences in electoral systems and why conflicting hypotheses are generated, let us assume that the expected utility (E(U)) gained through representation is the sum of the values (V) sought by the representative times the probability (P) of attaining the values.

$$E(U) = \Sigma \, PV$$

The advocates of ward elections are essentially arguing that the values (V) of at-large based representatives are different (e.g., they are less relevant to the minority community) from those of representatives from SMDs owing to the necessity of getting elected (i.e., positioning at the median voter). At-large advocates take a different view by noting that the descriptive representatives are still a numerical minority so that nonminority representatives can veto any prominority policies (i.e., that the value of P is close to zero).

To support the cause of at-large elections, the advocates contend that the probability (P) of achieving any representation values after election increases in at-large systems owing to the common constituencies and the potential for coalition partners. The ward advocates counter that the at-large minority representatives will hold values distinctly different from the values of their minority constituents so that any representational success will not be as closely linked to constituent values. In short, whether ward or at-large elections generate better substantive representation depends on whether the change in values (V) is greater or less than the change in the probability (P) of attaining the values. Both sides use the same assumptions and the same utility calculus but emphasize different parts of the equation. The two contradictory hypotheses, therefore, are the result of stressing either changes in values (wards) or changes in the probability of attaining these values (at-large). Substantive minority representation, as a result, can be greater (or smaller) in ward-based SMD systems than will the substantive representation in at-large systems depending on the relative change of values versus the relative change in probabilities. Our hypotheses can be stated as:

H_1 [The Ward Hypothesis] Minority representatives in ward-based SMD systems will be more likely to share the policy values of minority constituents; they will thus be more effective representing minority interests than will minority representatives in at-large systems, all other things being equal.

H_2 [The At-Large Hypothesis] Minority representatives in at-large systems will find it easier to craft majority coalitions and will thus be more effective in representing minority interests than will minority representatives in ward systems, all other things being equal.

Generalizing the preceding arguments further, the at-large hypothesis is essentially about the ability to gain support from like-minded individuals. Such allies might be generated with processes other than at-large elections. The argument for SMDs and descriptive representation relies on the assumption of racial polarization. If one relaxes the assumption of racial polarization, it means that some other political cleavage will be the determinant of election outcomes. Partisanship or ideology are likely candidates. Because the voting patterns for African Americans are so heavily Democratic, having white

Democrats either as constituents or as fellow elected officials should also be a way to increase the probability of attaining any representational values in the absence of racial polarization.[4] This logic suggest that the at-large hypothesis might be a special case of a more general hypothesis:

H3 [The Allies Hypothesis] Minority representatives in any electoral system will find it easier to craft coalitions when they have supportive allies. In jurisdictions with Democratic voting majorities, minority representatives will be more successful in representing minority interests.

Data

This chapter uses the same database that was introduced in Chapter 3; three original surveys generated data on school board representation, administrators, and teachers in 2001, 2004, and 2008 for all school districts with student populations more than five thousand. The demographic and socioeconomic information were from the 2000 US Census school district files, and the partisan distribution of school districts were estimated using data on elections returns for 2004 and 2008 presidential elections. The panel nature of the data set and potential problems were addressed with fixed effects for the individual years to deal with any trends over time, and standard errors are clustered by school district.[5]

This chapter examines allocative representation; policy representation will be addressed in Chapters 5 and 6. The two measures of allocative responsiveness are the percentage of African-American administrators and the percentage of African-American teachers in the school district. The process of hiring administrators and teachers varies enough so that it is quite possible that descriptive representation might affect one but not the other. Hiring teachers is generally more constrained with elaborate certification requirements imposed at the state level. Although there are alternative certification processes for teachers, these also have education requirements and include additional posthiring training. The implementation of quality teacher standards under No Child Left Behind has also placed a high premium on certified teachers (though exceptions were certainly made for many groups, including Teach for America affiliates). Administrators, particularly central office administrators, can be drawn from a range of professions, and thus, allow more flexibility in hiring.[6] The empirical evidence suggests hiring more African-American administrators is easier than hiring African-American teachers. In our sample, African Americans achieve

---

[4] Or it might be the case that partisanship is a measure of racial polarization given the collinearity of race and partisanship. Preuhs (2006) uses region as a measure of polarization at the state level, which is also highly collinear with partisanship.

[5] Including state fixed effects do not substantively change findings reported in the following text.

[6] Many states have qualification restrictions for principals, vice principals, and superintendents that require additional education or a given period of time in the classroom. A variety of other administrative positions are fairly open in terms of qualifications.

98 percent of the administrative representation their population would predict but only 73 percent of the teacher representation.[7] Specific hypotheses distinguishing between teachers and administrators are ambiguous; because hiring administrators is subject to fewer rules, one might expect that descriptive representation would have a stronger impact on administrators than teachers. Meier et al. (1989) found school board representation influenced the hiring of black administrators but only indirectly affected the hiring of black teachers (by increasing the number of black administrators; there were no direct effects). The logic of more committed values and greater allies, by contrast, are likely to be more valuable as processes get more difficult suggesting that structure might have a greater influence on the hiring of teachers.

Modeling Substantive Representation

An extensive literature in US politics uses the hiring of bureaucratic employees as a measure of the allocative dimension of substantive representation. Hiring public employees, however, is not an unconstrained task as it might have been during the patronage era but is subject to merit system rules and a variety of other constraints. The dominant determinant of minority hiring or any public employment position is the composition and qualifications of the labor pool. To that factor, we add variables measuring the political context and representation as it interacts with electoral structure. Parallel models for policy actions (Chapters 4 and 5) will include all of these factors plus the representation of black administrators and black teachers.

Representation and Structure

The theoretical argument linking descriptive representation as modified by structure to substantive representation requires an interaction between electoral structure and representation. African-American representation on the school board is measured as the percentage of school board members who are African American. As noted in Chapter 3, school boards in the United States use three types of selection plans – at-large elections in which all individuals are elected by the entire jurisdiction (59 percent of cases in this analysis), SMD elections in which individuals run within smaller wards with one representative per ward (29 percent), and appointed systems in which the school board is appointed by another elected official (3 percent).[8] The remaining school districts (9 percent)

---

[7] These figures are generated using a regression with African-American administrators (or teachers) as the dependent variable and African-American population as the independent variable. The administrator representation is also easier to affect because there are fewer of them. Teachers make up 50 to 60 percent of school district employees whereas administrations are generally less than 5 percent of the total.

[8] Appointed systems are used in dependent school districts where the school system is a unit of another local government such as the Chicago Public Schools. Appointed systems are also put in place temporarily when a school district is taken over by the state.

use a combination of these methods, the most common of which is electing some members at-large and some in SMDs. Most elections, regardless of structure, are organized as nonpartisan elections (87 percent); most school board candidates cannot explicitly identify with a political party. The electoral system variable will be operationalized as the proportion of members elected by SMDs and the proportion appointed (with those elected at-large as the excluded category) to retain the mixed systems in the analysis. These two variables will be interacted with the percentage of African-American school board members so as to permit comparing the effectiveness of representatives elected in pure at-large with those elected by pure SMD systems or appointed (see Engstrom and McDonald 1982; Meier et al. 2005).

The Political Context

The political context – a key contribution of this book – contains a set of factors that could facilitate or limit the ability of African-American representatives to be engaged in allocative responsiveness – partisanship and unionization. Democratic partisanship is likely to enhance the ability to hire additional minority teachers and administrators by providing allies in the political support for affirmative action policies. Liberal whites are viewed as a natural political ally of African Americans (Browning et al. 1984; Hajnal 2001; Sigelman et al. 1995) and are likely to share policy values with African Americans. This chapter uses the Democratic percentage variable estimated by presidential election returns for 2004 and 2008 with adjustments for the differences in school district and county demographics (see Chapter 3).

In addition to partisanship, we also control for the presence of unions, as these groups have long played a role in the politics of urban school districts (Katznelson 1981; Moe 2009). Although much attention has been paid to the role of teachers' unions in school board electoral politics, they can also influence hiring practices given their ability to negotiate for and engage in the protection of union members. Unions should essentially slow down the personnel process and make rapid changes in personnel less likely. Given the historical discrimination in hiring, this could result in a negative relationship with minority hiring. Our surrogate measure of unionization is the percentage of the workforce that was unionized in each state. This assumes that the presence of unions within a state is correlated with the level of teacher unionization and thus that teachers are more likely to be unionized. This also assumes that a relatively even proportion of teachers in all districts across the state are unionized.

Labor Pool Factors

The primary labor pool characteristic is the size of the minority population. This factor, operationalized as the percentage of the population in the school district that is black, is consistently the strongest predictor of minority employment in the bureaucracy (Eisinger 1980; Meier, O'Toole, and Nicholson-Crotty 2004;

Mladenka 1989; Sass and Mehay 2003). US education systems have elaborate certification processes for teachers and, to a lesser extent, educational administrators. Alternative certification processes have created some additional avenues to teaching positions, but a college degree is essentially required for teaching positions and virtually required for administrative ones; the qualifications measure is the percentage of the black population aged 25+ with a college degree. The attractiveness of a teaching position is also likely a function of the relative benefits of teaching versus alternative jobs, and this can be tapped by some economic factors. Models of teachers and administrators have used a measure of median black income to indicate the relative attractiveness of a teaching salary, a measure of black home ownership to indicate minority commitment to the community (Baretto, Marks, and Woods 2007), and a measure of white poverty to indicate the percentage of whites that may have a similar socioeconomic status to minority populations in the community. The labor pool characteristics should be considered controls to make sure the models are not underspecified and will not be given a great deal of attention in this analysis.[9]

Finally, a district can only hire African-American teachers and administrators if there are qualified individuals, generally graduates of schools of education. School districts in the South have an advantage in this regard for two reasons. First, by operating a segregated school system for many years, southern districts created a demand for African-American teachers for their segregated schools. Second, to meet this demand, many of the southern Historically Black Colleges and Universities had strong teaching programs that continue to produce large numbers of teachers today. We classified a district as southern if it was located in a state that operated a *de jure* segregated school system in 1954 when the Supreme Court declared such systems unconstitutional for the first time.

The Quality of Black Representation

Because the estimations that show the interactions of structure and representation are fairly complex, we will examine the determinants of bureaucratic representation in two steps. The first step will present some relatively underspecified models to show the determinants of representation without considering the influence of structure. The second step will include the structural interactions in the model, and the third step will probe the relationship of partisanship and how it enhances or limits representation in different cases.

Table 4.1 presents the initial determinants of African-American administrators. Column 1 presents the simple regression of African-American population on administrative representation and clearly demonstrates how much population size by itself contributes to representation. African Americans achieved fully 98 percent of the administrative representation that they would expect

---

[9] Income, home ownership, and white poverty are relatively rough proxies for the concepts they seek to measure but are frequently used in the literature.

TABLE 4.1. *Baseline Determinants of Black Administrators*

DV: % Black Administrators	Model 1	Model 2	Model 3
Intercept	-0.141	-0.276	-4.085*
	(0.192)	(0.186)	(1.043)
Black Population Percentage	0.982*	0.800*	0.812*
	(0.019)	(0.034)	(0.032)
Percent Black Board		0.212*	0.149*
		(0.026)	(0.023)
Black Education (College Percent)			-0.007
			(0.009)
Black Family Income (000s)			-0.031
			(0.024)
Black Home Ownership			0.009
			(0.006)
White Poverty Percentage			-0.188*
			(0.052)
District Democrat Percent			0.123*
			(0.015)
South			1.401*
			(0.508)
Unionization			-0.079*
			(0.037)
Year FE	Yes	Yes	Yes
N	4207	4078	3542
R^2	0.78	0.80	0.81
F	877.1	793.18	297.07

Standard errors in parentheses.
* $p < 0.05$; + $p < .10$

based solely on population (the intercept is insignificant indicating no thresh-old effect), and the regression coefficient is not statistically different from 1.0 or perfectly equitable representation. Although the level of prediction is rela-tively high (78 percent), just more than 20 percent of the variation remains unexplained.[10]

The second column of Table 4.1 adds school board representation to this equation and shows a statistically significant positive impact over and above the impact of black population. A 1 percentage point increase in black school board representation is associated with a .21 percentage point increase in black school administrators controlling for population. The striking aspect of this equation is that the regression coefficients are almost exactly equal to those reported in Meier et al. (1989, 73) for their 1986 data from a set of large school

---

[10] The first two models in Table 4.1 were also conducted with the restricted sample of the 3,542 cases in Model 3. Findings (not shown) remain robust and are not affected by the dropping of cases.

districts (see following text). The third column of Table 4.1 adds in the various labor pool factors and partisanship. Partisanship shows a strong positive relationship and has approximately the same level of impact on black administrative representation as school board representation does. This suggests that partisanship (or at least its correlated values) is associated with outcomes of a personnel process that is designed to be based on neutral merit system principles. From a representation standpoint, black representation's impact on allocative representative over and above the impact of partisanship is important, something that is rarely found in the legislative literature.

Labor pool factors have a series of modest influences on black administrative representation. Of note are the positive relationship of region (southern districts have on average 1.4 percentage points more black administrators) and that districts in more unionized states have fewer black administrators on average. The relationship between white poverty and black administrators is unexpected but its cumulative impact is modest. Overall the three key variables that influence the percentage of black administrators are black population size, black school board representation, and Democratic partisanship (there is also a slight upward trend in black administrators).

The determinants of African-American teachers are presented in Table 4.2 in a series of similar steps, with the exception that the percent of black administrators is added as a control variable in Model 3 because administrators should be able to directly hire more black teachers. The first column shows that African Americans are underrepresented in teaching population; a 1 percentage point increase in black population is associated with .73 percentage point increase in black teachers. This figure is highly consistent with the representation levels reported in Meier et al. (1989, 72). The underrepresentation is even more significant if the comparison is to the student population where the representation ratio drops to .50 (model not shown).

The second column of Table 4.2 adds school board representation to the equation; the coefficient is positive and significant. The inclusion of the political and labor pool factors in Model 3 illustrates why school board representation has no direct impact on teacher representation; that equation is dominated by two factors – black administrative representation and black population. School board representation influences the level of administrative representation that, in turn, affects the level of teacher representation. The impact of school board representation is indirect, working through administrative representation. This pattern of relationships mirrors the personnel selection process. There are fewer administrators and the board can directly determine the race of at least the top administrator; teacher hiring encompasses many more individuals and is highly regulated by both certification requirements and merit system rules.

Political and labor force factors retain some modest influences on the levels of teacher representation. Democratic partisanship and the southern region are positively associated with black teachers while unions are negatively associated with teacher representation. The substantive influence of partisanship is not

TABLE 4.2. *Baseline Determinants of Black Teachers*

DV: % Black Teachers	Model 1	Model 2	Model 3
Intercept	−0.856*	−0.818*	−2.421*
	(0.161)	(0.162)	(0.618)
Black Population Percentage	0.729*	0.631*	0.310*
	(0.020)	(0.029)	(0.027)
Percent Black Board		0.105*	0.013
		(0.021)	(0.016)
Percent Black Administrators			0.399*
			(0.027)
Black Education (College Percent)			0.022*
			(0.006)
Black Family Income (000s)			−0.004
			(0.014)
Black Home Ownership			0.005
			(0.004)
White Poverty Percentage			0.075*
			(0.027)
District Democrat Percent			0.038*
			(0.009)
South			0.622*
			(0.286)
Unionization			−0.098*
			(0.024)
Year FE	Yes	Yes	Yes
N	4465	4311	3494
R²	0.77	0.78	0.86
F	432.11	346.59	213.06

Standard errors in parentheses.
* $p < 0.05$; + $p < .10$

large and would thus have to exert itself through favorable community attitudes. This correlation along with the findings in Chapter 3 merit further investigation (see following text).[11] The percentage of black teachers also increases as the percentage of black college graduates increases and as the percentage of whites in poverty increases.

Electoral Structure and Representation

The central theoretical question this chapter addresses is the relationship between electoral structure and representation while taking into account the

---

[11] The size of the partisanship coefficient for black teachers is essentially one-fourth the size of the same coefficient for black administrators. The decline in partisan association as one moves further down the administrative hierarchy is consistent with how US merit systems are designed.

mediating effect of politics. There are theoretical reasons that argue for either at-large elections or SMD elections in generating conditions that enhance the ability of representatives to gain allocational benefits. Table 4.3 examines the impact of African-American school board members on the hiring of African-American administrators and teachers. For African-American administrators, population size, a basic labor pool characteristic, remains the predominant predictor.[12] This makes imminent sense in that one cannot generate bureaucratic representation if there is no population to represent. The interactive nature of the equation means that the regression results need to be reordered to get a clear view of how structure influences representation. The zero-order coefficients for African-American representation and the intercept are interpreted as the impact of representation in at-large systems because the ward and appointed terms are equal to zero as are the interaction terms (controlling for all other factors in the model). The impact of representation in ward and appointed systems can be calculated by simply substituting in the change in intercept and change in slope terms as follows:

At-Large Systems Administrators = –4.176 + .129 Representation

Ward Systems Administrators = (–4.176 + .176) + (.129 + .041) Representation

Or –4.0 + .170 Representation

Appointed Administrators = (–4.176 + 1.294) + (.129 + .052) Representation

Or –2.882 + .181 Representation

Although these equations suggest that representatives elected in SMDs or appointed are slightly more effective than those elected at-large, the interaction coefficients are not statistically different from zero.[13] The appropriate conclusion is that a 1 percentage point increase in African-American representatives is associated with a .13 percentage point increase in African-American administrators, and that how the representatives are elected has no impact on their allocative effectiveness.[14] Several of the control variables remain significant predictors with administrative representation positively associated with Democratic partisanship and Southern region and negatively associated with white poverty and unionization.

The second column of Table 4.3 presents a similar regression for the employment of African-American teachers with one exception – the inclusion of the percentage of African-American administrators as an independent variable to reflect that administrators hire teachers. The most important predictor

---

[12] Nonlinear tests for both the black population and black board members proved insignificant.

[13] The intercept terms are meaningful only if all other variables are set at zero, which is well outside the range of the data. The change-in-intercept terms, however, are meaningful because they indicate the difference in levels across the selection systems.

[14] Column 3 in Table 4.1 indicates that without the interaction terms in the equation, the best estimate of the representation impact is approximately .15 or slightly larger than the coefficient in Table 4.3.

TABLE 4.3. *Impact of Electoral Structure on Black Representation: Administrators and Teachers*

	DV: % Black Administrators	DV: % Black Teachers
Intercept	-4.176*	-2.519*
	(1.044)	(0.579)
Percent Black Administrators		0.390*
		(0.027)
Percent Black Board	0.129*	-0.038*
	(0.026)	(0.015)
Black Population Percentage	0.799*	0.282*
	(0.034)	(0.026)
Ward Elections	0.176	-0.573*
	(0.286)	(0.203)
Ward X Percent Black Board	0.041	0.139*
	(0.034)	(0.026)
Appointed System	1.294	-2.096*
	(1.527)	(0.818)
Appointed X Percent Black Board	0.052	0.140*
	(0.081)	(0.036)
Black Education (College Percent)	-0.007	0.017*
	(0.009)	(0.005)
Black Family Income (000s)	-0.027	0.004
	(0.024)	(0.013)
Black Home Ownership	0.009	0.005
	(0.006)	(0.003)
White Poverty Percentage	-0.189*	0.081*
	(0.052)	(0.026)
District Democrat Percent	0.124*	0.042*
	(0.015)	(0.008)
South	1.295*	0.604*
	(0.494)	(0.272)
Unionization	-0.077*	-0.077*
	(0.037)	(0.023)
Year Effects	Yes	Yes
N	3522	3476
R^2	0.81	0.87
F	229.6	204.7

Standard errors in parentheses.
* $p < 0.05$; + $p < .10$

of African-American teachers again is the percentage of African-American administrators, and population also has a strong and significant effect. The results of the structure representation interaction provide the first support for hypothesis 1. The relevant representation equations are as follows:

At-Large Systems Teachers = −2.52 − .038 Representation
Ward Systems Teachers = (−2.52 − .573) + (−.038 + .139) Representation
Or −3.09 + .101 Representation
Appointed Teachers = (−2.52 − 2.096) + (−.038 + .140) Representation
Or −4.616 + .102 Representation

In at-large systems, school board representation is not associated with more African-American teachers; it is significantly and *negatively* related although the impact is relatively small (a 10 percentage point increase is representation is associated with less than a half percentage point decline in teachers). Representatives elected in SMDs as well as appointed representatives have a positive impact (the coefficients are statistically distinct from both the at-large coefficient and from zero). In both cases a 10 percentage point increase in African-American representation is associated with a 1 percentage point increase in teacher representation. Given the elaborate merit system procedures for hiring teachers, this impact should be considered substantively significant. Further, as most school boards consist of seven to nine people, this level of change would be experienced given the election of one additional African-American member.

Examining the individual change coefficients reveals that in both cases the intercept for SMDs and appointed representatives becomes more negative. For the SMD representatives, the negative drop in intercept is compensated by the increase in slope when representation is greater than 4 percent; given the relative size of school boards (96.5 percent have nine or fewer members), this indicates that any representation at all in a ward system generates positive results. For appointed systems, the threshold is 15 percent representation, which suggests that a single person on an appointed school board is likely to have little impact and a critical mass could well be needed. Teacher representation remains positively associated with black education levels, Democratic partisans, white poverty, and the southern region and is negatively associated with union strength.

These results should not be taken to imply that representatives elected at-large are completely ineffective in gaining allocational representation at the street level, only that they have no direct impact. Similar to representatives elected through ward structures or who are appointed, representatives in at-large districts still have an indirect impact on the teaching population through their influence on the hiring of African-American administrators (column 1) who in turn are associated with more African-American teachers (column 2).

The results thus far support the first hypothesis and reject the second; African Americans elected in SMDs are associated with better allocational representation than are at-large members. These findings are consistent with the logic that the change in values is more important than the change in probability associated with coalition partners. These results, however, could be influenced by the small set of school districts where African Americans are a majority of the population,

TABLE 4.4. *Impact of Electoral Structure on Black Representation, Minority Districts*

	DV: % Black Administrators	DV: % Black Teachers
Intercept	−3.784*	−1.924*
	(1.040)	(0.552)
Percent Black Administrators		0.348*
		(0.024)
Percent Black Board	0.159*	−0.027+
	(0.026)	(0.014)
Black Population Percentage	0.782*	0.274*
	(0.031)	(0.026)
Ward Elections	0.561*	−0.213
	(0.272)	(0.159)
Ward X Percent Black Board	−0.007	0.104*
	(0.035)	(0.022)
Appointed System	0.376	−1.714*
	(1.098)	(0.645)
Appointed X Percent Black Board	0.105+	0.147*
	(0.055)	(0.030)
Black Education (College Percent)	−0.008	0.011*
	(0.009)	(0.005)
Black Family Income (000s)	−0.013	0.003
	(0.023)	(0.012)
Black Home Ownership	0.007	0.005
	(0.005)	(0.003)
White Poverty Percentage	−0.182*	0.074*
	(0.051)	(0.026)
District Democrat Percent	0.111*	0.032*
	(0.015)	(0.008)
South	1.190*	0.784*
	(0.474)	(0.237)
Unionization	−0.067+	−0.060*
	(0.037)	(0.019)
Year FE	Yes	Yes
N	3451	3405
R^2	0.77	0.83
F	225.28	207.24

Standard errors in parentheses.
* $p < 0.05$; + $p < .10$

which renders the coalitional argument moot. To investigate further, Table 4.4 presents the determinants of African-American administrators and teachers only for those districts where African Americans are less than 50 percent of the population. The results of Table 4.4 confirm those in Table 4.3; Figure 4.1 further

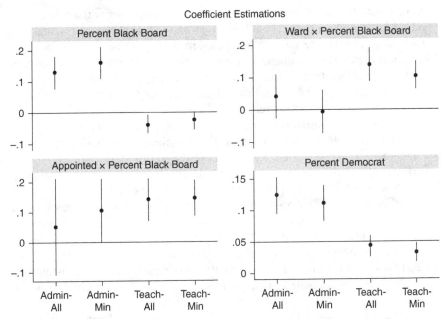

FIGURE 4.1. Black administrators and teachers, all districts and minority districts.

illustrates coefficient estimates for population, structure, and partisanship across Tables 4.3 and 4.4. The exception is in the administrative equation where the change in intercept term for SMDs is now positive and statistically significant. The impact is modest at best with an additional 0.56 percent African-American administrators in districts where the school board is elected in SMDs (the slopes do not change from one system to the other). The representational effectiveness of appointed African-American school board members also increases to .264 from .159, a statistically significant impact at the 0.10 level. That appointed board members appear more effective in jurisdictions where African Americans are a minority likely reflects the coalition composition of the appointing politicians. The second equation in Table 4.4 for teacher representation shows results that are highly consistent with Table 4.3, again indicating that African-American representatives elected from SMDs are associated with higher levels of allocative representation compared to those elected at-large.

The importance of partisanship in all models presented thus far stands in contrast to the general argument that education policy is nonpartisan. Browning et al. (1984) indicate an important role for partisanship in their study of urban politics; they contend that the presence of liberal whites is necessary for African Americans to be fully incorporated into a governing coalition. Quite clearly, liberal whites are more likely to be found in the Democratic Party than in the Republican Party. A substantial portion of liberal whites could well mean that some of the white school board members share the same policy values as the

African-American school board members and see themselves in the role of representing African Americans (see Selden 1997 on the role of the representative).

To further clarify the role of partisanship in the representation process, Table 4.5 presents the administrative and teacher equations for districts with a Democratic majority and for districts with a Republican majority; Figure 4.2 further illustrates the effects of representation, structure, and partisanship on administrators and teachers in these two contexts. Consistent with Table 4.3, at the administrative level, structure appears to matter very little; the interaction coefficients are statistically insignificant for both Republican and Democratic jurisdictions. One modest difference is that the effectiveness of African-American representatives in general appears to be higher in Democratic jurisdictions (.146) than in Republican ones (.101), although the two coefficients are not statistically different from each other. This lack of significance, however, is a function of including those districts with African-American population majorities. When the analysis is limited to those districts where African Americans are less than half of the population (Table 4.6), the representation coefficient in Democratic jurisdictions (0.206) is almost double that in Republican areas (0.102); and the difference is statistically significant. So while structure does not matter in this case, partisanship does.

The teacher regressions in Table 4.5 show the impact of the combination of electoral structure and partisanship. African-American representatives in at-large systems are not associated with any increase in African-American teachers regardless of which party is the majority. In both cases only representatives in either SMDs or appointive systems are associated with gains in allocative representation. For the SMD systems, the impact of partisanship is readily apparent. The size of the representation coefficient is three times larger in Democratic jurisdictions (.194) than it is in Republican ones (.060), and the difference is statistically significant (the relationship is unaffected by whether or not African Americans are a majority of the population; see Table 4.7). This indicates that, all other things being equal, black representatives elected from SMDs are significantly more effective in allocative representation than their counter parts in Republican districts.[15]

The best of all possible worlds in allocative representation is to achieve a voting majority in the legislature. Two percent of district years in our analysis have a school board with an African-American majority. Table 4.8 replicates the results of the teacher model in Table 4.3 but includes an interaction between African-American representation and a dummy variable for the cases in which African Americans control the school board.[16] Model 1 includes all districts in

---

[15] This finding also holds if one pools the equations and uses interaction terms to determine the relative impact of SMD representatives.

[16] The large negative intercept shift with majority black districts can be ignored because it is more than compensated for the 50 percent figure for black representatives. The actual intercept shift at a voting majority is approximately a 3.5 percent increase in African-American teachers.

TABLE 4.5. *Impact of Partisanship on Black Representation: Administrators and Teachers*

	DV: % Black Administrators		DV: % Black Teachers	
	Republican	Democrat	Republican	Democrat
Intercept	−3.613*	−5.500*	−2.853*	−2.651+
	(1.351)	(2.650)	(0.613)	(1.492)
Percent Black			0.352*	0.382*
Administrators			(0.026)	(0.041)
Percent Black Board	0.101*	0.146*	−0.025	−0.033
	(0.031)	(0.041)	(0.018)	(0.024)
Black Population	0.785*	0.787*	0.296*	0.286*
Percentage	(0.038)	(0.054)	(0.025)	(0.041)
Ward Elections	0.510+	−0.157	−0.010	−0.912*
	(0.304)	(0.547)	(0.158)	(0.412)
Ward X Percent Black	0.035	0.050	0.060*	0.194*
Board	(0.046)	(0.048)	(0.024)	(0.041)
Appointed System	1.048	1.152	−1.705*	−1.219
	(1.570)	(2.244)	(0.781)	(1.046)
Appointed X Percent	0.136	0.028	0.099*	0.131*
Black Board	(0.089)	(0.094)	(0.049)	(0.040)
Black Education	0.006	−0.023	0.011+	0.025*
(College Percent)	(0.010)	(0.015)	(0.005)	(0.009)
Black Family Income	−0.038	−0.039	0.007	−0.016
(000s)	(0.031)	(0.040)	(0.015)	(0.023)
Black Home Ownership	0.005	0.015	0.009*	0.001
	(0.007)	(0.009)	(0.004)	(0.007)
White Poverty Percentage	−0.135*	−0.275*	0.095*	0.036
	(0.058)	(0.105)	(0.028)	(0.059)
District Democrat Percent	0.122*	0.135*	0.034*	0.049*
	(0.026)	(0.036)	(0.012)	(0.020)
South	0.466	3.819*	0.427+	2.199*
	(0.507)	(1.030)	(0.224)	(0.654)
Unionization	−0.063	−0.047	−0.003	−0.100*
	(0.045)	(0.063)	(0.020)	(0.042)
Year FE	Yes	Yes	Yes	Yes
N	2107	1415	2080	1396
R²	0.76	0.84	0.84	0.9
F	144.46	135.00	145.58	137.28

Standard errors in parentheses.

* $p < 0.05$; + $p < .10$

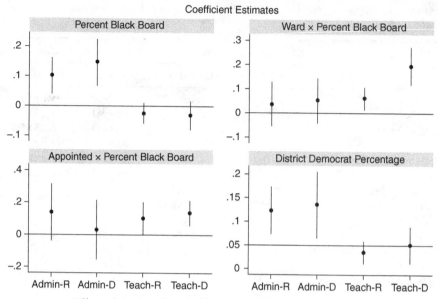

FIGURE 4.2. Effect of partisanship on black administrators and teachers.

our sample, and Model 2 includes only districts where African Americans are a minority population. The marginal effects of a 10 percentage point increase in black board representation for the various combinations of electoral structure and majorities on the board reveals the following in terms of hiring black teachers:

At-large minority of board members	−0.78
At-large majority of board members	+1.43
SMD minority of board members	+0.61
SMD majority of board members	+2.82
Appointed minority of board members	+0.19
Appointed majority of board members	+2.40

All marginal effects are statistically significant except for the appointive-minority case. Although the best possible cases for representation occur when there is a voting majority on the school board, this is an obvious and perhaps trivial case (but see the extensive literature on black mayors and city council majorities including Eisinger 1982; Gerber and Hopkins 2011; Keller 1978). The results clearly show how the values portion of the utility calculus dominates the relationship between representation and allocative responsiveness. SMD systems consistently produce better representation; this representational effectiveness is further enhanced when the jurisdiction has a Democratic majority. Appointive systems also have a positive interaction coefficient that is slightly larger than

TABLE 4.6. *Impact of Partisanship on Black Representation: Administrators, Black Minority Districts*

	DV: % Black Administrators	
	Republican	Democrat
Intercept	−3.622*	−4.0478
	(1.351)	(2.671)
Percent Black Board	0.102*	0.206*
	(0.031)	(0.041)
Black Population Percentage	0.783*	0.753*
	(0.039)	(0.052)
Ward Elections	0.531	0.480
	(0.304)	(0.528)
Ward X Percent Black Board	0.032	−0.022
	(0.047)	(0.053)
Appointed System	1.005	0.013
	(1.591)	(1.783)
Appointed X Percent Black Board	0.140	0.097
	(0.095)	(0.065)
Black Education (College Percent)	0.006	−0.023
	(0.010)	(0.015)
Black Family Income (000s)	−0.038	−0.007
	(0.031)	(0.035)
Black Home Ownership	0.005	0.011
	(0.007)	(0.009)
White Poverty Percentage	−0.135*	−0.271*
	(0.057)	(0.100)
District Democrat Percent	0.123*	0.107*
	(0.026)	(0.034)
South	0.472	3.271*
	(0.510)	(0.975)
Unionization	−0.064	−0.051
	(0.046)	(0.062)
Year FE	Yes	Yes
N	2102	1349
R^2	0.75	0.79
F	130.57	118.13

Standard errors in parentheses.
* $p < 0.05$; + $p < .10$

the ward coefficient in Republican majority jurisdictions and slightly smaller in Democratic ones.

The idea that Democratic partisans are allies of African-American school board members is not fully captured by the previous regression results. Those results essentially treated partisanship as a relative constant in the

TABLE 4.7. *Impact of Partisanship on Black Representation: Teachers, Black Minority Districts*

	DV: % Black Teachers	
	Republican	Democrat
Intercept	−2.820*	−0.897
	(0.612)	(1.446)
Percent Black Administrators	0.351*	0.321*
	(0.026)	(0.037)
Percent Black Board	−0.027	−0.008
	(0.018)	(0.022)
Black Population Percentage	0.301*	0.251*
	(0.025)	(0.044)
Ward Elections	0.016	−0.391
	(0.158)	(0.329)
Ward X Percent Black Board	0.055*	0.154*
	(0.024)	(0.041)
Appointed System	−1.648*	−1.437
	(0.817)	(0.895)
Appointed X Percent Black Board	0.116*	0.172*
	(0.048)	(0.040)
Black Education (College Percent)	0.011*	0.012
	(0.005)	(0.008)
Black Family Income (000s)	0.006	−0.008
	(0.015)	(0.020)
Black Home Ownership	0.009*	0.003
	(0.004)	(0.006)
White Poverty Percentage	0.094*	0.036
	(0.028)	(0.058)
District Democrat Percent	0.034*	0.021
	(0.012)	(0.018)
South	0.383+	2.539*
	(0.222)	(0.583)
Unionization	−0.007	−0.074*
	(0.020)	(0.034)
Year FE	Yes	Yes
N	2075	1330
R^2	0.83	0.85
F	142.10	98.08

Standard errors in parentheses.
* $p < 0.05$; + $p < .10$

representation process depending on whether the district has a Democratic or Republican majority. Theoretically, the presence of allies should augment the influence of representatives but how much should also depend on the level of representation. In short, the relationship between partisanship and black

TABLE 4.8. *Impact of Electoral Structure on Black Representation: Black Control of School Boards*

DV: % Black Teachers	All Districts	Minority Districts
Intercept	−2.132*	−1.861*
	(0.571)	(0.551)
Percent Black Administrators	0.385*	0.346*
	(0.026)	(0.024)
Percent Black Board	−0.077*	−0.035*
	(0.017)	(0.013)
Black Population Percentage	0.277*	0.272*
	(0.026)	(0.026)
Ward Elections	−0.449*	−0.181
	(0.177)	(0.157)
Ward X Percent Black Board	0.138*	0.102*
	(0.024)	(0.022)
Appointed System	−0.898	−1.580*
	(0.819)	(0.652)
Appointed X Percent Black Board	0.096*	0.144*
	(0.037)	(0.034)
Black Majority	−7.687	3.815
	(6.034)	(11.243)
Black Majority X Percent Black Board	0.221*	−0.032
	(0.097)	(0.189)
Black Education (College Percent)	0.012*	0.011*
	(0.005)	(0.005)
Black Family Income (000s)	−0.002	0.002
	(0.012)	(0.012)
Black Home Ownership	0.005	0.005+
	(0.003)	(0.003)
White Poverty Percentage	0.074*	0.073*
	(0.026)	(0.026)
District Democrat Percent	0.041*	0.032*
	(0.008)	(0.008)
South	0.859*	0.824*
	(0.256)	(0.234)
Unionization	−0.071*	−0.059*
	(0.021)	(0.019)
Year FE	Yes	Yes
N	3466	3395
R^2	0.87	0.83
F	221.83	184.32

Standard errors in parentheses.

* $p < 0.05$; + $p < .10$

TABLE 4.9. *The Role of Partisanship in Determining Black Administrator Representation*

DV: % Black Administrators	Model 1	Model 2
	Pure Ward	Pure At-Large
Intercept	−2.571	−3.825*
	(1.671)	(1.254)
Percent Black Board	−0.062	0.025
	(0.083)	(0.098)
District Democrat Percent	0.083*	0.104*
	(0.026)	(0.018)
Percent Black Board X Democrat Percent	0.005*	0.002
	(0.002)	(0.002)
Black Population Percentage	0.798*	0.802*
	(0.050)	(0.049)
Black Education (College Percent)	0.015	−0.012
	(0.027)	(0.008)
Black Family Income (000s)	−0.077	0.011
	(0.052)	(0.024)
Black Home Ownership	0.016	0.006
	(0.011)	(0.006)
White Poverty Percentage	−0.321*	−0.049
	(0.075)	(0.064)
South	2.558*	0.613
	(0.722)	(0.609)
Unionization	0.001	−0.090*
	(0.067)	(0.043)
Year FE	Yes	Yes
N	1009	2032
R^2	0.84	0.74
F	179.95	79.85

Standard errors in parentheses.
* $p < 0.05$; + $p < .10$

representation should be interactive. Because the existing equations already contain several interactions that create significant collinearity, we will hold constant the type of electoral structure (to eliminate a set of interactions) and examine the interaction of Democratic partisanship and black representation.

Table 4.9 shows the allocative representation results for the employment of African-American administrators. The first column shows the interaction of partisanship and representation in ward-based electoral systems and the second column shows a similar regression for at-large systems. The best way to view the impact of these two variables is to plot the marginal effects of the impact of black representation at various levels of Democratic partisanship

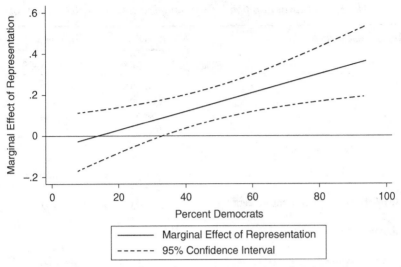

FIGURE 4.3. Marginal effect of representation on administrators as partisanship changes, pure ward districts.

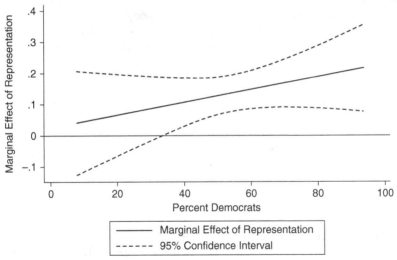

FIGURE 4.4. Marginal effect of representation on administrators as partisanship changes, pure at-large districts.

as in Figures 4.3 and 4.4. Both graphs clearly demonstrate that the relative efficacy of black representatives increases as the percentage of Democratic partisan increases, and that the marginal impact is statistically greater than zero at approximately 35 percent Democratic. Comparing the two figures, the

TABLE 4.10. *The Role of Partisanship in Determining Black Teacher Representation*

DV: % Black Teachers	Model 1	Model 2
	Pure Ward	Pure At-Large
Intercept	−2.214*	−0.833
	(1.107)	(0.531)
Percent Black Administrators	0.468*	0.314*
	(0.033)	(0.037)
Percent Black Board	−0.215*	−0.073
	(0.063)	(0.051)
District Democrat Percent	−0.012	0.018*
	(0.018)	(0.008)
Percent Black Board X Democrat Percent	0.005*	0.001
	(0.001)	(0.001)
Black Population Percentage	0.275*	0.263*
	(0.046)	(0.031)
Black Education (College Percent)	0.051*	0.000
	(0.016)	(0.005)
Black Family Income (000s)	0.009	0.008
	(0.035)	(0.013)
Black Home Ownership	0.005	0.004
	(0.007)	(0.003)
White Poverty Percentage	0.156*	0.054+
	(0.045)	(0.029)
South	0.841+	0.585*
	(0.484)	(0.282)
Unionization	−0.030	−0.066*
	(0.048)	(0.024)
Year FE	Yes	Yes
N	1000	2002
R^2	0.88	0.8
F	135.33	72.59

Standard errors in parentheses.
* $p < 0.05$; + $p < .10$

slope of the marginal effects line is much steeper in ward systems than in at-large systems generating the conclusion that representation in ward systems is more effective than representation in at-large systems at the same level of Democratic partisanship.[17]

The interactive impact of black representation and Democratic partisanship for teacher representation is presented in Table 4.10 and Figures 4.5 and 4.6. Again the figures provide the most direct and clearest picture of the

[17] The at-large systems are actually found in more Democratic areas. The average percent Democratic for pure systems is 49.6 percent for at-large and 43.1 percent for ward systems.

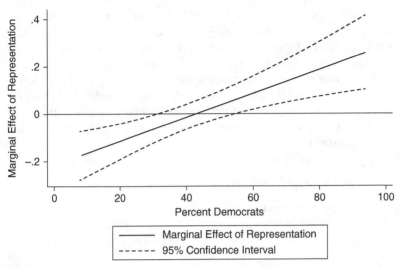

FIGURE 4.5. Marginal effect of representation on teachers as partisanship changes, pure wards.

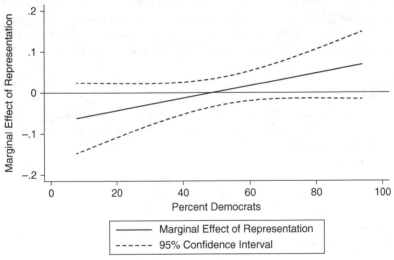

FIGURE 4.6. Marginal effect of representation on teachers as partisanship changes, pure at-large.

results. Although increases in Democratic partisanship increase the marginal effect of black representation in at-large systems, the overall impact is never statistically different from zero, a finding consistent with the earlier findings in this chapter. Figure 4.6 for ward systems shows that at low levels of Democratic partisanship, the impact of black school board representation on black teacher representation is negative, but that at higher levels of Democratic partisanship the relationship reverses and has a positive marginal effect. The marginal effects line crosses the zero point at approximately 42 percent Democratic. This finding essentially specifies the prior findings indicating that school board representation can penetrate to the lower levels of the bureaucracy only when there are ward elections (and the elected representatives closely share the values of their constituents) and where there are large numbers of Democratic partisans (allies who generally support greater bureaucratic representation).

Has Representation Changed Over Time?

Our snapshot comparison of large school districts in 1986 and 2008 shows some modest trends.[18] For these districts, the black representation on the school board increased from 15.8 percent to 19.8 percent, black administrative representation increased from 17.8 percent to 23.6 percent, but the percentage of black teachers dropped from 17.0 percent to 15.6 percent. The decline in black teachers represents the employment gains of the civil rights movement and the movement of individuals who would have opted to be teachers when schools were still segregated but now go on to law schools, business schools, medical schools, and other professions. Black administrators can increase at the same time that black teachers decrease simply because the number of administrators is much smaller and administrators are subjected to fewer restrictions in terms of educational background and licensing.

Comparing the 1986 sample of school districts with the same school districts in 2008 shows that the representation process has remained relatively similar. Table 4.11 predicts the level of black administrators (column 1) and the level of black teachers (column 2) with the percentage of black population and school board representation. By interacting these variables with a dummy variable for the year, one can tell whether or not the slopes were different in the two years. For black administrators, both population and school board representation are significant predictors, but none of the interaction terms reach statistical significance. The conservative conclusion is that the influence of both variables is no different in the two years (even though the population coefficient increases and the board representation coefficient decreases). For the black teacher equations, population dominates the regression, and school board representation is marginally significant (in 1986 but not in 2008). All the interaction terms are insignificant indicating the conservative conclusion is that representation remained the same in both years.

---

[18] Data from the 1986 analysis contained 174 total school districts. We were able to match 140 of these districts to data available in 2008. However, only ninety total districts have complete data for black board, administrator, and teacher representation for both years. As such, our snapshot multivariate analyses in this chapter only include the ninety direct matches.

TABLE 4.11. *Snapshot Comparison, Representation in 1986 and 2008*

	Model 1	Model 2
	DV: % Black Admins	DV: % Black Teachers
Intercept	1.018	0.210
	(0.705)	(0.698)
Black Population Percentage	0.798*	0.987*
	(0.079)	(0.071)
Percent Black Board	0.226*	0.011
	(0.061)	(0.061)
2008	1.296	−2.678*
	(1.058)	(0.875)
Black Population Percentage X 2008	0.159	−0.098
	(0.136)	(0.115)
Percent Black Board X 2008	−0.072	0.048
	(0.107)	(0.093)
N	180	180
R^2	0.86	0.87
F	163.47	150.94

Standard errors in parentheses.
* $p < 0.05$; + $p < .10$

It is important to note that this snapshot should be taken as simply a snapshot. Given the smaller number of cases and the low response rate in 1986 (67 percent), the comparisons likely illustrates the problems of small sample research that have limited previous studies. Similarly, a set of interactions of school board members times the type of representation system as in Table 4.3 (not shown) also showed none of the interactions in either 1986 or 2008 were statistically significant.

Table 4.12 shows an abbreviated regression for the influence of school board and administrative representation on teacher representation. As might be expected, school board representation has no direct impact, and the interactive coefficients show that the relationships for 2008 are no different statistically than in 1986. Despite the drop in the number of black teachers by 2008 (note the significant intercept for the year), the process of gaining representation is equally efficient in both years.

Conclusion

The theoretical motivation for this chapter was to examine the effectiveness of representation under different electoral systems. Research since the passage of the Voting Rights Act has focused largely on the differences in descriptive

TABLE 4.12. *Snapshot Comparison, Representation in 1986 and 2008, including Percent Black Administrators*

DV: % Black Teachers	Model 1
Intercept	−0.218
	(0.751)
Percent Black Administrators	0.405*
	(0.092)
Black Population Percentage	0.665*
	(0.097)
Percent Black Board	−0.080
	(0.062)
2008	−3.185*
	(0.829)
Black Population Percentage X 2008	−0.163
	(0.105)
Percent Black Board X 2008	0.077
	(0.089)
N	180
R^2	0.90
F	147.45

Standard errors in parentheses.

* $p < 0.05$; + $p < .10$

representation in at-large and SMD/ward electoral systems. While this extensive research has been useful in understanding the role of electoral structures for representation, it has often overlooked whether minority representatives, once elected, are able to secure policy benefits for the minority group they represent. Theoretically, we frame this in terms of how electoral structures affect either the values of the representatives or the probability that the representatives could attain their values. In terms of the values argument, this study finds that, in the context of local school districts, electoral structure matters little for increasing representation among school administrators but that SMD systems consistently produce better representation among teachers. In terms of the probability of attaining values, the more important variable was not structure but partisanship. Findings in this study show that the allocative effectiveness of representation is enhanced when the school district has a Democratic majority (potential allies), despite the partisan face-neutrality of school board elections. Partisan politics matters even where elections and related environmental contexts are intended to be nonpartisan.

That partisanship matters for achieving representation and policy benefits is perhaps not surprising but cannot be understated at the local level. Even in elections that are labeled as nonpartisan (87 percent of the districts in this study use nonpartisan elections), higher levels of Democratic voters are able to foster better representation for African Americans.[19] This is likely to produce further indirect and direct benefits for lessening the education gap between student majority and minority groups. Additional research linking representation to student achievement and educational equity can shed additional light on the influence of partisanship and electoral structure in education policy.

The theoretical focus on the direct effects of representation as they interact with structure downplays the basic substantive findings of this chapter. All political representation had a direct impact on administrative representation and, subsequently, greatly influenced teacher representation. Overall political representation matters a great deal. The impacts of electoral structure examined here show how structure affects this representation at the margins. Separate from the direct impacts of structure and partisanship demonstrated in this research, political representation always influences allocative representation and will also influence policy representation as demonstrated in Chapter 5.

In sum, Chapters 2 through 4 have illustrated that electoral structure and partisanship continue to matter, and that black access to education has changed little since questions related to equity resurfaced in the 1980s. Although this chapter only examined African Americans and one policy area, the expected utility logic of value congruence and the probability of attaining values should apply to other minority groups. It is also likely to apply in other local policy areas such as health, welfare, and public safety although the multifunctional nature of city and county governments might complicate the relationship between race, structure, and partisanship.

---

[19] Whether or not the elections are actually partisan does not appear to matter at all. I.e., replicating the results in this chapter for partisan and nonpartisan systems generates very similar conclusion. Although one might think a partisan system would facilitate the ability of the parties to shape allocative representation, that is not the case.

5

Partisanship, Teacher Representation, and Access to Education Opportunities

Politics and structure clearly shape the access of African Americans to policy-making positions in public education. Chapter 3 demonstrated the interaction of both electoral structure and partisanship and their combined influence on the ability of African Americans to gain access to seats on the school board. Chapter 4 traced both of these factors on the ability of African-American school board members to hire African-American administrators and teachers. Although electoral structure mattered in both chapters, the most important substantive finding was how partisanship permeated the entire process. Partisanship permitted blacks to overcome the biases of at-large elections and make such a system work for them rather than against them. Similarly, partisanship created allies (friends) that black politicians could rely on to gain allocative responsiveness in the form of more African-American administrators and teachers. These political and representational processes matter, however, only to the extent that they affect the educational experiences of African-American students. This topic is the subject of Chapters 5 and 6. This chapter will examine a set of processes within schools that are often associated with second-generation educational discrimination – access to gifted classes, assignments to special education, and the use of discipline. Chapter 6 will continue this process into the era of No Child Left Behind and high stakes educational testing to look at student performance on standardized tests and other educational outcomes. In both chapters the key explanatory variable will be African-American representation.

Similar to previous chapters, this chapter will continue to focus on both structure and partisanship; however, the focus on structure will shift from electoral structure to the broader structural dimensions of school district governance. Chapter 3 found that partisanship altered the intended influence of structures and that structural biases could be used to benefit African Americans when the partisan environment was favorable. Chapter 4 demonstrated that partisanship was more important than structure in enhancing the impact of political representation on allocative responsiveness. As analyses shift to policy outputs and outcomes, how school board members are elected has little direct influence on the representation process (other than by increasing the number of bureaucratic representatives).[1] The structures more likely to matter are those of the independent school district; these structures create distinct roles for school board members, school administrators, and teachers. Further, these structures enhance or reduce the relative ability of the three sets of representatives to influence student outputs in predictable ways.

Representation: School Boards

Representation that could benefit African-American students occurs in three different forums – among members of the school board, top-level administrators, and teachers. School boards are the legislative policy body for school districts and represent the avenue of the representation present in most of the traditional work in political science. The findings on racial representation in national and state legislatures has been, at best, mixed, in part because the overwhelming majority of minority legislators are Democrats and separating out the influence of party and constituency pressures from that of race is difficult. Studies consistently find that minority legislators engage in the *process of representation*; these individuals are more likely to sponsor legislation with racial aspects, speak on issues of race, and engage in a variety of interactions with constituents based on race (Banducci, Donovan, and Karp 2004; Broockman 2013; Grose 2005; Minta 2011; Preuhs 2006). Advocacy does not necessarily translate into policy and outcomes, however, so the impact of minority legislators on roll call votes is often not discernable (Bratton and Haynie 1999; Cameron, Epstein, and O'Halloran 1996; Lublin 1999). Studies at the state level indicate that minority representatives can influence policy when they operate in favorable institutional and partisan environments. For example, Preuhs (2006) finds that gaining positions of formal influence within a legislature and membership in the majority party combine with race to influence policy. Hicklin and Meier's (2008) study of college admissions shows that minority legislatures can influence public colleges and universities but only if the governance structure of higher education facilitates this influence.

Studies that examine the influence of minority legislators at the local level come to a more positive conclusion for both city councils and school boards. One consistent finding is that representation in local legislatures is positively associated with allocative responsiveness (minority employment in local

---

[1] We conducted analyses similar to the structural interactions in Chapter 4 on the dependent variables in this chapter and generally found that the electoral structure interaction with board representation had little influence.

government) for both city councils and school boards (Marschall and Ruhil 2007; Mladenka 1989; Saltzstein 1989). Research has also found that minority school board members have been associated with greater access of minority students to educational opportunities (Meier and England 1984; Pitts 2007; Roch, Pitts, and Navarro 2010). These policy representation studies, however, are often underspecified in that they do not consider bureaucratic representation and, therefore, cannot determine if the effect of representation is direct (such that board members influence policy) or indirect (through the hiring of black administrators and black teachers).

School board members do have ways to directly influence the performance of minority students if they opt to use them. School boards can set and fund policies that encourage the expansion of gifted classes or the use of advanced placement classes. They can establish disciplinary policies that either encourage the use of certain policies over others (e.g., in-school suspensions rather than out-of-school suspensions; see Roch et al. 2010) or prohibit their use all together (e.g., corporal punishment). Test scores are responsive to class size and instructional spending (Meier and O'Toole 2006; Mosteller 1995; Wenglinsky 1997), and school resources matter more for low-income and minority students who often lack educational resources in the home (Darling-Hammond 2007; Rumberger 2001).[2] Although school boards face limitations on their actions owing to state and federal laws and limits on taxes and revenues, they have substantial discretion over the funds they receive and also possess the discretion that is inherent in any implementation process (Mazmanian and Sabatier 1983).

Representation: The Bureaucracy

Representation is the *sine qua non* of legislatures; they are expected to represent and translate constituent interests into policy. Bureaucracies, in contrast, are not generally perceived as representative institutions by the public, but an extensive scholarly literature documents that bureaucracies can represent a constituent or stakeholder group under a set of specific conditions.[3] Bureaucratic representation requires both a correspondence of policy-relevant

---

[2] Hanushek (1996) has frequently made an argument that money does not matter in education based on examining trends over time. The literature cited here is only part of a substantial body of work that demonstrates positive correlations between resources and student performance particularly for African-American students.

[3] The representative bureaucracy literature focuses on representation by groups that generally lack political power. This focus detracts from the basic idea that all bureaucracies represent people although generally their missions are to represent individuals with political power. In the United States, the Department of Agriculture has always been asked to represent farmers and farm interests; the Departments of Labor and Commerce were created for similar reasons. In these cases, bureaucratic representation is expected by the political institutions; the representative bureaucracy literature deals with the more interesting cases in which political institutions have not necessarily authorized that representation.

identities and the discretion to act on the part of the bureaucrat. Despite the normative models of bureaucracy that hold that bureaucracies neutrally implement policy created by legislatures, the reality is that bureaucracies exercise vast discretion simply because legislatures cannot write legislation with sufficient detail to cover all circumstances (Meier and Bohte 2006; Rourke 1976). Programs also evolve over time as bureaucracies learn how to solve problems or as the environmental circumstances change. A classic example in both situations is the education of students with limited English proficiency. The influx of immigrants has rapidly changed the environment, and schools that once had no need to instruct limited English students are now held responsible for educating immigrant children. Similarly, as effective educational techniques are discovered and diffused, bureaucracies can choose to adopt them, exercising discretion in the process.

Discretion is ubiquitous in bureaucracy (Evans 2012; Lipsky 1993; Sowa and Selden 2003); if bureaucrats exercise their discretion, it will reflect their own values. For representative bureaucracy to occur, there must be a convergence of values and policy problems, that is, the identity of the teacher as an African American (or any other identity) must be relevant to the decision being made. This convergence of values and policy problems occurs naturally for an African-American teacher if there are African-American children in the school. A variety of other factors such as professionalization, hierarchy, critical mass, and political support all can enhance bureaucratic representation (Keiser et al. 2002; Nicholson-Crotty, Grissom, and Nicholson-Crotty 2011). This chapter will also consider the notion of a favorable political environment and examine how partisanship can support bureaucratic representation.

Cases of representative bureaucracy have been found in a wide variety of public organizations including the Equal Employment Opportunity Commission (Hindera 1993), the Farmers Home Administration (Selden 1997), local law enforcement agencies (Meier and Nicholson-Crotty 2006; Riccucci, Van Ryzin, and Lavena 2014), health care bureaucracies (Cooper and Powe 2004), the Veterans' Administration (Gade and Wilkins 2013), child support enforcement (Wilkins and Keiser 2006), welfare agencies (Davis, Livermore, and Lim 2011; but see Watkins-Hayes 2011) and fire departments (Andrews, Ashworth, and Meier 2014). Schools, because they vest extensive discretion in bureaucrats, particularly teachers, are viewed as a nurturing environment for bureaucratic representation (Grissom, Kern, and Rodriguez 2015). The literature on how students benefit or how they perform with same-race teachers is extensive and has been linked to measures of grouping, tracking, and discipline (Epps 1995; Meier, England, and Stewart 1989; Skiba et al. 2002), student performance in classes (Dee 2004, 2005; Egalite, Kisada, and Winters 2015; Meier and Stewart 1992), and even to issues such as teen pregnancy (Atkins and Wilkins 2013; Zhu and Walker 2013).

Despite the literature showing a positive relationship between minority teachers and minority students, the microtheory of exactly how the process works is not clear. Minority teachers can theoretically benefit minority students through four different but often overlapping processes. First, a minority teacher might teach a minority student differently compared to other students as the result of cultural sensitivity or other factors. This teaching influence might also occur through coproduction, or the ability of a minority teacher to interact with minority parents, encouraging parents to take a more active role in their child's education. Second, minority teachers might influence other teachers to change how they interact with minority students; this causal process would not necessarily require that a minority student be directly taught by a minority teacher.[4] Third, in the process of interacting with other teachers and administrators to deal with problems, minority teachers might generate discussions that lead to changes in policy that benefit minority students. As an example, Roch et al. (2010) find that schools with more diverse faculty tend to use ameliorative rather than punitive discipline (e.g., using in-school suspensions instead of out-of-school suspensions or expulsions). These ameliorative policies benefit minority students (and nonminority students) by limiting the negative consequences of disciplinary actions. Fourth, the teacher may not take any direct action while the minority student adopts the teacher as a role model and subsequently changes his or her own behavior.[5]

These processes of bureaucratic representation might seem a fair distance from such external influences as partisanship, yet no bureaucracy, no matter how well structured, is immune to political forces. Teachers who are interested in engaging a representative function should be well aware that local education issues can become highly salient to the general population. Similarly, the extent to which parents are satisfied with the school system can also translate into both greater public support for such things as bond issues, but also greater leeway and discretion for teachers as they operate in the classroom. Teachers can be expected to be attuned to the general ideological and partisan nature of the community. As such, they are likely to respond more positively in districts that support greater efforts in terms of race and education.

Representation: An Institutional View

The previous discussion suggests that the representation of black interests in education might take place in three different institutional settings – the school board (the legislature), the school administration (the agency level), and the teachers (the street level). The interaction of representation among these three institutional venues is virtually unexplored in the political science literature

---

[4] Schools of education spend a great deal of time teaching about multicultural education. The influence of minority teachers on nonminority teachers might thus be reinforced through the common educational training of the teachers.

[5] Keiser et al. (2002) refer to this as changing the relationship between the bureaucrat and the client simply as a result of shared identities. As an illustration of this process in criminal justice see Meier and Nicholson-Crotty (2006).

because the dominant theory is either overhead democracy or informed by the logic of principal-agent models. Both are top-down models that assume that policy is the domain of the political branches and that bureaucrats seek to avoid direction by political institutions (Moe 1985; Redford 1969; for an alternative view see Krause and Meier 2005). Principal-agent models assume that there is goal conflict between politicians (principals) and bureaucrats (agents), despite evidence that the degree of goal consensus is highly variable and that, in some cases, the politicians and bureaucrats operate with similar if not identical goals (Waterman and Meier 1998). In the present cases, assuming that black school board members, black school administrators, and black teachers share some common goals in regard to the education of African-American students is a reasonable position.

Assessing how representation plays out across these three venues needs to take into account how the structure of an independent school district[6] influences three characteristics – visibility, barriers to participation, and permanence. School boards are the most visible to the general public of the three forums; they hold regular meetings (and are limited in their ability to meet privately except for personnel issues) that are open to the public with an agenda that is publicized in advance. Barriers to participation exist, but they are low compared to the other two venues; individuals can attend board meetings and can address the board. Dissatisfied citizens can run for a position on the school board or back an alternative to the existing board. Finally, while the institution of the school board is relatively permanent (although school boards can be dissolved by the state and replaced by other elected or appointed officials), any action of the school board can be reversed by the same school board at a later time. The selection of board members by elections means additional instability, and local campaigns might well be based on previous school board decisions.

Administrators and their decisions are less visible than those of the school board. Unlike regulatory agencies, school administrators are not required to publish a notice of a pending policy decision and generally do not do so. The barriers to participation in administrative decisions by individuals who are not part of the organization are very high; the individual first has to find out that a policy decision is being made and when and then bear the cost of gaining sufficient technical expertise to participate in an effective way. Finally, superintendents work on multiyear contracts and the senior administrative staff are likely to be careerists who have spent their entire working life in the current school district or one very similar to it. Although the superintendent can be replaced by the school board, such a process is messy politically and reflects on the prior judgment of the school board. Essentially, bureaucracies in turn value permanence; the defining characteristic of bureaucracy is the creation of rules and structures to sort cases into similar groups that can be dealt with

---

[6] There are a small number of dependent school districts in this study. The logic discussed here also applies to such districts although less strongly than the independent school district.

in a consistent manner (Weber 2009). This sorting characteristic is especially applicable to the process of grouping and discipline in education.

Teachers are classic street-level bureaucrats (Lipsky 2010; May and Winter 2000) who operate with a great deal of discretion and only modest oversight. Teachers' actions, particularly in terms of instruction, are rarely visible either to the general public or to school administrators. The high costs of participation in a bureaucracy apply to those at the street level, particularly given the discretion that street-level personnel have in implementing or not implementing policy decisions. Street-level bureaucrats develop coping routines that transform policy decisions into manageable actions that are rarely open to review by upper administrators (Brehm and Gates 1997), let alone by the public. Further, complaints about bureaucracies being slow to change reflect, in part, the relative permanence of the standard operating procedures that characterize street-level bureaucracy.

Given the variance on these three structural dimensions, strategic decisions on how to engage in shared representation suggest that there are significant advantages in lodging the representation function at the street level of the bureaucracy. School board members with policy interests are quite likely to see that board policies are subject to change with elections (Moe 1989). They may seek to create, therefore, additional barriers to change by delegating the decisions to bureaucracy. In addition to reducing the visibility of the policy and vesting the decisions in bureaucrats with tenure, such actions take the advantage of the inherent information asymmetry in the principal-agent relationship. Bureaucrats have far greater expertise in terms of which policies might work and the process for translating a policy into specific actions within the bureaucracy. They can even embed such decisions in highly technical procedures (e.g., the classification of students into severity levels of special educational needs for grouping purposes) that are difficult to comprehend let alone challenge by elected officials or the general public. This advantage is further exacerbated by the part-time nature of school boards versus the full-time nature of the professional bureaucracy, which limits the time that school boards can spend on any individual issue.[7]

The logic of moving representation from the school board to the school bureaucracy also holds for moving representation from the school bureaucracy down to the street level. The decisions become less visible, costlier to reverse, and more resistant to change. This logic suggests that a coalition that advocates policies that will benefit any given group (in this case, African-American students) will favor lodging the representation and decision-making function as low in the bureaucracy as possible.

School administrators, especially minority administrators, have an additional reason to push representation to lower levels of the bureaucracy. School administrators have multiple roles; they need to interface with the school board,

---

[7] Board members can also blame the bureaucracy in individual cases for their own lack of action.

present the school system to the public, deal with state legislatures on funding issues, and entice local business and community leaders to support the school system. The ability to delegate their representation role or a portion of that role (Selden 1997) to teachers frees minority administrators to present themselves as advocating for all students. Minority administrators, in particular, might not need to aggressively advocate for minority students if teachers take cues about preferences from the race of administrators and anticipate how they should act.

The organizational structure of school districts further advantages street-level representation. The logic of the independent school district is a school board of part-time generalists who represent the views of the entire community. The school board's task is to set general policy and hire a professional administrator to operate the school system based on merit principles for administrators and teachers. The structure seeks to enshrine the traditional politics-administration dichotomy. Some states go even further in this separation and do not permit school board members to have direct contact with district employees except through the superintendent.

The preceding structural arguments indicate that a minority community would be rational to vest the representational function at the street level and have both the board and administrators perform other functions while giving tacit support to teachers. The relative advantages of street-level bureaucrats also indicate that they might simply be more effective representatives of minority student interests. Teachers have far greater contact with students than either administrators or board members. This is coupled with the fact that teachers are also the largest group of employees in the organization. Even as new accountability systems seek to impose external controls over school systems and teachers, teachers still have vast discretion in interactions with individual students; and discretion is considered a key variable in fostering bureaucratic representation (Keiser et al. 2002).[8] To the extent that teachers act as role models to students, no amount of external accountability is likely to dampen the relationship between black teachers and the performance of black students.

This discussion of the structural influences on the multiple levels of representation indicates that the generic hypothesis in current literature – that minority representation will be associated with greater outputs that will benefit minority clientele – should be modified in the case of school districts to the following:

H1 African-American representation among teachers will be more strongly associated with outcomes that benefit African-American students than will representation of African-American administrators or African-American school board members.

The preceding hypothesis should not be taken to indicate that either black school board members or administrators are irrelevant in the education of black

---

[8] See Sacks (2015) for one teacher's discussion about classroom discretion and the implication of Common Core standards.

students. Chapter 4 clearly demonstrates that black school board members are strongly associated with the hiring of black administrators and black administrators are the strongest correlate of hiring black teachers. Both board members and administrators have significant indirect influence on what happens to black students through the allocative responsiveness documented in Chapter 4.

Research comparing the relative efficacy of representation at different levels of a policy system is in its infancy. The only existing study is framed as an examination of the political control of bureaucracy and involves Latinos in school districts in Texas (Meier and O'Toole 2006). That study found that teacher representation had dramatically stronger associations with student outcomes than board representation (administrative representation had little direct influence).

Representation in the Bureaucracy: A Symbiotic View

The basic distinction between the managerial level of bureaucracy and the street level of bureaucracy may be problematic in the case of the policy outputs examined in this chapter. Teachers clearly cannot unilaterally assign a student to a gifted class or a special education program; nor are teachers generally involved in the actual administration of discipline. In all cases, teachers play a role by recommending a student to be assigned or tested for assignment to a class or in referring cases of misbehavior to the appropriate administrator. Reducing racial disparities in any of these categories clearly requires action by both teachers and administrators indicating that representation must occur in both groups to be effective. This logic implies that examining the interaction of black teachers and black administrators is required to gain a full understanding of the role of bureaucratic representation on black student access to education with following hypothesis:

H2 African-American students will receive more equitable educational outputs in districts where African Americans are represented among both teachers and administrators.

This hypothesis can be directly tested by interacting teacher representation and administrative representation to determine if this interaction term improves the predictive ability of the model.

Partisanship and Educational Outputs

The myth of education policy as nonpartisan is long-standing in American politics. The progressive reforms were directly targeted at patronage-ridden urban school districts, and they used at-large nonpartisan elections held in months other than November to disadvantage the existing political machines and advantage business and professional elites (Tyack 1991). The creation of merit systems for teachers and the hiring of professional administrators further reinforced this effort. Scholars of education, however, recognize that these reforms did not remove the politics from education but merely transformed it by advantaging a new set of interests and disadvantaging the political machines. Whether or not these reforms were successful in eliminating partisan politics at the turn of the twentieth century, the results of Chapters 3 and 4 demonstrate that partisanship has a dramatic influence on the election of African Americans to school boards and an equally significant impact on the allocative responsiveness of those representatives in terms of employing black administrators and black teachers.

Shifting from elections and "quasipatronage" areas to the education of children, however, moves from a process where elections are important to a bureaucratic process that is likely to be strongly influenced by professional norms. How is it that an assignment to gifted classes or the decision to suspend a student might be influenced by the partisan composition of the community? Studies of education politics concede that teachers are active participants in the politics of local school districts. This might be expected of individuals whose livelihoods can be directly affected by school board actions (Moe 2009). Teachers can easily see who supports school bond issues or the coalitions behind candidates that emphasize issues such as the teaching of creation science (Berkman and Plutzer 2010). Such activities provide clear signals as to the nature of the political environment and what the political environment expects of public education. On the racial issues involving education, ties to Democratic partisanship or its corresponding ideology should be readily apparent. Teachers can use these information signals to make judgments about their ability to use their discretion without fear of public consequences. In short, the representational job of the teacher becomes easier with a little help from his or her partisan friends.

This logic suggests that partisanship will enhance the influence of representation, generating the following testable hypothesis:

H3 Black teacher representation will have a larger substantive influence in Democratic majority school districts than in Republican majority school districts.

The hypothesis specifies teacher representation as the key representation variable because the preceding theoretical arguments pointed to teacher representation as the crucial node in influencing educational outputs and outcomes. The models will also test this interactive effect of partisanship for both black school board members and black administrators; but given the relative advantages of street-level bureaucrats in representation, we do not expect strong positive results for the administrators.

Partisanship might also have a more direct influence on educational outcomes of African-American children either through stronger support for programs focused on traditionally disadvantaged students or support for additional resources for the schools. To allow for this path of influence, the models will also test for a direct influence of partisanship composition on the various indicators of student outputs.

TABLE 5.1. *Mean African-American Student Ratios by Year*

Outcome	2002	2004	2006	2008	2011
Gifted	0.48	0.51	0.48	0.41	0.51
Expulsion	1.82	1.99	1.86	1.43	2.00
Suspension	1.86	1.96	1.83	1.72	1.88
Intellectual Disability	1.73	1.74	1.66	1.65	1.39
Emotional Disturbance	1.59	1.72	1.56	1.66	1.33
Learning Disability	1.33	1.40	1.33	1.41	1.38

Note: For districts with at least 5% black students.

Second-Generation Educational Discrimination: An Overview

This chapter will examine racial disparities in assignments to gifted classes and various categories of special education as well as in the application of discipline. Table 5.1 provides an overall snapshot of assignments for the five most recent Office for Civil Rights (OCR) surveys. OCR conducts a sample survey with weighting to include an oversample of large districts. The means for each year do not include the same school districts and should be viewed as estimates rather than actual numbers. The numbers in the table are odds ratios for districts with at least a 5 percent black student population. The odds ratio is simply the probability that a black student will be assigned to the category relative to his or her level of enrollment (i.e., the percentage of black students in the category divided by the percentage of black students in the school district). An odds ratio of 1.0 means that black students are represented in that category at the same levels of their share of the student population, and a ratio of 1.20 would indicate an overrepresentation of 20 percent in the category.

The pattern of ratios in Table 5.1 is consistent with past research and expectations. African-American students are assigned to gifted classes at a rate of about one-half of their enrollment figures and are overrepresented in all discipline and special education categories.[9] One striking finding is the consistency of the ratios over time; the gifted ratio ranges from .41 to .51, suspensions from 1.72 to 1.96, expulsions from 1.43 to 2.00, the intellectual disability category from 1.39 to 1.74, the emotional disturbance category from 1.33 to 1.72, and specific learning disabilities from 1.33 to 1.41. Changes in definitions for special education mean that comparisons of 2011 to prior years should be done with a greater deal of caution, particularly given the sampling error. Overall, there appear to be no real trends in the data to indicate either a decline or an increase in assignments.[10]

---

[9] OCR also reports data on corporal punishment, but most states ban corporal punishment; and many districts within states that allow corporal punishment also prohibit it.

[10] The gifted class ratios reported here are very similar to those reported by Meier, Stewart, and England (1989, 82) for their sample of larger districts. Their suspension ratios are also very

TABLE 5.2. *African-American Student Ratios by Partisan District Majority*

	Republican	Democrat
Gifted	0.44	0.76
Expulsion	1.43	1.10
Suspension	1.39	1.13
Intellectual Disability	1.37	1.09
Emotional Disturbance	1.14	1.04
Learning Disability	1.17	1.00

To illustrate the potential influence of partisanship, we also compared Democratic majority to Republican majority school districts in terms of these ratios (Table 5.2).[11] This comparison shows that African-American students in Democratic districts are 32 percentage points more likely to be assigned to gifted classes, 26 percentage points less likely to be suspended, 33 percentage points less likely to be expelled, 26 percentage points less likely to be classified as intellectual disabled, 10 percentage points less likely to be classified as emotionally disturbed, and 17 percentage points less likely to be classified as having a specific learning disability. Interpreting these same figures as relative odds ratios, an African-American student in a Democratic district is 73 percent more likely to be in a gifted class, 23 percent less likely to be suspended, 30 percent less likely to be expelled, 24 percent less likely to be classified as intellectual disabled, 10 percent less likely to be classified as emotionally disturbed, and 17 percent less likely to be classified as having a learning disability

similar but they report much higher expulsion ratios although expulsion ratios were declining rapidly during the time period of their study and current figures are within the range of that trend. Definitions for special education classes have changed since their study, and therefore, the special education ratios are not directly comparable.

[11] This chapter will rely on splitting the sample into majority Democratic and majority Republican districts rather than interacting partisanship with representation or other variables. We do this for several reasons. First, this approach essentially interacts with the partisan majority with every variable in the model. Although this reduces the degrees of freedom in the analyses, it also illustrates that many of the relationships vary in terms of the partisanship of the districts. In addition to the representation coefficients we are also very concerned with the coefficients for black enrollment, which indicate over- or underassignments. Second, we will be introducing additional interactions to test the symbiotic representation hypothesis, and interpreting three-way interactions is exceedingly complex. Third, we also do this for statistical reasons. The basic statistical test for determining whether or not two groups of cases should be analyzed separately or together is the Chow test, which essentially uses a single equation but interacts all independent variables with the criterion variable (in this case party majority) and asks whether the interacted coefficients are different from zero (or alternatively whether the two sets of coefficients are different from each other). The Chow tests in all six cases indicate that the Democratic and the Republican districts should not be pooled.

than a student in a Republican district. These differences are surprisingly large, especially given the traditional view of education policy as nonpartisan.

Methods

The basic modeling strategy will be to predict the percentage of black students in a given category with measures of black representation on the school board, among school administrators, and among teachers while controlling for the percentage of black students in the district and other factors likely to influence assignments. The advantage of predicting the percentage of blacks in a category with the percentage of black students as one of the controls is that it generates a rate of over- or underassignment without the extreme values that can be generated for representation ratios in districts with small black populations; such extreme values can easily bias the regression line. These coefficients can then be compared to see how much a set of variables either narrows or widens the racial gaps in these outputs. Because each of the representation measures is also a percentage, the regression coefficients are roughly comparable across the types of representation. The statistical controls include the percentage of black college graduates in the district, black home ownership, the black median income, white poverty, Democratic partisanship, the southern region, and the percent unionization variable. These controls seek to adjust for any of the economic or political factors that influence the educational outputs being examined. All models are estimated with fixed effects for the years and standard errors clustered by district. Because our interest is in the efficacy of representation, we will generally not interpret any of the control variable relationships unless they show an interesting theoretical or substantive result.

Gifted Classes

Table 5.3 presents three regressions for predicting gifted class assignments for all districts and also for districts with Democratic and Republican majorities. Column 1 shows that both school board representation and teacher representation matter for black gifted class assignments, but the substantive impact of teachers is more than six times the impact of school board members. Columns 2 and 3 show the school board impact is only statistically significant in cases with a Democratic majority (at the 0.10) level. Teacher representation matters in both types of districts, but the impact of black teachers is three times larger in Democratic districts than in Republican ones, all else equal. Administrative representation never matters.[12] Of substantive note from column 1 is the large

---

[12] This is not a function of collinearity. Even if administrative representation is the only representation variable included in the model, it does not produce statistically significant results in the predicted direction. The analysis in the following text, however, shows that administrative representation does interact with teacher representation to enhance educational outcomes for black students.

TABLE 5.3. *Effect of Representation on Black Percentage of Gifted Students*

	Baseline	Majority R	Majority D
	Model 1	Model 2	Model 3
Percent Black Board	0.058*	0.019	0.059+
	(0.025)	(0.020)	(0.036)
Percent Black Administrators	−0.034	0.058	−0.061
	(0.046)	(0.042)	(0.062)
Percent Black Teachers	0.392*	0.143*	0.450*
	(0.071)	(0.060)	(0.089)
Percent Black Students	0.440*	0.336*	0.533*
	(0.034)	(0.037)	(0.044)
Black Education (College Percent)	0.012	0.008	0.043*
	(0.009)	(0.006)	(0.018)
Black Family Income (000s)	0.046+	0.031	0.016
	(0.024)	(0.020)	(0.044)
Black Home Ownership	0.011+	−0.006	0.029*
	(0.006)	(0.005)	(0.011)
White Poverty Percentage	0.147*	0.048	0.367*
	(0.051)	(0.039)	(0.105)
District Democrat Percent	0.049*	0.022	0.085+
	(0.014)	(0.016)	(0.044)
South	−2.645*	−0.732+	−4.373*
	(0.444)	(0.387)	(0.927)
Unionization	0.072+	0.033	0.090
	(0.037)	(0.034)	(0.068)
Constant	−6.043*	−1.567+	−12.052*
	(1.009)	(0.877)	(2.910)
Year FE	Yes	Yes	Yes
N	3491	2165	1326
R^2	0.81	0.74	0.86
F	123.63	65.05	106.12

Standard errors in parentheses.
* $p < 0.05$; + $p < 0.10$
Note: Time points include 2002, 2004, 2006, and 2008.

negative impact in southern school districts and the small but positive impact of Democratic partisanship.[13] Striking in the partisanship equations is the difference in coefficients for black students; all things being equal, black students gain only 34 percent of the access to gifted classes that their numbers would suggest in Republican districts but 53 percent of the access in Democratic

---

[13] Comparing the equations indicates that the southern region is the most detrimental in school districts with a Democratic majority. That would be limited to major urban areas in the South that are operating districts composed of a large majority of minority students.

TABLE 5.4. *Effect of Representation on Black Percentage of Expelled Students*

	Baseline	Majority R	Majority D
	Model 1	Model 2	Model 3
Percent Black Board	−0.030	0.026	−0.060
	(0.059)	(0.077)	(0.090)
Percent Black Administrators	0.275*	0.157	0.321+
	(0.103)	(0.143)	(0.167)
Percent Black Teachers	−0.420*	−0.091	−0.419*
	(0.133)	(0.221)	(0.176)
Percent Black Students	1.267*	1.359*	1.179*
	(0.067)	(0.099)	(0.092)
Black Education (College Percent)	0.053	−0.002	0.111
	(0.045)	(0.042)	(0.089)
Black Family Income (000s)	−0.202+	−0.186	−0.132
	(0.119)	(0.139)	(0.218)
Black Home Ownership	0.008	0.023	−0.019
	(0.021)	(0.025)	(0.034)
White Poverty Percentage	−0.074	−0.129	−0.147
	(0.142)	(0.164)	(0.271)
District Democrat Percent	−0.026	−0.149+	−0.007
	(0.047)	(0.090)	(0.107)
South	3.871*	3.153+	−0.053
	(1.630)	(1.881)	(3.147)
Unionization	0.198	0.325+	−0.013
	(0.143)	(0.172)	(0.240)
Constant	6.854+	7.897	11.338
	(3.761)	(4.913)	(8.376)
Year FE	Yes	Yes	Yes
N	2199	1390	809
R^2	0.6	0.56	119.81
F	167.18	72.77	7233.018

Standard errors in parentheses.
* $p < 0.05$; + $p < 0.10$
Note: Time points include 2002, 2004, 2006, and 2008.

districts, an increase of 56 percent in the odds of a gifted class assignment (see following text).

Discipline
Racial disparities in discipline have long been a salient issue in education policy. Column 1 of Tables 5.4 and 5.5 show the determinants of expulsions and suspensions, respectively, and the patterns for representation are fairly similar. In both cases an increase in black teachers is associated with more equitable

TABLE 5.5. *Effect of Representation on Black Percentage of Suspended Students*

	Baseline	Majority R	Majority D
	Model 1	Model 2	Model 3
Percent Black Board	0.033	0.061*	0.029
	(0.026)	(0.028)	(0.037)
Percent Black Administrators	0.203*	0.141*	0.217*
	(0.040)	(0.053)	(0.055)
Percent Black Teachers	−0.396*	−0.149	−0.438*
	(0.071)	(0.092)	(0.087)
Percent Black Students	1.250*	1.295*	1.193*
	(0.037)	(0.049)	(0.050)
Black Education (College Percent)	0.003	−0.001	−0.007
	(0.018)	(0.018)	(0.034)
Black Family Income (000s)	−0.120*	−0.110*	−0.105
	(0.054)	(0.047)	(0.091)
Black Home Ownership	−0.035*	−0.035*	−0.033*
	(0.009)	(0.009)	(0.015)
White Poverty Percentage	−0.419*	−0.378*	−0.523*
	(0.054)	(0.058)	(0.097)
District Democrat Percent	−0.020	−0.014	−0.045
	(0.022)	(0.033)	(0.059)
South	5.055*	4.163*	4.600*
	(0.706)	(0.582)	(1.668)
Unionization	0.129*	0.113*	0.118
	(0.049)	(0.051)	(0.092)
Constant	9.638*	7.920*	13.259*
	(1.580)	(1.539)	(4.453)
Year FE	Yes	Yes	Yes
N	3673	2198	1475
R^2	0.89	0.9	0.89
F	520.41	304.76	322.41

Standard errors in parentheses.

* $p < 0.05$

Note: Time points include 2002, 2004, 2006, and 2008.

discipline for black students, but an increase in black administration is positively correlated with racial disparities in discipline. These patterns could reflect a balance of roles and identities in the two groups. Administrators are responsible for imposing discipline, and certain administrative positions (generally vice principal or assistant principal) are assigned to administer discipline. For vice principals, paths to promotion involve performing the functions assigned, and strong disciplinarians have a positive reputation in the general community (Bowen 1988; Losen 2011).

More important than the positive relationship for black administrators, however, is the relative impact of teachers' and administrators' representation. The negative coefficient for teachers is substantially larger than the positive coefficient for administrators and, given the high collinearity between two measures,[14] would generate an overall reduction in racial disparities from representation in most cases. The regression coefficients show the unique contribution of the two forms of representation controlling for all other factors; the shared variance of the two variables play no role in determining the regression coefficients. This means that black students might be worse off in terms of racial disparities in discipline in school districts with few black teachers and a large number of black administrators (see following text on the interaction of teacher and administrator representation).[15] This pattern often occurs in transitional districts with a large influx of black students because teaching faculty are relatively stable. Because there are far fewer administrators than teachers, it is much easier to increase administrative representation than to increase teacher representation. In this case, the representation might only be symbolic.

The regression results also show that racial disparities in discipline are more severe in the South. The coefficients greater than one for the black students' variable indicate that even with all the controls in the current models, black students are still overrepresented among students who are suspended or expelled.

Although partisanship does not matter in terms of racial disparities in discipline in the overall models in the first column, it clearly interacts with the representation variables and affects their relative efficacy. Neither black teacher nor black administrator representation matter for expulsions (Table 5.4, column 2) in Republican majority districts, but the strong competitive effects for administrators and teachers appear for districts with a Democratic majority (column 3). The pattern for suspensions is generally similar (stronger in Democratic districts) with some nuances (Table 5.5, columns 2 and 3). School board representation is significant in Republican districts, but the coefficient is very small. The largest change is that the efficacy of black teacher representation triples in Democratic districts relative to that in Republican districts and is approximately double the size of the administrator coefficient. The clear pattern in discipline disparities is that Democratic partisanship enhances the representative efficacy of black teachers.

Special Education

Special education classifications have undergone significant changes over the last several decades, including changes in the federal definitions for data collection. These changes have also affected the actual process of assignments

---

[14] The variance inflation estimates for black administrators is 8.21 and for black teachers is 7.17.
[15] The representation measures net to zero impact when there are 1.53 times more administrators than teachers proportionately for expulsions and 1.96 times as many administrators than teachers for suspensions.

TABLE 5.6. *Effect of Representation on Black Percentage of Intellectual Disability Students*

	Baseline	Majority R	Majority D
	Model 1	Model 2	Model 3
Percent Black Board	0.016	0.028	0.028
	(0.028)	(0.033)	(0.039)
Percent Black Administrators	0.180*	0.142*	0.165*
	(0.045)	(0.065)	(0.059)
Percent Black Teachers	−0.246*	0.046	−0.275*
	(0.068)	(0.101)	(0.075)
Percent Black Students	1.159*	1.168*	1.116*
	(0.036)	(0.053)	(0.047)
Black Education (College Percent)	−0.044*	−0.041*	−0.061*
	(0.015)	(0.016)	(0.027)
Black Family Income (000s)	−0.184*	−0.233*	−0.109
	(0.048)	(0.056)	(0.070)
Black Home Ownership	−0.001	0.014	−0.021
	(0.009)	(0.011)	(0.014)
White Poverty Percentage	−0.501*	−0.499*	−0.572*
	(0.064)	(0.073)	(0.094)
District Democrat Percent	−0.034	0.021	−0.126*
	(0.022)	(0.037)	(0.051)
South	5.215*	5.021*	3.125*
	(0.637)	(0.713)	(1.220)
Unionization	−0.066	−0.061	−0.171+
	(0.056)	(0.068)	(0.089)
Constant	12.701*	8.894*	21.651*
	(1.493)	(1.934)	(3.692)
Year FE	Yes	Yes	Yes
N	3589	2168	1421
R^2	0.88	0.87	0.9
F	531.65	284.72	347.29

Standard errors in parentheses.
* $p < 0.05$; + $p < 0.10$
Note: Time points include 2002, 2004, 2006, and 2008.

to special education by increasing the procedural rights of parents and children and also by moving away from general classifications such as intellectual disabled to specific learning disabilities. Tables 5.6, 5.7, and 5.8 present the regression results for racial disparities in intellectual disability, emotional disturbance, and learning disability classification. The results for all school districts (column 1) show that black teachers are associated with fewer black students assigned to all three of these classes. At the same time, an increase in black administrators is positively associated with black assignments to these classes.

TABLE 5.7. *Effect of Representation on Black Percentage of Emotional Disturbance Students*

	Baseline	Majority R	Majority D
	Model 1	Model 2	Model 3
Percent Black Board	0.106*	0.098*	0.135*
	(0.032)	(0.041)	(0.044)
Percent Black Administrators	0.214*	0.104	0.277*
	(0.048)	(0.066)	(0.070)
Percent Black Teachers	−0.173*	0.181+	−0.318*
	(0.070)	(0.107)	(0.083)
Percent Black Students	0.952*	0.910*	0.945*
	(0.036)	(0.057)	(0.049)
Black Education (College Percent)	−0.071*	−0.068*	−0.084*
	(0.017)	(0.020)	(0.031)
Black Family Income (000s)	−0.114*	−0.082	−0.141*
	(0.046)	(0.064)	(0.069)
Black Home Ownership	−0.036*	−0.037*	−0.045*
	(0.010)	(0.012)	(0.015)
White Poverty Percentage	−0.330*	−0.245*	−0.552*
	(0.078)	(0.098)	(0.123)
District Democrat Percent	0.041+	0.071+	−0.027
	(0.024)	(0.040)	(0.064)
South	1.517*	1.258	0.697
	(0.695)	(0.816)	(1.338)
Unionization	0.016	−0.059	−0.016
	(0.057)	(0.076)	(0.088)
Constant	9.431*	7.792*	16.330*
	(1.636)	(2.232)	(4.505)
Year FE	Yes	Yes	Yes
N	3586	2155	1431
R^2	0.83	0.77	0.87
F	415.63	160.63	291.65

Standard errors in parentheses.
* $p < 0.05$; + $p < .10$
Note: Time points include 2002, 2004, 2006, and 2008.

In terms of partisan splits, teacher representation only matters in Democratic school districts; administrative influence also increases in Democratic districts, but administrators are always associated with greater racial disparities. These results are generally consistent with the hypothesis that Democratic school districts enhance the representational effectiveness of black teachers.[16]

---

[16] The weak results for teachers in the specific learning disabilities model likely results because it is the largest category of special education and students can be placed in this category for myriad

TABLE 5.8. *Effect of Representation on Black Percentage of Learning Disability Students*

	Baseline	Majority R	Majority D
	Model 1	Model 2	Model 3
Percent Black Board	0.008	0.018	0.009
	(0.019)	(0.024)	(0.026)
Percent Black Administrators	0.172*	0.145*	0.163*
	(0.031)	(0.045)	(0.038)
Percent Black Teachers	−0.101*	0.056	−0.113+
	(0.049)	(0.075)	(0.059)
Percent Black Students	1.007*	1.047*	0.967*
	(0.027)	(0.036)	(0.036)
Black Education (College Percent)	0.028*	0.045*	−0.004
	(0.011)	(0.015)	(0.017)
Black Family Income (000s)	−0.055+	−0.072+	−0.023
	(0.029)	(0.041)	(0.041)
Black Home Ownership	−0.023*	−0.025*	−0.019*
	(0.006)	(0.007)	(0.008)
White Poverty Percentage	−0.196*	−0.131*	−0.374*
	(0.052)	(0.062)	(0.070)
District Democrat Percent	−0.063*	−0.091*	0.003
	(0.016)	(0.027)	(0.038)
South	2.213*	2.118*	0.707
	(0.425)	(0.456)	(0.892)
Unionization	0.157*	0.216*	0.085
	(0.035)	(0.046)	(0.053)
Constant	5.289*	4.099*	4.740+
	(1.058)	(1.394)	(2.564)
Year FE	Yes	Yes	Yes
N	3622	2179	1443
R^2	0.93	0.92	0.95
F	861.93	445.37	715.66

Standard errors in parentheses.
* $p < 0.05$; + $p < 0.10$
Note: Time points include 2002, 2004, 2006, and 2008.

Bureaucratic Representation as a Symbiotic Process

Examining the separate representational impacts of black school board members, black administrators, and black teachers in a single equation estimate was complicated by two factors. First, these three measures are highly

reasons. This heterogeneous grouping as well as parental demands for services using individualized plans could well mean that teachers' discretion is limited.

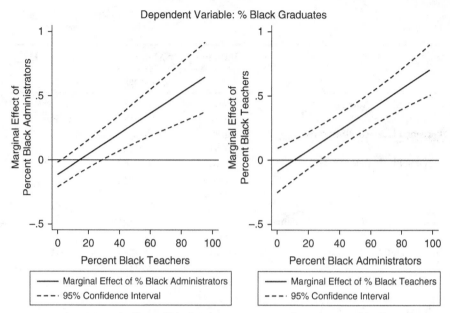

FIGURE 5.1. Marginal effect of black administrators and teachers on black graduation.

collinear; the highest correlation among them is between black teachers and black administrators (.914). In the various models, the black administrator covariate has a variance inflation factor (VIF) of 8.21 (10.04 in Democratic districts), and the black teacher covariate has a VIF of 7.17 (8.43 in Democratic districts).[17] The regression tables thus far provide the impact of teachers controlling for the influence of administrators (and other factors) and the impact of administrators controlling for teachers (and other factors). In short, the estimates are of the impact of each of these variables independent of the others even though these variables are not independent of each other. Theoretically, we made an argument earlier that black teachers and black administrators generally have a symbiotic relationship in educating black students. Teacher recommendations on class assignments or discipline also go through an administrative process. This suggests that the impact of black administrators and black teachers should interact and in combination generate better outcomes for black students.

Table A5.1 presents these interaction models for gifted classes, expulsions, and suspensions, and Table A5.2 presents the models for the special education assignments. Because interaction models are easier to interpret graphically, Figures 5.1 to 5.6 present the marginal effect graphs. As an example,

---

[17] School board representation has a relatively lower VIF of 3.10, which should not be as severe a problem.

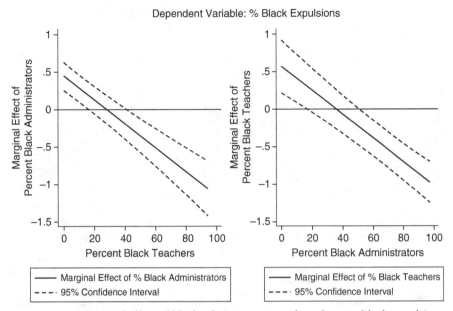

FIGURE 5.2. Marginal effect of black administrators and teachers on black expulsion.

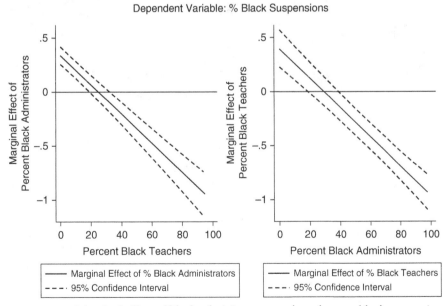

FIGURE 5.3. Marginal effect of black administrators and teachers on black suspension.

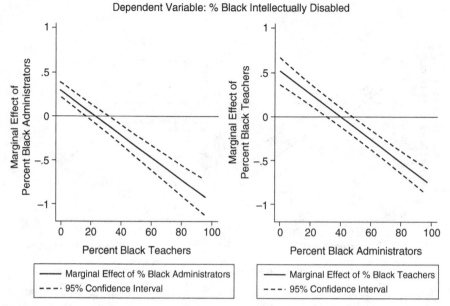

FIGURE 5.4. Marginal effect of black administrators and teachers on black intellectual disability (ID).

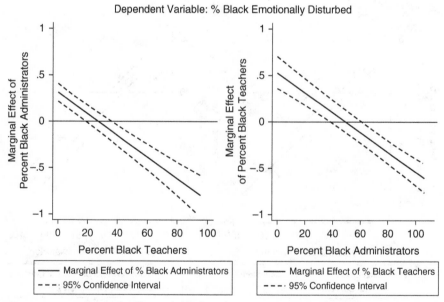

FIGURE 5.5. Marginal effect of black administrators and teachers on emotional disturbance (ED).

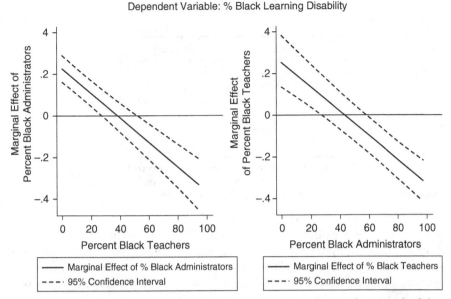

FIGURE 5.6. Marginal effect of black administrators and teachers on learning disability (LD).

Figure 5.1b examines the marginal effect of black teachers on black gifted class assignments at various levels of black administrators; the graph clearly shows that an increase in black teachers has little effect on the assignment of black students to gifted classes at low levels of black administrators (less than 10 percent). As the percentage of black administrators increases, the impact of black teachers is increasingly positive. Figure 5.1a shows a similar graph that demonstrates that the influence of black administrators on gifted class assignments also increases fairly dramatically as the percentage of black teachers increases, and the impact is positive not negative. These are the patterns that we would expect if the assignment of black students to gifted classes required black representation both among teachers and administrators.

The remaining figures illustrate similar patterns for both discipline measures and all three special education measures. Black teachers are more effective in reducing racial disparities in discipline and special education when they are in districts with more black administrators, and black administrators are more efficacious in limiting black student disparities in discipline and special education when they are in districts with more black teachers.[18] The different policy

---

[18] The symbiotic hypothesis does not resolve all the issues related to the complexities of race, partisanship, and education. It is also clear that teacher representation interacts with Democratic partisanship. At the same time, there does not appear to be a three-way interaction for teacher representation, administrative representation, and partisanship.

TABLE 5.9. *Black Student Outcomes in Democratic and Republican Districts*

Outcome	Democratic	Republican
Gifted	0.533	0.336
Expulsion	1.179	1.359
Suspension	1.193	1.295
Intellectual Disability	1.116	1.168
Emotional Disturbance	0.945	0.910
Learning Disability	0.967	1.047

Note: Numbers are the regression coefficients for percent black students from Tables 5.3 through 5.8 and can be interpreted as odds ratios after the adjustment for control variables. All are significant at $p < 0.05$.

indicators represent different levels of difficulty in translating administrative representation into policy outputs. Assignments to gifted classes become more equitable at lower levels of teacher (about 10 percent) and administrator representation (about 14 percent) than do suspensions and expulsions (25–35 percent) or for special education classes (23–46 percent).

These general patterns do not appear to be directly affected by the partisanship of the district; the set of interaction graphs for Democratic districts does not appear significantly different from those for Republican districts (results not shown). This does not mean that partisanship does not matter. As Chapters 3 and 4 demonstrate, partisanship plays a major role in the ability of African Americans to gain representation on the school board as well as the ability of school board members to hire black administrators and teachers. Democratic districts have larger numbers of black teachers and black administrators, all else equal, and so the marginal impact of both black teachers and administrators is further along the curves presented in this chapter.

Table 5.1 noted the racial gaps in all six policy indicators used in this chapter. By using measures of representation and various social and economic controls, Table 5.9 shows the remaining partisan racial gaps. For special education, where the gaps were generally smaller to start with, the gaps have essentially been closed. A black student enrolled in a school district with a Democratic majority, however, is still 56 percent more likely to have access to a gifted class, 9 percent less likely to be suspended, and 15 percent less likely to be expelled (all things being equal) than a black student enrolled in a Republican district. Clearly there are still other factors that are associated with partisanship and equal access to educational opportunities for black students that remain to be discovered.

Conclusion

Racial disparities in access to gifted classes or assignments to special education or in the administration of discipline are all indicators of limits to access to

quality education for African-American students. The stability of these disparities in discipline and gifted classes over the last thirty years indicates that little
has changed (the decline in disparities in special education may or may not be
meaningful given the changes in the definitions used for these classes). Racial
disparities on all the second-generation indicators vary greatly across school
districts, however, and declines in disparities are consistently linked to the proportion of African-American teachers in this district.

The effectiveness of black teacher representation stands in stark contrast to
the direct representational impacts of black school board members and black
administrators. Although teachers are associated with declines in racial disparities in gifted classes, suspensions, expulsions, and all three forms of special
education, school board members are only positively associated with greater
black student access to gifted classes, and that relationship is relatively modest.
Black school administrators are unrelated to gifted class access and are actually associated with greater racial disparities in both disciplinary actions and
special education assignments.

These blanket assessments, however, need to be qualified. The method of
analysis reveals the direct impacts of both administrators and school board
members but obscures their indirect impacts. African-American school board
members and school administrators are both highly correlated with the presence of black school teachers (see Chapter 4). The basic logic holds that black
school board members can influence the hiring of the black administrators
who are in turn the highest correlate of the hiring of black teachers. These indirect influences create the environment for effective street-level representation
by black teachers.

Creating an effective environment for representation is best shown by the
interaction effects of black teachers and black administrators. For all the indicators of access to education, the effectiveness of black teachers at reducing
racial disparities increases as the percentage of black administrators increases.
Similarly, black administrators actually have a positive impact on reducing
racial disparities when they are in districts with larger proportions of black
teachers. The student assignments are always more sensitive to the percentage
of black teachers, but black administrators also matter.

The differences in representational impact can be explain by a reliance on
Selden's (1997) concept of the representative role. Selden argues that some
bureaucrats adopt the role of a minority representative and others do not.
While adopting this role is associated with the race of the bureaucrat, the correlation is far from perfect and nonminority bureaucrats can also adopt that
role. Selden's concept of representative role needs to be expanded to deal with
the different roles that exist within an organization and how that role fits with
the ability to represent. Organizational roles are linked to the concept of discretion that plays a key role in the theory of representative bureaucracy. The scope
of discretion available to school board members, school administrators, and
school teachers varies. School board members are focused on policy issues and
broad advocacy roles. They cannot determine assignments to gifted classes or

who is suspended from school. They can advocate and fund limits on the size of various classes (although that is within the professional role of the school administrator to a greater extent) and they can advocate for greater representation among administrators and teachers (but other than for the superintendent, they have no direct role). These limits of discretion go a great distance in explaining the lack of impact of school board representation in this chapter.

Black school administrators also face role constraints that may limit representation. Administrators do not generally teach classes and, thus, their interaction is limited to students they come into contact with in their official duties. For many administrators, that might be in relationship to the administration of discipline or dealing with the procedures needed in assignments to classes. Most of these contacts will be filtered through teacher recommendations that could foreclose or limit the options that an administrator can take. The finding that black administrators play a positive role in reducing racial disparities when there are larger numbers of black teachers is consistent with this dependence on teacher referrals. The basic incentives of schools whereby administrative promotions are based on effective performance and most line administrators pass through a position such as vice principal that deals with discipline means that black administrators need to temper any racial representation with their own career objectives.

The contextual nature of teacher representation is perhaps most striking when considering the partisan environment. African-American teachers in school districts with a Democratic majority are always associated with fewer racial disparities in outcomes than are African-American teachers in Republican districts. At times, black teachers in Republican districts appear to have no influence whatsoever on racial disparities and even when their impact reaches statistical significance, the substantive impact is often only one-third or one-fourth the impact of their counterparts in Democratic districts. Partisanship's influence is not limited to augmenting the impact of black teachers. All other things being equal, Table 5.9 shows that a black student in a Democratic school district is far more likely to be in a gifted class and less likely to be suspended or expelled than a black student in a Republican district. Partisanship in effect has a double impact – it is generally associated with racial disparities and it enhances the ability of black teachers to reduce those disparities further. Chapters 3 and 4 also demonstrated that Democratic partisanship increased the level of school board representation and also then increased the association of board representation with the percentage of black teachers. This process generates a multiplier effect that reverberates through the entire school district with a variety of direct and indirect influences on the life chances of African-American students.

The implications of the partisanship findings cannot be understated. The simple fact of whether an African-American child attends school in a jurisdiction with a Democratic or a Republican majority profoundly shapes the education experience of that child and provides differences in human capital that are likely to greatly influence that child's future education, income, and social status. This is the partisan politics of education in the United States.

Appendix

TABLE A5.1. *Effect of Representation on Black Tracking and Discipline, Interaction of Administrators and Teachers*

	Gifted	Expulsions	Suspension
	Model 1	Model 2	Model 3
Percent Black Administrators	−0.114*	0.438*	0.343*
	(0.049)	(0.097)	(0.041)
Percent Black Teachers	−0.083	0.561*	0.403*
	(0.090)	(0.178)	(0.085)
Administrators X Teachers	0.008*	−0.016*	−0.014*
	(0.001)	(0.002)	(0.001)
Percent Black Board	0.069*	−0.023	0.007
	(0.021)	(0.055)	(0.022)
Percent Black Students	0.509*	1.106*	1.137*
	(0.034)	(0.069)	(0.036)
Black Education (College Percent)	−0.007	0.088*	0.033+
	(0.007)	(0.044)	(0.018)
Black Family Income (000s)	0.056*	−0.207+	−0.138*
	(0.023)	(0.117)	(0.051)
Black Home Ownership	0.009+	0.009	−0.032*
	(0.006)	(0.020)	(0.008)
White Poverty Percentage	0.133*	−0.057	−0.398*
	(0.046)	(0.135)	(0.048)
District Democrat Percent	0.041*	−0.033	−0.023
	(0.012)	(0.043)	(0.019)
South	−1.727*	1.599	3.335*
	(0.451)	(1.588)	(0.660)
Unionization	0.070*	0.217	0.138*
	(0.035)	(0.140)	(0.045)
Constant	−4.486*	4.444	7.754*
	(0.945)	(3.548)	(1.400)
Year FE	Yes	Yes	Yes
N	3545	2231	3727
R²	0.83	0.62	0.91
F	147.38	214.28	933.48

Standard errors in parentheses.

* $p < 0.05$; + $p < 0.10$

Note: Time points include 2002, 2004, 2006, and 2008.

TABLE A5.2. *Effect of Representation on Black Special Education, Interaction of Administrators and Teachers*

	Intellectual Disability (ID)	Emotional Disturbance (ED)	Learning Disability (LD)
	Model 1	Model 2	Model 3
Percent Black Administrators	0.299*	0.316*	0.226*
	(0.046)	(0.049)	(0.032)
Percent Black Teachers	0.518*	0.534*	0.259*
	(0.080)	(0.087)	(0.062)
Administrators X Teachers	−0.013*	−0.012*	−0.006*
	(0.001)	(0.001)	(0.001)
Percent Black Board	−0.005	0.069*	0.001
	(0.024)	(0.030)	(0.018)
Percent Black Students	1.056*	0.866*	0.949*
	(0.034)	(0.036)	(0.027)
Black Education (College Percent)	−0.014	−0.046*	0.038*
	(0.014)	(0.016)	(0.011)
Black Family Income (000s)	−0.201*	−0.129*	−0.058*
	(0.045)	(0.042)	(0.029)
Black Home Ownership	−0.000	−0.037*	−0.021*
	(0.008)	(0.009)	(0.006)
White Poverty Percentage	−0.477*	−0.311*	−0.184*
	(0.056)	(0.072)	(0.049)
District Democrat Percent	−0.037*	0.045*	−0.053*
	(0.019)	(0.021)	(0.015)
South	3.590*	0.170	1.497*
	(0.592)	(0.664)	(0.416)
Unionization	−0.057	0.025	0.157*
	(0.054)	(0.054)	(0.035)
Constant	10.973*	7.649*	3.982*
	(1.347)	(1.528)	(0.995)
Year FE	Yes	Yes	Yes
N	3642	3639	3675
R²	0.90	0.84	0.93
F	852.53	545.31	1049.83

Standard errors in parentheses.
* p < 0.05; + p < 0.10
Note: Time points include 2002, 2004, 2006, and 2008.

6

Race, Politics, and Student Learning

Politics, bureaucracy, and representation greatly affect the life chances of African-American students in our nation's schools. Chapter 5 demonstrates that bureaucratic representation and politics are associated with access to gifted classes, assignments to special education, and the administration of discipline. These policy outputs are considered indicators of equal access to quality education and are likely to affect the educational attainment of individual students and, subsequently, their long-term economic and social status (Gordon, Della Piana, and Keleher 2000; Kozol 1991; Mulkey et al. 2005). Although the policy debate at times focuses on these outputs, more discussion is centered on outcomes, predominately test scores, graduation rates, and preparation for higher education. Any assessment of educational outcomes, however, should recognize, first, that the political process has defined the goals of education and, second, that the existing definition of these goals is highly controversial (Smith 2003).

Public education can have numerous goals that are very general and somewhat ambiguous. In the broadest sense, the goal of public education is to produce effective democratic citizens – individuals who can participate in the political, social, and economic life of a polity (Gutmann and Ben-Porath 1987). Trying to measure the attainment of such a goal would require assessments of the relationship between education and political participation, social capital, crime, cultural development, economic growth, and many other facets of contemporary life. The political process in the United States has culled the various indicators of education to generally focus on test scores with some additional concern over graduation rates and movement into postsecondary education. Scholarly and parental resistance to standardized testing indicates that the narrowing of education goals has not gone uncontested (Bushaw and Calderon 2014; Strauss 2013; Valenzuela 2002, 2005; Wiliam 2010). Although this chapter will focus on test scores, graduation rates, and college preparation, we recognize these are only one set of goals in US education policy.

The narrowing of the mainstream educational policy debate has taken place in conjunction with the rise of the federal government as a major player in elementary and secondary education. K–12 education is traditionally a state function in which state governments delegate authority to local education agencies, primarily independent school districts.[1] This does not mean that the federal government has played no role in education policy; federal actors have periodically created incentives or provided resources in order to shape overall policy. Starting with the Northwest Ordinance of 1787 that required new territories to set aside lands for the support of public education and continuing through the adoption of the Elementary and Secondary Education Act of 1965 and the federal role in school desegregation, there has always been some federal presence in public education.

With the publication of *A Nation at Risk* in 1983, the federal government's role in K–12 education shifted. Led by Secretary of Education Terrel Bell (though initially unsupported by the White House), *A Nation at Risk* examined data on international comparisons of student performance as well as College Board scores and concluded that the nation's school systems were failing (Manna 2006).[2] The report concluded that the nation's economic competitiveness was threatened by this decline in education and that major reforms were needed. *A Nation at Risk* received wide national coverage and, consequently, initiated renewed federal government involvement in setting the educational agenda and added support to an extensive wave of reform by states that adopted higher standards for graduation (in terms of numbers of courses in various areas) and teacher training (many of these state efforts began even before this document gained national attention, see Manna 2006). As implemented, these higher standards were often accompanied by statewide standardized testing for students and additional funding incentives for local schools (McGuinn 2006).

Among the 1980s initiatives were the Perot-White[3] restructuring efforts in Texas that appeared to generate major gains in student performance and provided the platform for George W. Bush's education reform effort that

---

[1] The extent of delegation varies by state and can take the form of control over state funding or simply the addition of state requirements that all districts need to meet (see Wong 1999).

[2] The conclusions of *A Nation at Risk* are not unchallenged. A report produced by Sandia National Laboratory at the request of Energy Secretary James Watson concluded that the reported decline in SAT scores simply reflected the increased number of students taking the exam and that, within any individual group of students, scores had increased over time (Stedman 1994). Comparisons based on international test scores can also be problematic owing the different timing patterns in national curriculum and the inherent difficulties of measurement in cross-national contexts (Goldstein 2004; Prais 2003). See Berliner and Biddle (1995) for additional discussion.

[3] So named because Governor Mark White enlisted H. Ross Perot to spearhead the reform effort in Texas. The reforms also provided large increases in state aid to local school districts and some efforts at financial equalization that continued through the governorship of George W. Bush.

culminated in the passage of No Child Left Behind (NCLB). NCLB then triggered a massive set of state reforms with additional incentives provided by the federal government to improve education (e.g., the Race to the Top, see McGuinn 2012). Altogether, these changes resulted in a mix of federal guidelines and policies alongside state-level standards that created significant barriers to creating a national database that could link student performance across individual districts in a uniform manner. These changes did, however, generate a more concerted focus on racial and income gaps in education, and the available data can be used to provide some insight into questions of race, partisanship, and representation in the United States.

Comparing Student Performance across States

This chapter will examine three education policy outcomes – test scores, graduation rates, and preparation for further education. These outcomes have been defined as important politically and have been incorporated in the various incentive systems that currently govern K–12 education. Political compromises in the adoption of NCLB meant that each state was allowed to set its own educational standards and create its own standardized exam as long as certain federal requirements were met. Similarly, each state continues to define high school graduation requirements and standards for college readiness. The National Assessment of Educational Progress (NAEP), often termed the "Nation's Report Card," is currently the only comparable national test available (though there is also the more recent, controversial push for the Common Core State Standards Initiatives). Even this exam is designed to only generate representative samples at the state level (or for a few large districts) and is not universally administered; before requirements set by NCLB to receive federal dollars, NAEP tests were administered on a voluntary basis often with more than forty states opting to participate. Analyses similar to that found in previous chapters using the NAEP, as a result, would be quite difficult.[4] These data limitations required the adoption of two second-best solutions in order to build on the prior analysis and to examine policy outcomes in a significant enough number of cases to be sure that our findings are relatively general. The first approach consists of empirical case studies of four large states to examine the role of teacher representation in these different contexts. The second approach converts state-level data from the ten largest states with available data to a common (standardized) metric; this metric is merged with our existing database to examine policy outcomes further.

---

[4] The NAEP is also not conducted every year, which creates problems of matching these test results with the cases and years in our study. Our attempt to create an NAEP data set for large school districts eventually resulted in only thirty-one total district-years. The small number of cases and the unrepresentative nature of the cases that were included led us to conclude that any results generated would not add significantly to the overall findings in this chapter.

Both approaches can be encompassed with a common general analytical model even though the components of the model will vary in implementation. Educational outcomes, test scores, graduation rates, and preparedness for future education are not completely under the control of the school systems. A variety of other factors such as the family characteristics, income levels, instructional technology, improvement in the economy, and other factors also influence education outcomes. In all cases, the analyses will create an education production function whereby the education output is a product of school district factors such as representation as well as a series of local resources (education levels, state funding, teacher credentials, school type) and constraints (poverty, non-English proficiency).

Approach 1: Four Case Studies

The first set of studies changes our focus from the national level to examine four large individual state systems – California, Florida, Ohio, and Texas. The selection of states was based on two criteria. First, the state had to have a significant African-American population and vary on other important characteristics such as region, income levels, partisanship, and efforts at education policy reform. Equally important, the state had to maintain an accessible, quality database (Table A6.1 provides descriptive statistics on the four states).[5] This strategy lets the state define the performance indicators and will cover approximately 28 percent of the districts used in our study (and 37 percent of the total enrollment). All four states provide standardized test scores and graduation rates; California and Texas also collect measures of college readiness. Because the databases are not designed to be used together, there will be four separate analyses that will be forced to use the varying set of control variables that are provided by the state in question. Importantly, one key variable is not included in these databases – the racial composition of school administrators. By contrast, because teacher representation had the strongest influence on other educational factors, focusing solely on teacher representation will still provide valuable information. In addition, racial disparities in terms of gifted classes, special education assignments, or discipline, all of which can affect educational outcomes, are not consistently available in these state databases.

Conducting the analysis at the state level also truncates some key explanatory variables and thus could change the results. Texas, for example, is a very red state while California is a very blue state. As such, school districts with a Republican majority are the norm in Texas but are less common in California.

---

[5] The passage of NCLB and the imposition of standardized testing should have created a large number of quality databases on education. State departments of education, however, vary in their ability to create and maintain databases on student performance. Some states will only provide data for a limited number of years even based on specific requests (e.g., in 2015 Georgia could provide no data that predated 2005). Other states only collect some of the control variables needed for analysis.

This lack of variation could limit the explanatory power of partisanship. Data availability also means that the years covered differ in the four states (the data are as follows: California 2006–2010, Ohio 2007–2008, Florida 2011–2013, and Texas 1999–2010).

Approach 2: Merging State Data into the National Data Set

The second set of studies will collect student standardized test scores from the ten states with the largest number of school districts in our data set: California, Florida, Georgia, Indiana, Massachusetts, New Jersey, North Carolina, Ohio, Pennsylvania, and Texas.[6] These ten states contain 49 percent of the districts in our overall study and approximately 54 percent of the students covered in the national study. The state test scores will be standardized (see following text). This essentially means that we have a state fixed effect that controls for both the mean and the variance within a state. This creates a comparison within the states but does not permit comparison across the states because the standardization turns all scores into comparisons with the average test score in the state.

The second database will have the advantage of having measures of all the variables previously examined and, therefore, be able to generate a full set of controls as well as including all three representation measures. This will also allow us to include measures of grouping, tracking, and discipline as intermediary variables in the analysis. The limitation of this data set is that by focusing on the within-state variation, the range of the independent variables is truncated. In combination, the two approaches, although not perfect, should provide significant leverage on the role that representation and partisanship place in reducing the racial gaps in US education. Graduation data and advanced placement (AP) classes and exam results from the Office for Civil Rights (OCR) surveys will provide additional policy outcomes for the national data set.

A Tale of Four States

States exercise a great deal of autonomy in the governance of public education. As a result, it is not surprising that each of the four state cases have slightly different backgrounds in the development of state accountability and testing standards. The state contexts including different racial, geographic, and economic factors also play a role in setting the tone of school standards.

California, the most Democratic of the four states (with 60.2 percent of the state's votes cast for Barack Obama in the 2012 election; Leamon and Bucelato 2013), is racially mixed. While the state has a smaller African-American population (6.2 percent) than the total US population (12.6 percent), it has a larger

---

[6] New York and Illinois were also in this group of states with a large number of students in our data. New York only provided applicable data for New York City, and Illinois data had a high rate of missing variables for the indicators needed for this analysis.

share of individuals who identify as Asian only (13 percent in California vs. 4.8 percent in the United States) or Hispanic/Latino (37.6 percent in California vs. 16.3 in the United States) (US Census 2010). Districts across California have used their own exit exams since at least 1978. Additional statewide tests, including the California Assessment Program (CAP), California Learning Assessment System (CLAS), and California Standards Tests (CSTs), have evolved over time. State laws also required School Accountability Report Cards (SARCs) in 1988, making the state a relatively early mover on accountability in the country. The purpose of SARCs was to provide parents and surrounding communities with information; report cards include information on demographics, safety, completions, teacher and staff characteristics, curriculum, college preparation programs, and expenditures (California Department of Education 2014). Following the SARC requirements, the legislature passed additional guidelines for standardized testing in the form of the Standardized Testing and Reporting (STAR) Program for grades two through eleven. The test was implemented in 1998 and operates alongside the CAHSEE (California High School Exit Exam) for students intending to graduate from high school. The STAR Program consists of multiple CSTs that include English language arts, mathematics, science, and history/social science (Education Data Partnership 2014). Not all students take all tests (e.g., history/social science is not administered to every grade); all tests are scored along five ranges of proficiency, ranging from advanced to far below basic (Education Data Partnership 2014).

While the STAR Program was still in the early stage of implementation, the legislature passed the Public Schools Accountability Act (PSAA) to fully develop a system that would hold students and schools accountable for performance (California Department of Education 2015). The cornerstone of the PSAA is the assignment of an API (Academic Performance Index) to each school; the API is the performance indicator used in the analysis in the following text. The API can range from two hundred to one thousand and is primarily determined by STAR and CAHSEE results (although there are periodic changes to how various tests are weighted in the API calculation); other components – such as those related to staffing or graduation – were intended to be used in addition to test scores but data in these area have not yet been deemed reliable (California Department of Education 2014). API scores operate on a two-year cycle so that year one provides a base score while year two provides a growth score. Using the API, schools are compared to other schools of the same type (e.g., elementary, high school) and are also compared to one hundred other schools in the state that have comparable student populations (California Department of Education 2014). The API system helped California to prepare and provide information for the Adequate Yearly Progress requirements of NCLB. Although some evidence exists of student improvement on exams – English proficiency has increased from 35 percent to 56 percent and math proficiency from 35 percent to 51 percent between 2003 and 2013 – new standards for state exams were passed in 2014 (California Assessment of

Student Performance and Progress) (Education Data Partnership 2014). This change was partially the result of the state's request to be waived from NCLB requirements as well as state adoption of the Common Core State Standards.

On the other side of the country, Florida's history of education accountability shares some similarities and differences with California. Demographically, Florida has the highest percentage of African Americans (16 percent) of the four case studies; individuals who identify as Hispanic or Latino also slightly outpace the national average (22.5 percent vs. 16.3 percent) (US Census 2010). Individuals who identify as other races comprise quite small shares of the state. Politically, Floridians are quite split, with 50 percent of the 2012 vote for Barack Obama and 49.1 percent for Mitt Romney (Leamon and Bucelato 2013).

Similar to California, Florida begin expanding K–12 education data tracking in the mid-1980s as the *A Nation at Risk* report gained nationwide attention. The legislature wanted to increase the ability to track student performance over time and began developing Sunshine State Standards (SSS) in 1993; these standards were subsequently adopted by the Florida Board of Education in 1996 and have been updated over time. SSS provides students, parents, and teachers specific benchmarks that students in each grade should achieve in eight subject areas (Florida Center for Instructional Technology 2015).[7] To measure progress toward these SSS benchmarks, the state implemented its version of standardized testing in the Florida Comprehensive Assessment Test (FCAT) (earlier standardized tests, including the State Student Assessment Test (SSAT) and the High School Competency Test (HSCT), were present in the state) (Florida Department of Education 2015). FCAT reading and math exams are required for grades three through ten while other subject areas (science and writing) are administered in select years.

FCAT scores provide the basis for the state's A+ Plan (established in 1999) that awards letter grades (A–F) to individual schools (Peterson 2006). Like the report card system in California, the purpose of establishing these grades was to provide information to the community about how well schools were performing. Although grades were initially assessed by comparing schools primarily through FCAT scores, they eventually included assessments based on school improvement from the previous year. Specifically, elements of the grading system include student test performance, learning gains in reading and math (with particular attention to improvement of students who were previously in the lowest 25 percentile), accelerated courses, and graduation rates. Unlike some states, grades are associated with clear positive and negative consequences related to oversight and funding, for example. Generally, 70 percent of schools score As and Bs while 10 percent score Ds and Fs (Foundation for Florida's Future 2015).

---

[7] E.g., for grade 1, six standards exist that contain subcategories. For the standard of "Developing and understanding of whole number relationships, including grouping by tens and ones," students are to "compare and order whole numbers at least to 100," among other points (Florida Center for Instructional Technology 2015).

More recently, in 2010 Florida was one of twelve states selected for federal Race to the Top funding, which spurred changes in three areas. First, the state created a new system for teacher and principal performance. In 2011, Senate Bill 736, or the Student Success Act, moved the state accountability system toward a more specific value-added model[8] by evaluating teachers on data including student learning growth. The new, and controversial, evaluation system essentially terminated tenure for teachers and created a salary structure determined in part by market forces (Florida Education Association 2015). Second, the state has been shifting toward the implementation of Common Core standards. Schools begin testing using the Florida Core Standards in the 2014–2015 academic year (this coincides with Next Generation SSS) (O'Connor 2014). Finally, the state is working to develop new methods for the use of performance data information that will improve classroom instruction and, subsequently, school performance.

Within the four cases considered, Ohio is most like Florida in terms of the political nature of the state. In the 2012 presidential election, 50.7 percent voted Democrat while 47.7 percent voted for Republican (Leamon and Bucelato 2013). By contrast, the population of Ohio is more homogenous compared to other states. While Ohio has the second-highest level of African Americans of the four states and reflects the national average for this group (12.2 percent in the state vs. 12.6 percent in the country), there exist no other sizeable minority racial or ethnic group, including those who identify as Hispanic or Latino (3.1 percent) (US Census 2010).

In terms of school accountability, in 1987 the Ohio legislature approved high-stakes ninth-grade proficiency exams in reading, writing, mathematics, and citizenship beginning with the graduating class of 1994 (Ohio Department of Education 1998). In addition to this graduation test, the Ohio Achievement Assessment (OAA) tests were developed throughout the early and mid-1990s. These tests are administered across grades three through eight and include tests in reading, mathematics, science, social studies, and writing. These tests were not linked to specific academic standards until new legislation was passed in 2001 (the new system was implemented in 2003) (Porter-Magee 2011). Additional test improvements were made in 2009, and in 2010, the State Board of Education voted to replace the state standards with the Common Core standards in math and English language arts. This move has also strengthened two points of high-stakes testing – value-added systems for teachers and reporting the performance of schools and districts (Hansen and Urycki 2013). First, Ohio has implemented a "Third Grade Reading Guarantee" such that students must pass a specific reading test in the third grade in order to be promoted. Students must also pass all five Ohio Graduation Tests (OGTs) to receive their diploma. Standardized tests will also align with the Common

---

[8] Value-added measures seek to evaluate teachers based on how much their students' performance improved in one year over performance in the previous year as well as compared to other students in the same grade, usually in reference to standardized test scores.

Core and have been deemed "New Ohio Tests" in the state. Second, similar to changes in Florida, OAAs are used to create value-added measures to evaluate teachers (this system was fully implemented in the 2013–2014 school year) (Hansen and Urycki 2013). Finally, the state has further developed a yearly report card system. Although districts initially were placed into categories (i.e., "Continuous Improvement"), letter grades will be used beginning in the 2015–2016 school year (these letter grades began being phased in during the 2012–2013 school year). Report cards include information related to performance (using standardized testing), value-added progress, achievement gaps, and graduation rates (Bloom 2013).

Of the states in the selected case studies, Texas arguably has the longest history with standardized testing and was widely cited as a role model for NCLB, in part because George W. Bush moved from being Texas governor to president. As measured by the 2010 Census, the state was 11.8 percent African American as well as 10.5 percent "Other Race" while 37.6 percent identified as Hispanic or Latino (this share is equal to that of California) (US Census 2010). Texas has the largest share of Republicans of the four case studies; 57.2 percent voted for Mitt Romney in 2012 while 41.4 percent voted for Barack Obama (Leamon and Bucelato 2013).[9]

In 1979, Senate Bill 350 required every district to administer test in grades three, five, and nine. The Texas Assessment of Basic Skills (TABS) was first administered in 1980. In 1983, the state began publishing test results by student groups for public consumption and, subsequently, placing more pressure on schools to perform. The test changed to TEAMS (Texas Educational Assessment of Minimum Skills) in 1985; this update expanded testing to include grades one, seven, and eleven, and remediation was made mandatory for students who did not pass the exam (Cruse and Twing 2000). The test was again revised as the Texas Assessment of Academic Skills (TAAS) in 1990 and the Texas Assessment of Knowledge and Skills (TAKS) in 2003. The TAKS test was aligned with state learning standards (Texas Essential Knowledge and Skills), and students in grades three, five, and eight were required to pass TAKS for promotion to the next grade. In 2011, the fifth version of the exam, the State of Texas Assessments of Academic Readiness (STAAR), required a series of new tests for high school students (these include algebra, biology, chemistry, and others) (Texas Education Agency 2015).

In addition to these standardized tests, Texas has maintained an Academic Excellence Indicator System (AEIS) – now Texas Academic Performance Reports – since 1990 (though an earlier version was started in 1988). These reports are available by school and district and provide information related to

---

[9] Portions of education policy in Texas have a clear ideological dimension. The elected Texas State Board of Education has presided over well-publicized fights regarding the content of textbooks as conservative members have pushed to restrict the teaching of evolution and global warming. Similar efforts have been present to alter the content of history and government texts.

student performance, staffing, finance, and additional programs. Subsets of the AEIS form school and district accountability ratings (available since 1994) as well as report cards (available since 1997) (Texas Education Agency 2012).

Unlike other cases considered, Texas stands out for its lack of interest in pursuing Race to the Top federal funding dollars (only Alaska, North Dakota, Texas, and Vermont did not submit applications) as well as its stance against the adoption of the Common Core standards (Smith 2011). In 2013, the legislature prohibited school districts from using the Common Core, and both Governor Rick Perry and Governor Greg Abbott have spoken against the standards (Bidwell 2014). The state has, however, recently moved toward approving a new A–F rating system for schools and districts and may also allow high school students intending to graduate to fail up to two standardized tests without penalty.

The development of school accountability and standardized testing across the four cases can be compared to some extent using the NAEP within the Department of Education. As compared to the national average, NAEP ratings list California tests as largely lower than average while Ohio, though mixed, is largely above average (NAEP 2014). Florida tests have a wide range (including some tests that are below, no different from, and higher than average) while Texas is largely no different than average. These testing differences may have some effect in the following analyses.

Modeling the State Cases

Three measures of education policy outcomes will be examined in the four state case studies – black student test scores, black graduation rates, and the preparation of black students for college. The test score measure is the percentage of black students who pass all tests administered by the state in question except for California.[10] California calculates an API that ranges between two hundred and one thousand and is based on the state standardized test and the California High School Exit Exam. In all states black students, on average, score well below white students. The pass rates for black students compared to whites are 15 percentage points lower in California, 45 points lower in Florida, 19 points lower in Ohio, and 25 points lower in Texas for the years in this study. In terms of difficulty of state exams, a National Center for Education Statistics (2011) study based on 2009 state standards found that none of the four states set especially high standards (see Table 6.1). All four states have reading standards below the national "basic" level (the lowest federal standard in the NAEP) in grade four and slightly above the basic level at grade eight except for Texas whose standards in reading rank thirty-ninth for grade four and last for grade eight. Math standards are generally at the national basic

---

[10] For Florida and Ohio, we averaged the student performance on the math and reading exams to create a single score. In Florida the measure is the percentage of students who score a grade of three or better on the exams.

TABLE 6.1. *NAEP Equivalents of State Standards*

	Reading		Math	
	Grade 4	Grade 8	Grade 4	Grade 8
National Standard "Proficient"	238	281	249	299
National Standard "Basic"	208	242	214	262
California	202	259	220	n/a
Florida	206	262	225	266
Ohio	192	251	219	265
Texas	188	201	214	275

Note: California did not administer the NAEP Grade 8 math test for the time period covered by the Department of Education study.

level or slightly higher. None of the states have standards that approach the higher national "proficient" level. None of the states could be considered a leader in setting high standards; Massachusetts comes closest to matching the national proficient standard.[11]

The black graduation rate is taken from state records and reflects the specific definitions of graduation applied within the state. The black-white gap across the four states for graduation ranges from 9 to 20 percentage points (66 percent vs. 86 percent in California, 64 percent vs. 80 percent in Florida, 61 percent vs. 86 percent in Ohio, and 84 percent vs. 93 percent in Texas), which is somewhat less than the gaps present in test scores. The second set of analysis with additional states will use graduation data provided by the OCR and will be more comparable across states than this measure. The college readiness measure in Texas is based on college admissions exams, specifically the percentage of students who score above 1110 on the SAT or its ACT equivalent (or in the top 20 percent nationwide). The California standard is the percentage of twelfth grade students who have completed all the course requirements needed for admission to the University of California or the California State University systems.

The key representation variable in the four state cases is the percentage of African-American teachers. Many of the school districts analyzed are not part of our large national study; and, therefore, we do not have school board representation or administrator representation for these school districts. To generate results that correspond to our national sample, all analyses will also be run on school districts with 5,000+ student enrollment. As our national survey was conducted in 2002, 2004, and 2008, we merge each survey year with two subsequent years of state data (the 2002 survey with 2003 and 2004; the 2004 survey with 2005 and 2006; and the 2008 survey with 2009 and 2010).

---

[11] In order from lowest to highest, standards can be ranked as below basic, basic, and proficient (see, e.g., rankings in Bandeira de Mello 2011).

TABLE 6.2. *Variables by State*

California	Texas
Percent Black Teachers	Percent Black Teachers
Percent Black Students	Percent Black Students
Percent English Learners	Percent Low-Income Students
Charter School (0,1)	Percent Bilingual Students
Percent Free and Reduced Lunch	Student-Teacher Ratio
Percent Teachers with Full Credentials	Charter School (0,1)
Percent Parents with College Education	Average Teacher Salary (1,000s)
School Type (Elementary, Middle, High)	Operating Expenditures/Student (log)

Ohio	Florida
Percent Black Teachers	Percent Black Teachers
Percent Black Students	Percent Black Students
Percent English Learners	Percent English Learners
All Disciplinary Actions per 100 Students	Attendance Stability Rate
Average Years of Teacher Experience	Percent Free and Reduced Lunch
Percent Core Courses Taught by Certified Teacher	Percent Highly Qualified Teachers
Average Teacher Salary (1,000s)	Teacher Median Salary (1,000)
Expenditures/Student (logged)	Instruction/Student (log)

Note: Charter schools in California and Texas are coded as a district. Thus, we include a bivariate measure that controls for whether a district is considered a charter or not.

To understand the influence of representation, it is also important to control for the quality of the district in which students learn; all analyses will include an independent variable measuring the performance of non-Hispanic white students.[12] The inclusion of this control will essentially mean that results should be interpreted as defining how much representation affects the test score gap between African-American and white students. As noted in the preceding text, test scores, similar to other education system outcomes, are determined by a wide variety of factors other than the school. These can essentially be divided into resources and constraints. Resources include both school resources (e.g., instructional expenditures, teacher salaries, class size) and community resources (parental education). Constraints include such factors as poverty and language.[13] Table 6.2 lists the control variables used in each of the state analyses. An effort was made to be as comprehensive as possible within each of the states rather

[12] The exception here is for standardized test scores in Texas where there are a significant number of school districts with so few non-Hispanic white students that their scores are not reported. In that case we controlled for the test scores of the students who were not African American.
[13] California also has some noncomprehensive school districts, i.e., districts that do not have all K–12 grades. Because test scores generally are higher in elementary grades, this required a set of controls for the grade distribution in the school district.

TABLE 6.3. *Test Scores Model Summaries*

	Model 1: Baseline		Model 2: Large Districts		Model 3: Partisanship	
	Coef.	t	Coef.	t	Coef.	t
California						
Percent Black Teachers	0.588+	1.83	0.611+	1.86	0.793*	2.27
Percent Democrat					−0.721*	−2.25
Ohio						
Percent Black Teachers	.727*	2.17	2.092*	3.28	2.023*	3.22
Percent Democrat					−0.087	−1.03
Florida						
Percent Black Teachers	0.388+	1.85	0.459+	1.98	0.443+	1.77
Percent Democrat					−0.077	−1.05
Texas						
Percent Black Teachers	0.090*	3.92	0.077	1.20	0.092	1.50
Percent Democrat					0.121*	2.85

* p < .05; + p < 0.10

Note: Regressions include only districts that have >1 and <50 percent black students.

than to limit the analysis to only those variables that were collected in all four states. Whether or not these different specifications somehow bias the results can be determined from the second set of analyses in the following text that will use the national data set with its consistent set of control variables. All models will also include fixed effects for years in order to deal with the inevitable creep in test scores over time (and changes in the nature of the test) and standard errors clustered by case. The analysis for each state and variable will be examined across three regressions. The first will include all school districts in the state with at least 1 percent black students and less than 50 percent black students, the second will include only those districts from the first model with more than five thousand students to try to match our national sample, and the third regression will add our partisanship measure as a control.

Representation and Test Scores

Because our concern is with representation and partisanship, we will focus on those variables rather than the various controls. Table 6.3 presents a summary of the four state models for the representation and the partisanship measure; the full regressions appear in the Tables A6.2–A6.11. Model 1, which includes both small and large districts, shows that the presence of black teachers is associated with narrowing the test score gap between black and white students in all four states. Limiting the analysis to districts with 5000+ students (Model 2) shows similar relationships between representation and black student performance

TABLE 6.4. *Graduation Model Summaries*

	Model 1: Baseline		Model 2: Large Districts		Model 3: Partisanship	
	Coef.	T	Coef.	T	Coef.	t
California						
Percent Black Teachers	0.042+	1.70	0.055*	2.13	0.053+	1.88
Percent Democrat					−0.027*	−2.00
Ohio						
Percent Black Teachers	0.451*	2.32	1.266*	5.56	1.437*	7.76
Percent Democrat					0.094+	1.90
Florida						
Percent Black Teachers	−0.010	−0.09	−0.087	−1.20	−0.121+	0.063
Percent Democrat					−0.047+	−1.97
Texas						
Percent Black Teachers	0.077+	1.69	0.010	0.160	0.011	0.14
Percent Democrat					0.051	0.84

* $p < .05$; + $p < 0.10$

Note: Regressions include only districts that have >1 and <50 percent black students.

in California, Florida, and Ohio, and in all cases the size of the coefficient increases in size. The relationship for Texas drops and fails to reach statistical significance. The impact of partisanship (Model 3) is mixed; it is associated with wider racial gaps in California and narrower gaps in Texas. Given the truncated nature of this variable within states (as opposed to across states), the most reasonable conclusion is that the results do not provide any evidence to support that there is a direct relationship between partisanship and the racial gap in test scores. An indirect relationship likely exists, however, based on the association between partisanship and representation revealed in Chapter 4 and the partisanship correlates of educational outputs in Chapter 5 (see following text for an assessment of the linkage through educational outputs).

Owing to the lack of comparability of the test scores across states without further adjustment, interpreting the substantive impact of black teacher representation on black student test scores will need to wait until they are further transformed into standardized units that can be compared (see Tables 6.7 and 6.8).

High School Graduation Rates

Table 6.4 examines the association of black teachers with graduation rates for black students in the four states. For the full set of school districts (Model 1) black teacher representation is associated with higher black graduation rates in California, Ohio, and Texas but not in Florida. When the analysis is restricted

TABLE 6.5. *College Readiness Model Summaries*

	Model 1: Baseline		Model 2: Large Districts		Model 3: Partisanship	
	Coef.	t	Coef.	T	Coef.	t
California						
Percent Black Teachers	0.720*	8.85	0.745*	9.43	0.771*	10.04
Percent Democrat					-0.291*	-2.39
Texas						
Percent Black Teachers	-0.013	-0.43	0.078	1.37	0.094	1.55
Percent Democrat					0.131*	3.02

* $p < .05$.
Note: Regressions include only districts that have >1 and <50 percent black students.

to larger districts (Model 2), the Texas relationship declines to insignificance, but the Ohio and California relationships become slightly larger (the Florida relationship remains insignificant). Partisanship continues its mixed pattern of direct relationships with a positive association in Ohio and a negative one in California, but again the truncated nature of this variable and the focus on only the direct influence of partisanship urges caution.

The case of Florida is clearly interesting because black teachers are associated with higher levels of test scores but no impact on graduation rates. Given that Florida is a high-stakes testing state that requires students to pass various tests in order to be promoted or to graduate from high school, one would expect that factors that increase test scores would also be factors that increase high school graduation rates.

College-Ready Students
The creation of a college-ready standard is an effort to establish an additional quality indicator for high school education based on preparation of college education. State standardized tests are criticized, often justifiably, for setting a low-performance bar and not being linked to preparedness for future education or the job market. Texas and California take different approaches to this question, with Texas relying on college entrance exams and California using the completion of a set of high school classes. The California standard is less stringent than the Texas standard; the mean black college-ready percentage is 30.4 in California versus 6.2 percent in Texas. Because the California standard is based on classes completed, it also falls under the control of the school system more so than do the college entrance exams used in Texas.

Table 6.5 shows that black teacher representation in California is positively associated with the percentage of black students meeting the college-ready standard for all districts (Model 1), for larger districts (Model 2), and in the presence of controls for partisanship (Model 3). In Texas, there is no relationship between black teachers and college readiness in the full set of districts, but a positive relationship in larger districts that holds up with controls for partisanship. Comparing the teacher effects in Texas across the three equations shows a pattern whereby relationships exist for test scores and graduation rates for all districts but not for the largest districts, but the impact on college readiness exists only for the large districts. Although this might relate to job markets and educational aspirations in rural versus urban areas of Texas, investigating this pattern is beyond the scope of the current research.

The mixed pattern for partisanship again is present in Table 6.5. For California, a Democratic state, an increase in Democratic partisanship is associated with declines in black college-ready attainment. In Texas, a Republican state, an increase in Democratic partisanship is correlated with an improvement in black student performances on the college boards. This pattern is consistent with our earlier findings, but given the truncation of the partisanship variable, this finding is not as robust as those presented in the following text.

Generalizing from the Four States

The examination of teacher representation and its association with black student performance provided some reasonable but not universal support for a positive link between the two variables. Although these were not independent tests given the nesting of the models, the empirical analysis examined thirty different possible relationships and found twenty-two significant results that all indicated that black student performance was higher in districts with more black teachers. The lack of completely consistent results might well be a function of the truncated variables, including both race and representation that occurs when the analysis is within a single state. If such effects are subject to diminishing marginal returns, for example, states that are further along the curve will show weaker or even statistically insignificant results. The absence of relationships in the eight cases out of thirty could also mean that teacher representation interacts with other variables (such as administrative representation, see Chapter 5) and without these other factors included, the models are underspecified. Underspecification could also occur simply because the different states do not include a full set of socioeconomic controls that commonly appear in education production functions. These limits highlight the need for additional tests using the full national data set.

The National Data

Comparing state test scores across the states is problematic given that state exams vary in both overall difficulty and in how much variation there is across students. The latter is especially problematic because the analyst does not know if this variation reflects actual differences among the students or if it is a function of the exam. Because there is no obvious way to solve the problem of comparability for the states included in the analysis in this section, we opt for a measure that will essentially create comparisons to the state mean test score. This means that the analysis will not account for any variation in the average quality of student performance across the states and thus is likely to limit the influence of key independent variables that also vary across the states (such as black representation). All test scores are standardized within states by subtracting the grand mean from the test score and dividing by the standard deviation. To illustrate, if this value were +0.5 for one group of students, it would indicate that the group scored, on average, one half of a standard deviation above the mean for the state. Negative values would indicate the group scored below the state mean. Across all ten states, African-American students produced an average score of −0.74, or .74 standard deviations below the all-student mean; white students had an average score of +0.65, or .65 standard deviations above the mean. This figure shows a substantial racial gap in test scores that is consistent with data from the NAEP and other sources.

The overall mean values mask a great deal of variation. Table 6.6 shows the means and racial gaps for each state. The important take-away point from Table 6.6 is that in every case African-American students score lower on the state standardized tests than white students. The extent of the gap, however, is influenced by a variety of factors. Some of the variation in scores and racial gaps reflects the differences in the racial compositions of state populations; Latinos comprise a large portion of many states as do Asians or Native Americans in other states. Some of the differences are also related to how easy or how difficult the test is. In cases in which the state tests are relatively easy, a ceiling effect reduces the overall range of the data and will artificially reduce the size of a gap between any two groups. This measurement concern suggested that all models should be tested for state fixed effects in order to determine if the findings are robust. Although the state fixed effects are frequently significant and absorb some of the cross-state variation in key independent variables (e.g., teacher representation varies by state simply because it reflects the racial distribution if the population), they do not affect either the substantive or statistical significance of the findings presented in this section.

The analysis of test scores will use the same models and control variables that were used to examine second-generation educational discrimination indicators in Chapter 5. All three measures of black representation (school board, administrators, teachers) are included as well as controls for percent black students, black education levels, black income levels, black home ownership, white poverty, and Democratic partisanship. Because union membership and the southern region are state-level variables and there are only ten states in the model, the two variables are too collinear to include in the analysis.[14] The models also

---

[14] The variables for South and unionization have variance inflation factors of greater than twenty-three when included in these models. They essentially represent deviations by two states (unionization is also measured only at the state level) and both coefficients drop from any significance in the presence of state fixed effects.

TABLE 6.6. *Ten-state Overview of Racial Gaps*

Variable	Mean	SD	Min	Max
California				
Standardized Black Test Score	−0.600	0.682	−2.667	1.853
Standardized White Test Score	0.495	0.600	−1.633	1.967
Florida				
Standardized Black Test Score	0.203	0.875	−1.576	2.271
Standardized White Test Score	3.439	0.821	0.967	5.080
Georgia				
Standardized Black Test Score	−0.679	0.952	−3.603	1.970
Standardized White Test Score	1.035	0.617	−1.315	2.178
Indiana				
Standardized Black Test Score	−1.763	0.966	−3.449	0.618
Standardized White Test Score	0.242	0.816	−1.925	1.839
Massachusetts				
Standardized Black Test Score	−1.806	0.841	−3.329	−0.616
Standardized White Test Score	−0.175	0.864	−2.094	1.573
New Jersey				
Standardized Black Test Score	0.072	0.944	−2.811	1.751
Standardized White Test Score	1.998	0.691	0.227	3.217
North Carolina				
Standardized Black Test Score	−0.896	0.989	−2.011	0.999
Standardized White Test Score	0.979	0.677	−1.852	2.150
Ohio				
Standardized Black Test Score	−2.189	1.340	−5.105	0.496
Standardized White Test Score	0.042	1.211	−3.362	1.836
Pennsylvania				
Standardized Black Test Score	0.079	0.894	−2.624	2.388
Standardized White Test Score	1.550	0.817	−2.555	2.748
Texas				
Standardized Black Test Score	−0.696	0.747	−3.398	1.725
Standardized White Test Score	0.518	0.504	−1.978	1.664

include non-Hispanic white test scores to control for the quality of education in the district and to allow the representation coefficients to be interpreted as the impact of a given variable on the black-white test score gap. Models include fixed effects for years, and standard errors are clustered for districts.

Test Scores
The first column of Table 6.7 indicates that the quality of the school district (measured by white student test scores) is the largest influence on black student test scores followed by indicators of wealth in the black community (income

TABLE 6.7. *Estimating Standardized Test Scores in Ten States, Baseline*

	Model 1	Model 2	Model 3
	All Cases	R Majority	D Majority
Percent Black Board	−0.005*	−0.008*	−0.002
	(0.002)	(0.003)	(0.002)
Percent Black Administrators	−0.007+	−0.000	−0.015*
	(0.004)	(0.005)	(0.005)
Percent Black Teachers	0.016*	0.007	0.024*
	(0.005)	(0.008)	(0.007)
Percent Black Students	−0.011*	−0.008+	−0.014*
	(0.003)	(0.004)	(0.004)
Black Education (College Percent)	0.006+	0.004	0.006
	(0.003)	(0.003)	(0.005)
Black Family Income (000s)	0.038*	0.050*	0.031*
	(0.007)	(0.010)	(0.011)
Black Home Ownership	0.001	−0.000	0.004*
	(0.001)	(0.001)	(0.002)
White Percent Poverty	−0.001	0.006	−0.006
	(0.008)	(0.010)	(0.015)
District Democrat Percent	−0.004*	−0.003	−0.009*
	(0.002)	(0.004)	(0.004)
Standardized White Scores	0.540*	0.570*	0.495*
	(0.025)	(0.033)	(0.039)
Constant	−1.408*	−1.524*	−0.973*
	(0.128)	(0.182)	(0.300)
Year FE	Yes	Yes	Yes
N	2696	1590	1106
R^2	.60	.58	.62
F	106.37	74.80	50.60

Standard errors in parentheses.
* $p < 0.05$; + $p < 0.10$

and home ownership). Black teacher representation is the next most influential variable with a positive association with test scores; at the same time black administrator representation shows a negative relationship (significant at the 0.10 level) consistent with the findings in Chapter 5 and black school board representation shows a marginally significant and very small negative influence on the test scores. Additional analysis to determine if the forms of representation interacted as in Chapter 5 such that representation among teachers and administrators generated more positive results than either type of representation by itself showed that there was no such interaction in the case of test scores within the meaningful range of the data.[15]

---

[15] There was a significant interaction at the extremes of the data but, given the small number of cases involved, this finding was not considered robust.

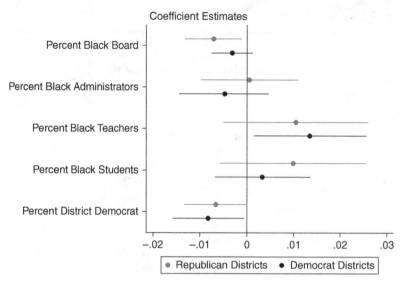

FIGURE 6.1. Black standardized test scores in ten states.

The teacher representation coefficient shows that a 1 percentage point increase in black teachers is associated with .016 standard deviation gain in black test scores relative to white test scores, all other things being equal. To provide a more substantive interpretation of that effect size, one needs to compare this to overall test score gap between blacks and whites that, in the current database, is 1.380. A 1 percentage point gain in black teachers is associated with a reduction of 1.2 percent in the black-white test score gap. Hypothetically, this could be a substantively large impact; a 10 percentage point increase in black teachers would be associated with a 12 percent reduction in the black-white test score gap. Because this is only the direct impact of black teachers and black teachers might have additional impact through their influence on grouping, tracking, and discipline (see following text), the overall impact could also be significantly greater. Practically, however, the number of black teachers available to be hired is a small and declining percentage of the overall labor pool. Further, the geographic concentration of these teachers also limits greater hiring in many states. A 10 percentage point increase in the number of black teachers, as a result, could be well beyond the capability of most of the school districts in the analysis.

Columns 2 and 3 of Table 6.7 split the districts into two groups based on partisanship; Figure 6.1 further displays whether Republican and Democrat districts are different from each other. Although partisanship has a very small negative relationship with overall test scores, similar to the other assessments of representation, partisanship's real influence is the impact that it has on the effectiveness of black representation. In Republican majority school districts, black teachers and black administrators have no association with black student test scores; in short, there is no bureaucratic representation, a finding consistent with Chapter 5. In Democratic majority school districts both teacher representation (positive) and administrative representation (negative) are significantly related to test scores with the larger influence from teacher representation, again a pattern very consistent with that found for grouping, tracking, and discipline. A 1 percentage point increase in black teachers in Democratic majority school districts is associated with a reduction in the black-white test score gap of 1.7 percent, all other things being equal.

The partisan results also show that black school board representation is negatively associated with black student performance in Republican school districts and unrelated in Democratic districts. Given the overwhelming Democratic Party affiliation of African Americans, black school board members in Republican districts are very likely to be in the minority and have difficulty in influencing school board actions.

If the patterns of grouping, tracking, and discipline examined in Chapter 5 create a systematic limitation on the access of African-American students to quality education, it is possible that they also will be reflected in test scores. Since the OCR survey has substantial missing data on some of the items, we will limit our analysis (Table 6.8) to three policy output measures – the percentage of gifted students who are black, the percentage of intellectually disabled students who are black, and the percentage of students receiving suspensions who are black.[16] If these measures reflect access to quality education as we have argued in the preceding text, we would expect that gifted class assignments would be positively associated with test scores and special education and suspensions to be negatively associated. The first column of Table 6.8 shows that all three of the second-generation measures are associated with test scores in the predicted direction.

The inclusion of the educational policy outputs reduces the impact of black teachers on test scores; a 1 percentage point increase in black teachers is now associated with only a 0.8 percent decline in the black-white racial gap in test scores. Fully half of the original teacher influence appears to operate through teachers' association with more equitable educational outputs rather than directly on test scores. The anomaly of black administrator representation is also explained by these results. Black administrators are no longer directly linked negatively to black test scores; the influence on black administrators on test scores is solely a function of their association with greater black suspension rates. This finding is consistent with the notion of role specialization in K–12 education and the responsibility of discipline being held by administration.

---

[16] The OCR data set does not include every district in each time period. If gifted, suspension, or special education information was not recorded for a district in 2004 but was recorded in the 2006 survey, these data were substituted.

TABLE 6.8. *Estimating Standardized Test Scores in Ten States, Policy Output Measures*

	Model 1	Model 2	Model 3
	All Cases	R Majority	D Majority
Percent Black Board	−0.005*	−0.007*	−0.003
	(0.002)	(0.003)	(0.002)
Percent Black Administrators	−0.001	0.001	−0.005
	(0.004)	(0.005)	(0.005)
Percent Black Teachers	0.011*	0.010	0.013*
	(0.005)	(0.008)	(0.006)
Percent Black Students	0.007	0.010	0.003
	(0.004)	(0.008)	(0.005)
Black Education (College Percent)	0.007*	0.007*	0.006
	(0.003)	(0.003)	(0.006)
Black Family Income (000s)	0.030*	0.039*	0.022*
	(0.007)	(0.010)	(0.011)
Black Home Ownership	0.001	0.000	0.003*
	(0.001)	(0.001)	(0.002)
White Percent Poverty	−0.002	0.010	−0.018
	(0.009)	(0.010)	(0.017)
District Democrat Percent	−0.004*	−0.006+	−0.008*
	(0.002)	(0.003)	(0.004)
Standardized White Scores	0.584*	0.621*	0.542*
	(0.025)	(0.031)	(0.043)
Percent Black Gifted	0.010*	0.022*	0.010*
	(0.004)	(0.007)	(0.005)
Percent Black Suspension	−0.007*	−0.008*	−0.008+
	(0.003)	(0.003)	(0.005)
Percent Black Special Education	−0.013*	−0.014*	−0.012*
	(0.003)	(0.003)	(0.005)
Constant	−1.213*	−1.299*	−0.768*
	(0.137)	(0.187)	(0.299)
Year FE	Yes	Yes	Yes
N	2181	1314	867
R²	.60	.61	.60
F	.57	.55	.59

Standard errors in parentheses.
* p < 0.05; + p < 0.10

The second two columns of Table 6.8 again divide the sample by partisan majority. The measures of representation for black students in gifted classes, in special education classes, and among suspensions show a consistent pattern of relationships with test scores whether in Democratic or Republican school districts. Again the key finding is that teacher representation is significantly related to test scores only in Democratic districts although the difference is more modest when the actual coefficients are compared. Similarly, school board representation is only negatively linked to test scores in Republican majority districts.

Graduation Rates

Combining the OCR data with our national surveys also permits a second look at high school graduation rates as a policy outcome. This allows us to use the full national data set, and this nationwide sample should provide a broader view than the earlier four-state case studies or even the ten-state analysis of case studies. The national data set also allows for the use of the more elaborate set of controls for socioeconomic status. Table 6.9 presents the baseline national findings in column 1. Black teacher representation shows a strong positive relationship with black graduation rates; all other things being equal, a 1 percentage point increase in black teachers is associated with a .22 percentage point increase in black graduation rates. Given that black students graduate at approximately 80 percent of the white student rate, this suggests a 10 percentage point increase in black teachers would be associated with a decrease of about 10 percent in the black-white racial gap in graduation rates. Similar to the very parallel findings in test scores, this statement should be qualified by the highly constrained supply of black teachers.

African-American school board representation also shows a direct positive influence on African-American graduation rates, although the substantive effect size is only about one-third that of black teachers. Black administrators are essentially uncorrelated with black student graduation rates. The direct impact of partisanship is positive although very small. Examining the interactive effect of partisanship and representation is needed given the strength of this finding in representation as well as the determination of other policy outputs and outcomes.

Columns 2 and 3 of Table 6.9 and Figure 6.2 show the familiar pattern of Democratic partisanship enhancing the influence of African-American representation. For both school boards and teachers, the influence of representation on high school graduation rates is approximately double in size in Democratic majority school districts than in Republican majority districts. Representation on the school board and among teachers remains statistically significant in Republican majority school districts unlike the previous findings for test scores and grouping, tracking, and discipline. These results suggest that board members and teachers are associated with some factor that influences black graduation rates and is separate from testing or grouping, tracking, and discipline. Whether this is the result of teachers acting as role models or some other type of symbolic representation cannot be determined with the current data set and should be the subject of future research.

Graduation rates should also be influenced by earlier decisions to group, track, and discipline students. Access to gifted classes, for example, might serve as a general indicator of African-American student access to quality education,

TABLE 6.9. *Estimating Black Graduation Rates, Baseline*

	Model 1	Model 2	Model 3
	All Cases	R Majority	D Majority
Percent Black Board	0.062*	0.041+	0.076*
	(0.018)	(0.021)	(0.028)
Percent Black Administrators	0.021	0.074	−0.027
	(0.032)	(0.044)	(0.041)
Percent Black Teachers	0.218*	0.149*	0.260*
	(0.046)	(0.063)	(0.059)
Percent Black Students	0.800*	0.770*	0.825*
	(0.024)	(0.032)	(0.033)
Black Education (College Percent)	−0.014+	−0.008	−0.019
	(0.008)	(0.010)	(0.013)
Black Family Income (000s)	0.089*	0.093*	0.096*
	(0.026)	(0.036)	(0.039)
Black Home Ownership	0.007	0.003	0.013
	(0.005)	(0.007)	(0.008)
White Percent Poverty	0.104*	0.038	0.241*
	(0.048)	(0.041)	(0.112)
District Democrat Percent	0.037*	0.009	0.021
	(0.016)	(0.017)	(0.044)
South	−0.885*	−0.317	−1.589
	(0.397)	(0.446)	(0.813)
Percent Unionization	−0.094*	−0.110*	−0.109*
	(0.033)	(0.043)	(0.054)
Constant	−1.381	0.876	−1.675
	(1.181)	(1.380)	(3.246)
Year FE	Yes	Yes	Yes
N	3244	1889	1355
R^2	0.89	0.87	0.91
F	851.58	531.82	524.40

Standard errors in parentheses.
* $p < 0.05$; + $p < 0.10$

which should in turn link to graduation rates. The relationship between disparities in discipline or special education assignments to graduation rates are more ambiguous. Greater discipline disparities have been associated with the concept of "push out" whereby minority students are encouraged to drop out of school (Marchbanks et al. 2014). Or, one might argue that a lack of discipline in schools will adversely affect learning environments. Similarly, special education assignments, particularly given the more recent requirements of specificity and limited removal from regular classes, could positively affect graduation rates. However, if implemented in a discriminatory way, special

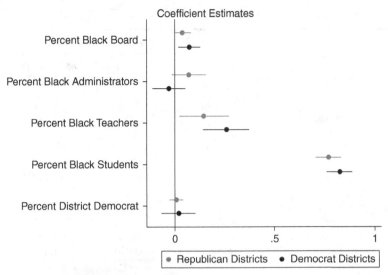

FIGURE 6.2. Black graduation rates.

education classification gaps could well have detrimental effects (Artiles and Trent 1994; Harry and Klingner 2014).

Table 6.10 adds measures of assignments to gifted classes, special education, and disciplinary actions to the high school graduation equation.[17] The addition of these policy outputs reduces the size of the representation coefficients, but both the school board and the teacher representation variables remain statistically significant (see column 1). Some of the influence of both the board and the teachers occur through the ability to influence tracking and discipline decisions. Gifted class assignments show a strong, positive influence on graduation rates as hypothesized. Other than black student enrollment, this factor is the strongest statistical influence on African-American graduation rates. The suspensions variable is also positively related to graduation rates consistent with the arguments that discipline will contribute to educational attainment. The much weaker substantive impact of the suspensions variable suggests that other factors (such as the type of discipline, see Roch and Pitts 2012) likely condition this relationship. The special education relationship is positive but does not attain statistical significance.

The final two columns in Table 6.10 present the results for partisanship and student assignments. The addition of measures of gifted classes, special

[17] The measures of assignments in this equation are highly collinear with each other and the percentage of black students. This primarily affects the black student coefficient because the coefficients only show the influence of the unique variation. We also residualized the gifted, special education, and suspension data and got results that matched those in Table 6.10 except for the black student coefficient and its standard error.

TABLE 6.10. *Estimating Black Graduation Rates, Policy Output Measures*

	Model 1	Model 2	Model 3
	All Cases	R Majority	D Majority
Percent Black Board	0.038*	0.026	0.050+
	(0.016)	(0.020)	(0.026)
Percent Black Administrators	0.003	0.061	−0.052
	(0.031)	(0.045)	(0.041)
Percent Black Teachers	0.165*	0.142*	0.196*
	(0.040)	(0.060)	(0.052)
Percent Black Students	0.460*	0.535*	0.415*
	(0.068)	(0.071)	(0.102)
Black Education (College Percent)	−0.018*	−0.010	−0.032*
	(0.009)	(0.010)	(0.016)
Black Family Income (000s)	0.110*	0.112*	0.125*
	(0.031)	(0.038)	(0.053)
Black Home Ownership	0.005	0.003	0.008
	(0.006)	(0.007)	(0.010)
White Percent Poverty	0.145*	0.081+	0.245+
	(0.055)	(0.047)	(0.139)
District Democrat Percent	0.023	−0.002	0.013
	(0.016)	(0.018)	(0.043)
South	−0.678	−0.775	−0.095
	(0.446)	(0.490)	(0.842)
Percent Unionization	−0.132*	−0.132*	−0.121*
	(0.037)	(0.047)	(0.061)
Percent Black Gifted	0.320*	0.250*	0.350*
	(0.041)	(0.064)	(0.058)
Percent Black Suspension	0.110*	0.057+	0.157*
	(0.039)	(0.032)	(0.062)
Percent Black Special Education	0.036+	0.046*	0.011
	(0.019)	(0.023)	(0.032)
Constant	−0.822	1.045	−1.348
	(1.236)	(1.499)	(3.206)
Year FE	Yes	Yes	Yes
N	2914	1771	1143
R^2	.90	.88	.92
F	881.94	435.40	593.55

Standard errors in parentheses.
* $p < 0.05$; + $p < 0.10$

education, and suspensions does not alter the basic findings on partisanship and representation. African-American representatives, be they on the school board or at the street level in bureaucracy, consistently get by better with help from their friends. Black representatives are always more effective in districts with a Democratic majority and less effective or even not effective at all in districts with a Republican majority. The influence of both gifted classes and suspensions also appears to be enhanced in Democratic majority jurisdictions although why that might be is not evident from the data at hand.

College Readiness: Advanced Placement Classes

The OCR began collecting data on AP classes in 2006. AP classes are designed to be the equivalent of college-level courses and many universities give college credit to students who take such classes and then pass the national exam. The ability to earn college credits while in high school should be *prima facie* evidence that a student is prepared for higher education. In our sample of school districts, the odds ratio of 0.76 show that black students are 24 percent underrepresented in taking one or more AP classes (non-Hispanic whites are 47 percent overrepresented). The odds ratio for passing at least one AP exam (0.54) indicates that black students are underrepresented by 46 percent in this category (the non-Hispanic white odds ratio is 1.64).

Students who take an AP class benefit from the experience whether or not they actually take and pass the exam. AP students are exposed to more challenging material and get acclimated to the pace of college classes; both are likely to translate into benefits in college. Table 6.11 presents our models for taking one or more AP classes. Although the size of the black student body and the relative socioeconomic status of the black community matter a great deal, black students are more likely to take AP classes in districts with more black teachers (column 1). A 1 percentage point increase in black teachers is associated with a .43 percentage point increase in black students enrolled in at least one AP class, all other things being equal. Neither school board representation nor administrative representation are associated with the percentage of black students taking AP courses.[18] As might be expected, the measures of black community socioeconomic status are all positively linked to greater participation by black students in AP classes.

Columns 2 and 3, accompanied by Figure 6.3, again divide the sample into Republican and Democratic majority districts and the pattern revealed is consistent with previous results for graduation rates and test scores and myriad other factors. The influence of black teachers on AP enrollments is twice as large in Democratic districts as it is in Republican districts (a statistically significant increase).[19] The coefficients for percent black students also indicates that with all the controls in the model, black students are more likely to take an AP class

---

[18] If the second-generation discrimination measures are entered into this equation, much of the influence of African-American teachers operates through their association with increases in gifted class enrollments although there remains a significant direct effect for teacher representation.

[19] The representation results are not a function of splitting the sample rather than simply interacting a Democratic majority with just the percentage of black teachers. In that case, the regressions show that the presence of black teachers is highly significant in Democratic districts (slope = 0.54, t = 7.61) and insignificant in Republican districts (slope = 0.001, t = 0.02).

TABLE 6.11. *Estimating Black AP Test-taking Rates*

	Model 1	Model 2	Model 3
	All Cases	R Majority	D Majority
Percent Black Board	0.019	−0.022	0.034
	(0.038)	(0.031)	(0.051)
Percent Black Administrators	−0.003	0.049	−0.044
	(0.065)	(0.062)	(0.079)
Percent Black Teachers	0.433*	0.195+	0.484*
	(0.097)	(0.102)	(0.115)
Percent Black Students	0.463*	0.351*	0.574*
	(0.047)	(0.054)	(0.054)
Black Education (College Percent)	0.037*	0.022+	0.064*
	(0.012)	(0.013)	(0.020)
Black Family Income (000s)	0.088*	0.168*	0.011
	(0.042)	(0.049)	(0.049)
Black Home Ownership	0.021*	−0.007	0.035*
	(0.008)	(0.008)	(0.013)
White Percent Poverty	0.151+	0.246*	0.013
	(0.083)	(0.118)	(0.133)
District Democrat Percent	0.006	−0.012	0.035
	(0.019)	(0.031)	(0.055)
South	−2.263*	0.272	−4.189*
	(0.660)	(0.585)	(1.431)
Percent Unionization	0.016	0.032	−0.037
	(0.054)	(0.052)	(0.092)
Constant	−4.905*	−2.857	−7.050
	(1.515)	(1.938)	(4.021)
Year FE	Yes	Yes	Yes
N	1440	826	614
R^2	0.78	0.63	0.85
F	70.79	40.57	73.86

Standard errors in parentheses.
* $p < 0.05$; + $p < 0.10$

in a Democratic district than in a Republican one ($\beta = .57$ vs. $\beta = .35$) all other things being equal.

The analysis of African-American students passing one or more AP exams (Table 6.12 and Figure 6.4) shows results very similar to those for taking AP classes (although the level of explained variation drops significantly as one might expect going from a measure of taking classes to passing exams). A 1 percentage point increase in African-American teachers is associated with a 0.25 percentage point increase in black students passing AP exams, all other things being equal. In Democratic majority school districts, this association increases to 0.36, and in Republican majority school districts, the association is essentially zero.

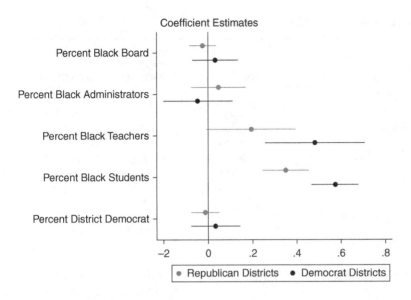

FIGURE 6.3. Black AP test taking.

Conclusion

The transition from policy outputs (assignments to classes and discipline) to policy outcomes (test scores, graduation rates, college preparedness) is often difficult in practice simply because policy outputs can be affected by a wide variety of factors outside the control of school boards, administrators, and teachers. The findings of this chapter, however, indicate that the politics of policy outcomes in race and education closely follow the pattern established in the analysis of policy outputs. Both are essentially the story of the interplay of representation and partisanship. African-American students do better in school districts that have more African-American teachers, and these direct teacher impacts are far stronger in school districts with a Democratic population majority.

This chapter examined student test scores, graduation rates, and preparation for higher education using four states as case studies and also using the national database. The analysis of test scores focused on the gap between black and white test scores. The national database, which included test scores from ten states, found a strong positive association between black teacher representation and a narrowing of the black-white test score gap (three of the four state case studies were also consistent with these findings). Similarly, the national analysis of graduation rates found its strong linkages between black teacher representation and black student graduation rates (the four case studies were generally consistent with these findings but show some variations across the states).

TABLE 6.12. *Estimating Black AP Test-passing Rates*

	Model 1	Model 2	Model 3
	All Cases	R Majority	D Majority
Percent Black Board	−0.010	−0.021	−0.010
	(0.053)	(0.036)	(0.081)
Percent Black Administrators	−0.071	−0.087	−0.078
	(0.085)	(0.078)	(0.127)
Percent Black Teachers	0.252*	−0.062	0.358*
	(0.098)	(0.118)	(0.122)
Percent Black Students	0.391*	0.391*	0.442*
	(0.066)	(0.059)	(0.088)
Black Education (College Percent)	0.024+	0.006	0.060*
	(0.015)	(0.015)	(0.024)
Black Family Income (000s)	0.072+	0.077	0.012
	(0.040)	(0.053)	(0.052)
Black Home Ownership	0.020*	0.025*	−0.000
	(0.010)	(0.009)	(0.019)
White Percent Poverty	−0.017	0.061	−0.234
	(0.090)	(0.101)	(0.178)
District Democrat Percent	0.030	0.089+	0.073
	(0.025)	(0.049)	(0.072)
South	−1.361	−0.559	−2.267
	(0.867)	(0.659)	(2.051)
Percent Unionization	−0.024	−0.124+	0.036
	(0.071)	(0.063)	(0.134)
Constant	−3.612+	−3.719+	−6.933
	(1.861)	(2.081)	(5.432)
Year FE	Yes	Yes	Yes
N	1195	674	521
R^2	0.5	0.34	0.59
F	20.47	12.45	17.13

Standard errors in parentheses.
* $p < 0.05$; + $p < 0.10$
Note: Dependent variable (DV) is percent of AP test takers who passed at least one test who are black.

Contemporary public education is frequently criticized for its focus on standardized testing and at times is charged with an excessive focus on average and below-average students to the detriment of better students. This study incorporated three different measures of preparation for college in an effort to determine if the politics of race and education are similar for high achieving students – College Board scores in Texas, class completions required for admission to a university in California, and AP classes in our national data set. All three analyses showed highly consistent results. African-American students in

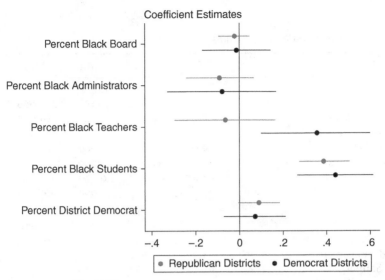

FIGURE 6.4. Black AP test passing.

school districts with more African-American teachers performed better on each of these indicators of college-ready performance.

The strong consistent influence of African-American teachers stands in contrast to the lack of direct relationships for African-American school board members and school administrators. School board members and school administrators are not without influence on the outcomes of African-American students, but their influence is indirect. They play a major role in the recruitment and retention of African-American teachers and through that process indirectly influence the education of African-American students.

All of the representational influence of teachers is dramatically influenced by the partisanship of the school district. Consistent with the notion of allies who can provide both direct support and a favorable organizational environment, the association between black teacher representation and black student performance was always stronger, sometimes dramatically so, in school districts with Democratic majorities than in districts with Republican majorities. In many cases in Republican districts, black teachers were not associated with positive performance by black students.

Partisanship also appeared to influence the relationships between black student enrollment and various outcomes. Black students generally had higher test scores (relative to whites), higher graduation rates, and better college-ready indicators in districts with Democratic majorities, all other things being equal. The full meaning of these partisanship relationships remain to be explored, but the idea that partisanship plays no role in the education of African-American students is simply a myth, an enduring myth, but a myth nonetheless.

Appendix

TABLE A6.1. *Descriptive Statistics by State*

Variable	Mean	SD	Min	Max
California				
Percent Black Teachers	9.869	11.930	0.362	100.000
Percent Black Students	8.430	8.875	1.000	49.908
Percent English Learners	23.255	18.639	0.000	100.000
Charter School (0,1)	0.067	0.239	0.000	1.000
Percent Free and Reduced Lunch	43.858	32.693	0.000	100.000
Percent Teachers with Full Credentials	94.271	8.878	0.000	100.000
Percent Parents with College Education	29.917	22.335	0.000	100.000
Florida				
Percent Black Teachers	7.974	5.996	0.000	26.874
Percent Black Students	16.970	9.751	2.500	46.960
Percent English Learners	4.790	4.638	0.000	20.100
Attendance Stability Rate	96.160	2.433	87.300	99.900
Percent Free and Reduced Lunch	53.920	12.286	18.920	100.000
Percent Highly Qualified Teachers	94.520	4.750	62.200	100.000
Teacher Medial Salary (1,000s)	40.959	3.908	30.251	55.396
Instruction/Student (log)	8.890	0.100	8.689	9.309
Ohio				
Percent Black Teachers	2.276	2.748	0.000	17.400
Percent Black Students	7.683	9.509	1.000	49.657
Percent English Learners	2.379	3.108	0.219	27.548
All Disciplinary Actions per 100 Students	22.604	23.981	0.000	163.400
Average Years of Teacher Experience	14.395	2.895	6.000	22.000
Percent Core Courses Taught by Certified Teacher	99.121	1.385	88.000	100.000
Average Teacher Salary (1,000s)	51.454	6.139	33.681	72.266
Expenditures/Student (logged)	8.932	0.170	8.564	9.623
Texas				
Percent Black Teachers	5.728	11.007	0.000	100.000
Percent Black Students	12.023	10.669	2.000	49.000
Percent Low–Income Students	50.741	19.518	0.000	100.000
Percent Bilingual Students	5.991	7.822	0.000	94.000
Student-Teacher Ratio	13.214	3.135	2.1	50.1
Charter School (0,1)	0.134	0.34	0	1
Average Teacher Salary (1,000s)	37.6	5.402	0	91.795
Operating Expenditures/Student (log)	8.888	0.295	5.547	11.267

Note: California data is reported by school; other states reported by district. Only schools (CA) and districts (FL, OH, TX) included that have >1 and <50 percent black students.

TABLE A6.2. *California API Test Scores*

	Model 1	Model 2	Model 3
Percent Black Teachers	0.588	0.611	0.793*
	(0.320)	(0.328)	(0.350)
Percent Black Students	−2.237*	−2.319*	−2.123*
	(0.511)	(0.521)	(0.446)
Percent English Learners	−1.204*	−1.159*	−0.903*
	(0.338)	(0.352)	(0.319)
Charter School	−7.985	−2.831	0.218
	(7.583)	(7.410)	(6.804)
Percent Free and Reduced Lunch	−0.234	−0.252*	−0.370*
	(0.119)	(0.124)	(0.130)
Percent Teachers with Full Credentials	1.326*	1.150*	0.895*
	(0.342)	(0.341)	(0.375)
Percent Parents with College Education	0.120	0.133	0.261
	(0.212)	(0.216)	(0.221)
White API Scores	0.490*	0.482*	0.499*
	(0.070)	(0.070)	(0.062)
Elementary School	52.494*	51.938*	49.626*
	(8.025)	(7.937)	(7.349)
Middle School	19.141*	16.893*	15.104*
	(4.812)	(5.002)	(5.369)
High School	−4.181	−6.340	−9.082
	(5.311)	(5.575)	(5.935)
Percent District Democrat			−0.721*
			(0.320)
Constant	197.460*	222.132*	268.061*
	(80.416)	(82.043)	(86.793)
Year FE	Yes	Yes	Yes
N	2143	2048	2001
F	100.35	107.77	110.91
R^2	.69	.69	.70

Standard errors in parentheses.

* $p < 0.05$

TABLE A6.3. *Ohio Proficiency Test Scores*

	Model 1	Model 2	Model 3
Percent Black Teachers	0.727*	2.092*	2.023*
	(0.334)	(0.639)	(0.629)
Percent Black Students	−0.199*	−0.289*	−0.213
	(0.082)	(0.138)	(0.146)
Percent English Learners	−0.264	−0.512	−0.513
	(0.170)	(0.312)	(0.326)
Disciplinary Actions/100 students	−0.078*	−0.060*	−0.072*
	(0.024)	(0.020)	(0.022)
Average Teacher Experience (years)	−0.415	−0.304	−0.230
	(0.291)	(0.245)	(0.252)
Percent Courses Taught by Certified Teacher	−0.145	0.165	0.080
	(0.389)	(0.471)	(0.449)
Average Teacher Salary (1,000s)	0.052	0.217	0.273
	(0.145)	(0.136)	(0.142)
Expenditures/Student (logged)	−1.514	−13.070*	−11.588*
	(4.348)	(4.934)	(5.273)
White Proficiency	0.724*	1.145*	1.169*
	(0.117)	(0.115)	(0.123)
Percent Democrat			−0.087
			(0.084)
Constant	38.168	61.112	53.906
	(59.656)	(68.373)	(67.614)
Year FE	Yes	Yes	Yes
N	207	47	47
F	28.97	58.5	53.65
R^2	.54	.94	.94

Standard errors in parentheses.

* $p < 0.05$

TABLE A6.4. *Florida FCAT Test Scores*

	Model 1	Model 2	Model 3
Percent Black Teachers	0.388	0.459	0.443
	(0.209)	(0.233)	(0.250)
Percent Black Students	−0.426*	−0.473*	−0.427*
	(0.139)	(0.144)	(0.142)
Percent English Learners	−0.344*	−0.403*	−0.325*
	(0.148)	(0.156)	(0.162)
Attendance Stability Rate	−0.158	−0.244	−0.295
	(0.233)	(0.262)	(0.268)
Percent Free and Reduced Lunch	0.056	0.064	0.063
	(0.089)	(0.101)	(0.099)
Percent Highly Qualified Teachers	−0.134	−0.196	−0.249
	(0.139)	(0.173)	(0.189)
Teacher Medial Salary (1,000)	−0.039	−0.052	−0.001
	(0.187)	(0.209)	(0.211)
Instruction/Student (log)	−10.866	−9.305	−9.577
	(6.469)	(7.123)	(7.567)
White FCAT	0.706*	0.713*	0.726*
	(0.141)	(0.171)	(0.173)
Percent Democrat			−0.077
			(0.074)
Constant	122.457*	123.230	134.611
	(55.724)	(61.733)	(67.508)
Year FE	Yes	Yes	Yes
N	169	155	150
F	120.9	100.64	79.7
R^2	.73	.70	.70

Standard errors in parentheses.

* $p < 0.05$

TABLE A6.5. *Texas TAKS/TAAS Test Scores*

	Model 1	Model 2	Model 3
Percent Black Teachers	0.090*	0.077	0.092
	(0.023)	(0.064)	(0.062)
Percent Black Students	−0.088*	−0.081	−0.106*
	(0.024)	(0.050)	(0.051)
Percent Low-Income Students	0.099*	0.128*	0.145*
	(0.017)	(0.031)	(0.030)
Percent Bilingual Students	0.099*	0.058	−0.007
	(0.037)	(0.066)	(0.065)
Student-Teacher Ratio	0.438*	0.765*	0.698*
	(0.111)	(0.325)	(0.326)
Charter School	4.877*		
	(1.024)		
Average Teacher Salary (1,000s)	0.133*	0.162	0.052
	(0.067)	(0.152)	(0.154)
Operating Expenditures/Student (log)	2.546	0.012	−2.651
	(1.367)	(4.594)	(4.419)
All Pass Rate	1.046*	1.106*	1.129*
	(0.022)	(0.069)	(0.067)
TAAS Test	0.715	−0.648	−3.907
	(1.144)	(2.473)	(2.473)
Percent Democrat			0.121*
			(0.042)
Constant	−56.706*	−43.874	−19.766
	(12.889)	(42.506)	(40.733)
Year FE	Yes	Yes	Yes
N	7945	1544	1520
F	465.62	332.35	307.21
R^2	.66	.82	.83

Standard errors in parentheses.

* $p < 0.05$

TABLE A6.6. *California Graduation*

	Model 1	Model 2	Model 3
Percent Black Teachers	0.042	0.055*	0.053
	(0.025)	(0.026)	(0.028)
Percent Black Students	0.881*	0.877*	0.879*
	(0.023)	(0.024)	(0.024)
Percent English Learners	−0.042*	−0.041*	−0.038
	(0.018)	(0.019)	(0.020)
Charter School	−0.148	−0.309	−0.277
	(0.613)	(0.673)	(0.685)
Percent Free and Reduced Lunch	0.019*	0.017*	0.015
	(0.008)	(0.008)	(0.008)
Percent Teachers with Full Credentials	−0.022	−0.029	−0.033
	(0.027)	(0.028)	(0.028)
Percent Parents with College Education	0.018*	0.019*	0.025*
	(0.007)	(0.007)	(0.008)
White Graduation Rate	−0.032*	−0.030*	−0.036*
	(0.007)	(0.008)	(0.008)
High School	−0.153	−0.229	−0.294
	(0.600)	(0.669)	(0.671)
Percent Democrat			−0.027*
			(0.013)
Constant	2.881	3.288	5.245
	(2.481)	(2.539)	(2.843)
Year FE	Yes	Yes	Yes
N	3233	3004	2951
F	247.24	263.85	244.55
R^2	0.76	0.76	0.76

Standard errors in parentheses.
* $p < 0.05$

TABLE A6.7. *Ohio Graduation*

	Model 1	Model 2	Model 3
Percent Black Teachers	0.451*	1.266*	1.437*
	(0.194)	(0.228)	(0.185)
Percent Black Students	0.435*	0.617*	0.532*
	(0.105)	(0.094)	(0.102)
Percent English Learners	−0.136	0.354*	0.332*
	(0.110)	(0.152)	(0.123)
Disciplinary Actions/100 Students	0.029*	0.028	0.046
	(0.011)	(0.030)	(0.031)
Average Teacher Experience (years)	−0.084	−0.103	−0.171
	(0.091)	(0.145)	(0.104)
Percent Courses Taught by Certified Teacher	−0.272	−0.570*	−0.557
	(0.170)	(0.256)	(0.272)
Average Teacher Salary (1,000s)	−0.196*	−0.251	−0.248
	(0.084)	(0.139)	(0.155)
Expenditures/Student (logged)	2.839	3.223	−0.236
	(2.771)	(3.360)	(3.538)
White Graduation Rate	−0.329*	0.038	0.052
	(0.137)	(0.090)	(0.075)
Percent Democrat			0.094
			(0.050)
Constant	44.297	37.008	61.899
	(37.492)	(41.439)	(44.239)
Year FE	Yes	Yes	Yes
N	150	43	43
F	146.63	347.08	658.98
R^2	.95	.99	.99

Standard errors in parentheses.

* $p < 0.05$

TABLE A6.8. *Florida Graduation*

	Model 1	Model 2	Model 3
Percent Black Teachers	-0.010	-0.087	-0.121
	(0.113)	(0.073)	(0.063)
Percent Black Students	0.793*	0.879*	0.912*
	(0.077)	(0.051)	(0.045)
Percent English Learners	-0.346*	-0.148	-0.096
	(0.164)	(0.086)	(0.080)
Attendance Stability Rate	0.170	0.226*	0.184*
	(0.171)	(0.085)	(0.081)
Percent Free and Reduced Lunch	0.045	0.037	0.021
	(0.036)	(0.022)	(0.020)
Percent Highly Qualified Teachers	-0.125*	-0.106	-0.182*
	(0.059)	(0.064)	(0.068)
Teacher Medial Salary (1,000)	-0.104	0.004	0.048
	(0.082)	(0.069)	(0.062)
Instruction/Student (log)	9.249	0.729	-0.816
	(5.257)	(3.657)	(2.690)
White Graduation Rate	-0.148	-0.083*	-0.090*
	(0.076)	(0.036)	(0.036)
Percent Democrat			-0.047
			(0.024)
Constant	-69.545	-11.832	13.777
	(46.629)	(33.351)	(22.517)
Year FE	Yes	Yes	Yes
N	178	159	153
F	144.82	209.96	281.97
R^2	0.93	0.96	0.97

Standard errors in parentheses.

* $p < 0.05$

TABLE A6.9. *Texas Graduation*

	Model 1	Model 2	Model 3
Percent Black Teachers	0.077	−0.010	−0.011
	(0.046)	(0.101)	(0.100)
Percent Black Students	0.064	0.037	0.031
	(0.042)	(0.065)	(0.065)
Percent Low-Income Students	−0.014	−0.038	−0.032
	(0.027)	(0.031)	(0.031)
Percent Bilingual Students	−0.144*	−0.012	−0.036
	(0.061)	(0.076)	(0.080)
Student-Teacher Ratio	−0.232	0.458	0.357
	(0.192)	(0.537)	(0.549)
Charter School	−17.535*		
	(3.927)		
Average Teacher Salary (1,000s)	−0.136	0.327	0.287
	(0.111)	(0.200)	(0.199)
Operating Expenditures/Student (log)	−2.049	−6.998	−8.231
	(4.265)	(5.480)	(5.299)
White Graduation Rate	0.768*	0.669*	0.663*
	(0.066)	(0.075)	(0.076)
Percent Democrat			0.051
			(0.051)
Constant	41.683	64.312	76.480
	(33.280)	(50.262)	(48.854)
Year FE	Yes	Yes	Yes
N	4129	1303	1284
F	157.82	27.39	26.27
R^2	0.59	0.36	0.36

Standard errors in parentheses.

* $p < 0.05$

TABLE A6.10. *California College Readiness*

	Model 1	Model 2	Model 3
Percent Black Teachers	0.720*	0.745*	0.771*
	(0.081)	(0.079)	(0.077)
Percent Black Students	−0.994*	−1.002*	−0.935*
	(0.131)	(0.133)	(0.154)
Percent English Learners	0.144	0.086	0.146
	(0.097)	(0.102)	(0.112)
Charter School	0.768	1.239	1.812
	(1.875)	(1.944)	(1.638)
Percent Free and Reduced Lunch	0.133*	0.147*	0.135
	(0.065)	(0.068)	(0.076)
Percent Teachers with Full Credentials	−0.257	−0.297	−0.350*
	(0.162)	(0.175)	(0.162)
Percent Parents with College Education	−0.384*	−0.395*	−0.328*
	(0.058)	(0.064)	(0.071)
White College Readiness Rate	−0.325*	−0.319*	−0.357*
	(0.066)	(0.069)	(0.056)
High School	−4.020*	−4.488*	−4.560*
	(1.674)	(1.771)	(1.877)
Percent Democrat			−0.291*
			(0.122)
Constant	78.495*	83.066*	102.482*
	(16.843)	(18.322)	(18.335)
Year FE	Yes	Yes	Yes
N	2631	2443	2406
F	54.94	60.17	56.89
R^2	0.60	0.60	0.62

* $p < 0.05$

TABLE A6.11. *Texas College Readiness*

	Model 1	Model 2	Model 3
Percent Black Teachers	−0.013	0.078	0.094
	(0.031)	(0.057)	(0.061)
Percent Black Students	−0.043	−0.126*	−0.146*
	(0.023)	(0.040)	(0.044)
Percent Low–Income Students	−0.119*	−0.144*	−0.138*
	(0.019)	(0.026)	(0.024)
Percent Bilingual Students	0.040	−0.015	−0.079
	(0.032)	(0.051)	(0.058)
Student-Teacher Ratio	−0.171	−0.685*	−0.870*
	(0.160)	(0.328)	(0.331)
Charter School	6.071		
	(3.717)		
Average Teacher Salary (1,000s)	0.429*	0.279*	0.180
	(0.064)	(0.106)	(0.113)
Operating Expenditures/Student (log)	−2.066	1.290	−1.789
	(1.645)	(5.404)	(5.107)
White College Readiness	0.161*	0.163*	0.152*
	(0.018)	(0.032)	(0.031)
Percent Democrat			0.131*
			(0.043)
Constant	13.291	1.139	29.182
	(14.797)	(46.557)	(44.330)
Year FE	Yes	Yes	Yes
N	3087	1417	1398
F	16.68	8.16	7.37
R^2	0.27	0.30	0.31

* $p < 0.05$

7

Can You Beat the Ovarian Lottery?

Although it has ebbed and flowed in salience, the issue of equal access to educational opportunities for African Americans has been on the national agenda for more than a century and a half. This study examined the current status of African-American education and the politics that influences it by analyzing the 1,800 largest school districts in the United States. The portrait painted by the empirical results shows that, in terms of student outcomes, the gap between the quality of education afforded to black students versus white students remains troublesome. Whether examining test scores from the National Assessment of Educational Progress (NAEP) or the various indicators used in this book's analysis, there remain large and persistent gaps in educational access and attainment for black and white Americans. Both the NAEP scores and the historical comparisons provided in this text show that the reduction in these gaps has stagnated.

The basic theme of this study is that racial inequities in education reflect, in part, racial inequities in political power. This contention does not mean that politics is the sole determinant of racial differences in education; a wide variety of other factors such as income, housing, health, and past historical levels of education also play a role.[1] If political disparities affect educational disparities, then changes in the politics of education hold some promise for reducing the level of educational disparities. Complicating the linkage between politics and education are the historical changes in the politics of race and education. The initial attempt to gain access to education evolved into efforts to eliminate, first, segregation and, later, second-generation educational discrimination. Now, the accountability era is focused on racial gaps in test scores and other educational outcomes. We have learned that formal desegregation is only the first in a series

---

[1] Inequities in political power, of course, also play a role in racial inequities in income, housing, health, and past levels of education.

of steps to equal access to quality education. In all cases of policy change in this area, the limits of effective implementation of policy become a key policy problem.

Politics is about advocacy that, in turn, requires representation. Using the concept of African-American representation, this study examined different forms of representation (legislative, bureaucratic) at different stages of the policy process (getting elected; recruiting administrators and teachers; making decisions about class assignments and discipline; and producing educational outcomes such as test scores, graduation rates, and college preparation). Before addressing the policy implications of this study, reviewing the major scholarly themes that have emerged is merited. The primary finding of this study is that political representation reduces the racial disparities in education. The effectiveness of African-American representatives, however, is affected by both political structures (type of election, the independent school district) and partisanship. The locus of the representational role shifts depending on the types of outputs and outcomes examined, but in every case representation is enhanced or limited by differences in political structures and even more so by political partisanship.

Partisanship Fundamentally Shapes African-American Education Policy

Few myths in American politics are as deep-seated as the notion that education policy is nonpartisan. Structurally, this myth is bolstered by the fact that the vast majority of school board elections are contested on nonpartisan ballots. Yet in contemporary education politics, several issues have distinct partisan dimensions. US political parties have long been divided on fundamental questions such as the size of government; these disputes further solidified after the tax revolts of the 1980s and the rise of tea party activists in the Republican Party. This partisan divide affects education in three ways. First, it generates Republican support for local control of education and Republican opposition to federal influence (such as national standardized tests) and, at times, opposition to federal incentives such as the Obama administration's Race to the Top. Second, arguments for lower taxes do not exempt local governments, and public schools absorb a large portion of state and local revenues. Third, the rise of more polarized groups in the Republican Party has placed divisive issues such as creation science, abstinence only, and the content of textbooks on the education agenda, which can overshadow other concerns.

The analysis in this book has shown that partisanship permeates the entire process of local education policy so much so that, at times, it overwhelms factors such as structure or representation. Partisanship has transformed an electoral structure that is designed to underrepresent minorities, into one that actually overrepresents African Americans. In at-large elections where African Americans are a minority of the population, they are overrepresented compared to their population numbers if the school district has a Democratic voting majority; representation levels in Democratic jurisdictions are 28 percentage points higher than representation in Republican majority districts. Even in single member district (SMD) elections, partisanship matters with African Americans gaining an additional 17 percentiles in representation in Democratic districts (106 percent vs. 89 percent relative to population).

That Democratic partisanship enhances the ability of African Americans to get elected to school boards or any other office is not surprising. African Americans are the most monolithic voting group in the United States, often casting more than nine out of ten votes for Democratic candidates; the overwhelming majority of African-American elected officials are also Democrats. White Democrats are an obvious coalition partner for African Americans in terms of contesting elections and pursuing policy goals. In combination these factors provide a strong base for linking African-American school board elections to Democratic partisanship.

Partisanship also plays a role in how effective school board members are in being allocative representatives, specifically in hiring African-American school administrators and teachers. Although African-American school board members have only a modest direct effect in hiring black administrators in Democratic districts regardless of structure for all districts, this changes in districts with populations that are less than 50 percent African American. In these black minority districts, a black school board member in a Democratic jurisdiction is twice as effective as one in a Republican jurisdiction in increasing the number of African-American administrators.

African-American school board members find it easier to influence the composition of school administrators than to influence the racial distribution of the teachers. There are fewer administrators such that a few targeted hires can have a meaningful impact. In addition, teachers are subject to extensive licensing requirements and are generally hired by a separate personnel department using merit procedures. As a result, having a representational impact on school administrators is easier than influencing the racial composition of the teaching faculty. Although the predominant predictor of black teachers is the percentage of black administrators, black school board members elected from SMDs (who are more likely to share values with black constituents) are associated with larger percentages of black teachers. Partisanship again conditions this influence; if African Americans are a minority of the population, the impact of African-American school board members on the hiring of African-American teachers is three times larger in Democratic jurisdictions than in Republican ones.

More surprising than partisanship's influence on electoral results and allocative representation is how deeply it permeates into the school system. An African-American student in a Democratic majority school district is 73 percent more likely to be in a gifted class, 23 percent less likely to be suspended, 30 percent less likely to be expelled, 24 percent less likely to be classified as intellectually disabled, 10 percent less likely to be classified as emotionally disturbed, and 17 percent less likely to be designated as having a specific learning disability. A portion of these differences remain for gifted classes and the discipline measures even after controlling for socioeconomic factors and the representation process. Similar partisan gaps remain for educational outcomes. All other things being equal, African-American students in a Democratic majority school district are about 7 percent more likely to graduate from high school, 64 percent more likely to take an advanced placement class, and 13 percent more likely to pass an advanced placement exam.

These partisan differences in educational outputs and outcomes would be even more dramatic if partisanship did not also greatly influence the representation process. African-American teachers were consistently more effective in generating positive outcome for African-American students in Democratic majority school districts than in Republican ones. In many cases, African-American teachers had no impact at all on African-American students in Republican districts, but were only able to act as representatives in Democratic ones.

These stunning racial differences in effect show the partisan version of a dual school system. That where an African-American child is born and goes to school greatly affects the child's life chances has been well documented in the literature given the income and other correlates to quality schooling. That partisanship also plays a role in racial disparities in education is less commonly recognized and is often entirely ignored. The fundamental unfairness of a process that disadvantages an African-American child just because of the school district he or she lives in is self-evident. The partisan dimension of this ovarian lottery contributes a great deal to limiting the future life's chances of African-American children.

Why Democratic school districts appear more beneficial for African-American students has not been the focus of this study, but several possibilities exist. In the current polarized partisan environment, educational issues such as creation science, decentralization, and opposition to the Common Core standards are supported by Republicans on the far right. The traditional partisan disputes on size of government can also be overlaid on educational issues simply because the largest share of state and local government expenditures are devoted to education. Any serious attempts to reduce tax levels at the state or local level has to consider expenditures on public education. These more recent educational issues are reinforced by the current civil rights movement and its association with the far left portion of the Democratic Party.

The most obvious way that partisanship translates into issues of educational equity is by providing a positive environment for public education and equal access to quality education. Bureaucrats take advantage of diffuse public support to gain both resources and autonomy in the use of those resources (Rourke 1976). A rational teacher committed to creating a more racially equitable process is likely to be willing to take more chances if she or he perceives a supportive political environment. Because we expect teachers and administrators to be active participants in local school politics, we would expect them to be well aware of the political opportunities and constraints in the local environment.[2]

A more direct reason for the partisan differences could well be funding. Comparing the districts in our study for the years 2004, 2006, and 2008, we found that Democratic majority school districts spent approximately 23 percent more per student than Republican school districts (about $2,700). With fixed effects for states to control for the dramatically different levels of education funding across the states, Democratic school districts still spent 11 percent more per student than did Republican districts. Although these spending differences likely reflect factors such as income levels; state and federal programs targeted at disadvantaged students; and a wide variety of other factors, they translate into a large difference in resources. The existing educational literature is consistent in its findings that additional resources in education matter more for disadvantaged students (Boreman and Rachuna 2001; Hedges, Laine, and Greenwald 1994; Wenglinsky 1997). Because African-American students are more likely to be disadvantaged, these spending differences could play a major role in reducing educational disparities.

Structure: Election Rules Matter

All politics takes place within the rules of the game that essentially create a playing field that is unlikely to be equitable. Any set of actors designing a governance structure for an electoral system or for a school district is likely to consider how the structural rules might produce results that they favor. Contemporary education politics takes place in a set of nested structures that greatly influence both the type of politics and what groups are advantaged in the process. The creation of the independent school district as a form of governance sought to isolate school politics from the urban politics and political machines of the time. This isolation took two forms – a separate governing structure and the elimination of the currency of patronage (jobs) through the creation of a merit system for hiring and retention of employees.

The independent school district was further isolated from the partisan and machine politics of the day by a system of at-large elections held at times that did not coincide with the regular partisan election cycle and with party labels banned from the ballot. These structures sought to enshrine a form of gentile politics that advantaged business and professional elites by increasing the costs to partisan machines (nonpartisan elections in the spring) and to ethnic and political minorities (at-large elections). Although a modest number of large city school districts avoided these reforms in whole or in part, the overwhelming majority of school systems adopted this governance structure.

---

[2] Qualitative studies of black teachers in different party majority school districts are needed to determine the exact way that party majorities influence teacher decisions.

What the reformers overlooked was that rules create incentives but do not necessarily lock in a permanent set of winners and losers. This study clearly demonstrated that the majoritarian bias in school board elections has shifted from one of race to one of partisanship. African Americans now do better in at-large elections than their numbers would imply when a school district has a Democratic voting majority. Partisanship now matters more than structure. This finding means that much of the previous work on race and electoral structure and on the structural influences on school board elections are probably underspecified (see Anzia 2011; Leal, Martinez-Ebers, and Meier 2004; Meier, Stewart, and England 1989). As noted in the preceding text, African Americans gain an additional 28 percentage points in representation in Democratic compared to Republican districts with at-large elections. For SMDs, the corresponding partisanship gain drops to 17 percentage points. These differences occur in an electoral system where African Americans have, on average, reached representational parity.

The change in the influence of electoral structure does not mean that structure is no longer important or that at-large elections cannot be used to limit the representation of racial minorities. There are numerous districts in our study where African Americans are significantly underrepresented on school boards. Many of these districts meet the requirements of underrepresentation accompanied by racial polarization in the electorate. Given the degree of racial polarization between the two political parties, an area with a Republican majority is quite likely to have greater racial polarization in voting. The findings of this research also only apply to African Americans. Latinos are clearly disadvantaged by at-large elections (Leal et al. 2004), and partisan biases are not sufficient to overcome this disadvantage (Meier and Molina 2015). The logic of at-large elections as majoritarian biases could also apply to Asian Americans, Native Americans, or other minorities. Further, nothing in this study undercuts the need for enforcement of the Voting Rights Act (VRA).

Electoral structure also has some influence on the ability of school board members to be effective representatives in allocative terms. Election from a SMD versus at-large implies a tradeoff between sharing the values of the minority African-American constituency and being able to form coalitions with others who share constituents. Although partisanship has a much larger impact on allocative representation, Chapter 4 demonstrates that SMDs enhance representation effectiveness, all else equal. The impact of SMDs is strongest when the jurisdiction has a Democratic voting majority and when African Americans constitute a majority of the school board.

Structure: The Independent School District

The independent school district is an attempt to create the intellectual politics–administration dichotomy in the real world of governance. Part-time school boards that represent the entire community are to set policies; these policies are to be implemented by professionally trained administrators with elaborate merit system protections. This governing structure influences representation as much as or more than electoral structure by defining specific roles for school board members and school system employees.

School board members collectively can set general policy, hire the superintendent, and express district goals linked to questions of equity. Board members do not teach any students and thus are limited to general actions that must, by definition, rely on administrators and teachers to implement. The primary method of influence documented in this study was the relationship between school board representation and administrative representation. Beyond that allocative action, there were few direct relationships between representation on the school board and actions that affected African-American students. When such relationships existed, they were subject to specific conditions. As an example, African-American school board members were associated with more African-American teachers if they were elected from SMDs and the overall school district had a Democratic voting majority. In short, the representation occurred when the match between board members and constituent's values were strongest (SMDs) and when the board members had political allies to support them (a Democratic majority). In other cases, the structural rules governing the hiring and retention of teachers limited the translation of school board representation into teacher representation.

Within the structure of the independent school district, African-American school administrators serve as a link between the political function of the school board and the street-level bureaucrats (teachers) who actually implement policy. This linkage process includes two distinct roles. First, administrators are in charge of running the school system and meeting the demands of the various education stakeholders. These stakeholders include not just African-American school board members but also other school board members, students, parents, the business community, local residents, state and federal officials, and additional stakeholder groups. Within the current accountability system, school administrators are held responsible for the performance of all students not just African-American students. In this role, administrators frequently perform a buffering role whereby they absorb the environmental demands and screen the teachers from them so that they can focus on instruction (Meier and O'Toole 2006). Second, within the primary role of running the school system, administrators have some opportunities to act as representatives in hiring teachers, making decisions on discipline and tracking, adjusting curriculum, and countless other activities.

In considering the representational role of administrators, these roles and the context in which administrators operate need to be considered. Administrators often know their teachers, and when teachers are acting as representatives, administrators may not need to represent and can perform their other roles. African-American administrators also have an advantage in dealing with issues such as discipline; they generally will not be accused of racial discrimination if they enforce discipline in a manner that rests more heavily on African-American students (for similar results in terms of police and racial profiling see Wilkins and Williams 2008). This means that African-American administrators can play the bad cop in terms of discipline and perhaps even tracking knowing that teachers will deal with the majority of the cases in a positive manner.

The mix of roles is consistent with the empirical findings in this book. African-American administrators are the major determinant in the hiring of African-American teachers. They are equally effective in the process regardless of the partisan makeup of the school district. In this sphere administrators clearly act as bureaucratic representatives. In the areas of discipline and special education assignments, African-American administrators play a counterbalancing role that moderates the impact of teachers at lower levels of representation. When school districts have a large percentage of both African-American administrators and African-American teachers, the administrators again take on the representation role.

The independent school district structures the representative role of the teachers. For bureaucrats to represent, they must have discretion and the ability to match their demographic identity with a corresponding policy outcome. Teachers have vast discretion even in this era where state accountability standards seek to create more uniform curricula and external standards for performance. That a large percentage of the documented cases of representative bureaucracy involves teachers is not surprising. Teachers interact on a daily basis with students in the classroom. They are likely to make initial recommendations in terms of academic grouping and discipline. They can encourage students to take more demanding classes such as advanced placement classes or to take the college boards and think about higher education, or they might simply serve as positive role models.

In all the indicators of African-American student assignments and performance, African-American teachers were far more influential than either school board members or school administrators. In some cases, they were the only point of representation that mattered. African-American teachers were associated with fewer African-American students disciplined or assigned to special education classes. African-American teachers were also associated with more African-American students in gifted classes and advanced placement classes, more African Americans graduating from high school, and more African-American students being prepared for higher education.

Partisanship conditioned the role of African-American teacher representation in ways that were not expected in an independent school district. African-American teachers were more effective in Democratic majority districts than in Republican majority districts in reducing racial disparities in almost every indicator linked to African-American students. At times, the representation process in Republican districts was so small that it was not statistically significant in our models.

Overall, representation can take many forms and occur in a wide range of institutional settings. This study took a broad view of representation and examined it in the bureaucracy as well in the more traditional legislative setting (i.e., local school boards). A reasonable metaphor for race and representation in school politics is that of a cascade effect whereby changes in representation on the school board cascade downward through changes in administration to changes at the classroom level. School boards can make broad policy changes and hire a superintendent who supports such changes, but the actual implementation of policy is done in the classroom.

The Study of Representation

These findings have implications for the general study of representation. Representation is a function of the identities an individual actor (legislator, bureaucrat, teacher) holds and the discretion that they have to act. All the actors in this study have multiple identities. School board members can also be parents, women, African Americans, supporters of school choice, or advocates of specific curriculum, among others. Teachers have identities as teachers, subject specialists, men, and more. Multiple identities are ubiquitous among policy makers. A member of Congress might perceive herself as a Democrat, a Latina, a child of immigrants, a liberal, an advocate of tax reform, and so forth. Using race as the identity in question creates a situation in which the identity is highly salient and applicable to a wide range of situations.

Discretion has played a major role in the study of bureaucratic representation and was instrumental in sorting out the various representation roles. School board members have discretion over certain areas, school administrators over others, and teachers over yet others. Representatives can have a direct impact only in those areas where they possess discretion; in other arenas, their influence must be indirect. School board members, for example, have discretion over funding issues (see Theobald 2007) but far less, if any, influence over assignments to gifted classes. School administrators have extensive influence over teacher hiring and the application of discipline but less discretion in the day-to-day interaction of teachers with students. Teachers exercise vast discretion over student referrals for discipline or for grouping assignments and directly affect student learning, but any influence they have over school funding or policy will be indirect.

Discretion as a concept should play a larger role in other studies of representation. If one takes a cross-national view, the variance in legislator discretion correlates strongly with legislator representation. In a strong party system such as the House of Commons, legislators have little discretion (except on a few votes) to allow any of their identities to come to fore, and so a study of racial representation or even of constituency representation makes little sense. Only when legislative and party rules permit discretion should one expect to see representation of any individual identities.

This study also gave a great deal of attention to policy implementation rather than policy adoption. Few policies are self-implementing and the relationships found here should also apply to other policy areas and other levels of government. Legislative representatives at the local, state, and federal level should be cognizant of the ability of bureaucrats to further representational functions. The classic literature on iron triangles in political science documents a very similar process in areas that are not linked to race. The interaction of structures and partisanship (or ideology) that were documented in this study are also likely in both different institutional settings and in different policy areas.

Limitations

Before moving to our policy recommendations, we should note some of the limitations of this study. First, our analysis only examined African-American education. Although we think that the influences of structure and representation apply to all minorities, empirical research on Latinos, Asian Americans, Native Americans, and other groups is still needed. Each group has a unique political history and different educational issues (e.g., language). The relative distribution of other minority groups across the two political parties is also likely to play a role in local education politics and policy. One might hypothesize that partisanship would not play as strong a role for other minority groups who vote in less cohesive blocks, but that is a hypothesis open for further study.

Second, this study examined school districts with 5,000+ students. Although this includes the overwhelming majority of African-American students in the United States, we cannot say anything about the status of African-American education or the representation process in smaller communities. Smaller communities have norms and processes that likely differ substantially from large districts, so no argument can be made that our findings are generalizable to these smaller districts.

Third, our analysis focused on averages to provide an overall generalization of the status of African-American education politics. There would be much to be gained by focusing on both high-performing and low-performing schools and districts. Clearly the averages mask a great deal of variation and, within that variation, there are likely additional policy instruments that could be transplanted to other school districts. Individual case studies of those districts that do better than our regressions predict can yield useful insights.

Fourth, our analysis was almost exclusively quantitative; this analysis found interesting new relationships but was not able to fully probe the causal linkages underlying these relationships. In particular, the reasons why Democratic school districts enhance African-American representation need to be examined. Is it the result of teachers' perceiving a more favorable political environment and acting accordingly? Or do Democratic school districts somehow enhance the coproduction process by which schools and communities educate children? These are questions that can only be answered with additional qualitative research.

Policy Recommendations

This study has clearly illustrated that racial educational gaps remain, and that all is not equal. In fact, little has changed over the last few decades in terms of achieving this goal in the United States as a whole. Following our analyses in this research, we offer the following policy recommendations. The policy recommendations are focused on getting to scale, that is, policy actions that can be applied at the district level.

Recruit more African-American teachers

The findings in this book provide strong support for the idea that more African-American teachers are needed in the classroom; however, a key obstacle is that there is currently a shortage of black teachers. At the present time, few African Americans are majoring in education in postsecondary institutions. In 2006, for example, African Americans earned close to 10 percent of total degrees awarded, but only 6 percent of education degrees (Snyder and Dillow 2012). This low level of representation is due to a number of factors, including perceptions of low prestige and low salary figures for teaching as compared to other options. Other obstacles include difficulties in passing exams required for teacher certification and the cost of entering the field of teaching (through exams, required courses, and state fees).

To combat the low levels of African Americans entering the teaching field, multiple policies can be expanded and new initiatives can be considered. Among existing policies, the TEACH (Teacher Education Assistance for College and Higher Education) grant can be bolstered. This federal grant program offers $4,000 to college students who plan to teach in low-income schools upon graduation for four years (these individuals must also spend 51 percent of their time teaching a high-need subject). The program might also waive requirements of what these individuals are required to teach or could consider offering larger monetary incentives should funding become available (possibilities here might include partnerships with funding organizations like the Gates or Lumina foundations). This program can be publicized to high school students making decisions about college as well as to college students through career services programs and third-party organizations. While this targeting would require the investment of time and funding, the effect on student achievement could be substantial.

Beyond the TEACH program, federal and state aid efforts also include loan forgiveness and loan cancellation for qualified candidates (i.e., teachers must work in certain high-poverty schools for a certain period of time). These incentives might act as a recruitment mechanism for the teaching profession if marketed well. Though the policy may be helpful to those who know about it, efforts to make these programs more salient can make the teaching profession more attractive to African Americans.

At the local level, districts could pursue partnerships with colleges and universities to host job fairs and Q&A seminars that can address common negative perceptions related to the teaching field while also illustrating the need for minority teachers in the classroom. Districts can also consider certain pay incentives that will allow the teaching professions to compete in a larger market. These incentives can also be used to retain African-American teachers once they are recruited to the profession.

The proposals on attracting more black teachers might be framed more broadly to stress more inclusive definitions of teaching quality and the attraction of talented individuals to the teaching profession. The case of New Orleans provides an example of what parents expect from a school district and the role that black teachers play in an urban area. After Hurricane Katrina, the state of Louisiana created a process that shut down most New Orleans schools, fired many teachers, and moved to a charter school–based system of delivery. Although the district is widely lauded by policy makers (including former Secretary of Education Arne Duncan) as a stunning success, there is substantial dissatisfaction among local parents. Some of this dissatisfaction is linked to the dramatic decrease in the number of black teachers in local schools (see Berkshire 2015; Brown 2015; Munguia 2015).[3] Also among parent concerns are excessive discipline, lack of cultural awareness, and the inability to relate to poor, black students.

The New Orleans discussion might be framed in more general terms that are not race specific. Improving the status of teachers, recognizing the full range of activities that teachers contribute to student learning (and moving away from qualifications criteria that cannot be linked to a wider range of student outcomes), and reducing the level of teacher turnover can be applied to the teaching profession in general, not just to the inability of attract African Americans to public school teaching.

Expand options for teacher certification

In addition to recruiting African Americans to be interested in the field of teaching through both monetary and nonmonetary incentives, the path to becoming a teacher can also be reconsidered. This starts with encouraging institutions of higher education and state and national certification agencies to work with school districts in at least two ways. First, African Americans often have the highest risk of leaving college before degree completion. Colleges should work to help students understand when and how to transfer credits from one institution to another in order to minimize the confusion that comes with the process. Next, African Americans have often been eliminated from the field of teaching

---

[3] The public pronouncements of success stand in contrast to the lack of scholarly examinations of New Orleans. Only a single peer-reviewed manuscript exists (Sacerdote 2012) that shows decidedly mixed results. The examination of the New Orleans program is limited by the state of Louisiana raising and then lowering the definition of acceptable performance and the limited access that has been allowed to scholars by the school system.

due to unsuccessful attempts to pass teacher certification tests, even when they have high grade point averages and SAT scores (Green 2004; Nnazor, Sloan, and Higgins 2004). In 2011, the passing rate for the Praxis I exam (the exam used by many states) was 82 percent for white candidates and only 46 percent for black candidates (Nettles et al. 2011). While these state certification tests are intended to ensure the quality and training of teachers before they can enter the classroom, they are also acting as barriers of entry for African-American candidates. For those who do make it to the classroom, failure to pass later tests can also mean that they are forced to leave the classroom, further diminishing the number of black teachers available to teach black students (Cochran-Smith 2000).

Colleges of education can offer more extensive test-preparation courses for these types of tests. States can also be proactive in this area; the Illinois Board of Education, for example, voted to end a policy that set a limit on the number of times prospective teachers were allowed to take the basic skills test in 2014 in order to remove barriers for underrepresented college students (Sanchez 2014). The state will also waive the licensure tests altogether if candidates scored above set thresholds on the ACT or SAT within the last ten years. In general, states should establish more reciprocity programs so that individuals who become licensed in one state might be able to transfer to other states without the need to retake tests given that states generally require different tests and different passing scores. They might also consider accepting substitutes for traditional licensure exams, such as the American Board of Certification of Teacher Excellence, which tests on subjects as well as pedagogy and advocates for a national passing cut score (meaning a national minimum test score as opposed to minimums that vary by state).

Use incentives to attract teachers to specific locations

At all levels of governance, incentives can also be used to attract teachers to specific locations that have a high demand for black teachers. This might look similar to a tactic used in higher education to attract professors. The state of Texas has a loan repayment program for student loans for individuals from disadvantaged high schools who earn PhDs and then teach in Texas universities. The same tactic can be scalable to school districts although state or federal support might be needed where resources are tight. Teachers from disadvantaged backgrounds, including African-American teachers who work in high-need areas, might be offered incentives such as student debt assistance, housing packages, or targeted mentoring from other teachers. Such a program could supplement the existing federal loan forgiveness programs for teachers. The nation's schools need a better funnel to (1) build interest among African Americans to enter the teaching profession, (2) lessen mechanisms that bar African Americans from getting into the classroom even when they do want to teach, and (3) recruit and retain African-American teachers, especially in areas where they are most needed.

Expand gifted and advanced placement curriculum as well as
access to college preparation for black students
Beyond addressing the importance of recruiting and retaining African-American
teachers, additional steps can be taken to ensure that African-American students are receiving equal access to educational opportunities that have both
short- and long-term benefits. African-American students should be allowed
the same access to gifted, advanced placement, and International Baccalaureate
(IB) courses as their peers as well as specific exposure to college preparation
seminars. This might occur through programs such as AVID (Advancement
Via Individual Determination), which targets average or below-average students. AVID students are often first generation and are from low socioeconomic families. The program seeks to close the achievement gap and is often
funded through federal and state funding. While the program currently serves
eight hundred thousand students in forty-four states (AVID 2015), many more
students can be exposed to AVID or similar programs.

Beyond offerings in schools, local colleges and universities can use specific
programs to prepare minority students for college. These might include local
sessions related to completing college applications or the Free Application for
Federal Student Aid. Students might also be encouraged with a free trip to tour
local campuses where admission to the event is free but requires that the student has worked to submit a college application.

Aside from these targeted programs, states can rethink how to approach
access to advanced placement or similar courses. As reported by Dounay
(2006), states offer various opportunities through few, some, or nearly all of
the following:

- State mandate for advanced placement course offering;
- State provision of financial incentives for advanced placement courses;
- State accountability incentives for advanced placement courses;
- State programs and funding for teacher training;
- State subsidies for advanced placement testing fees;
- State scholarship incentives for achieving certain advanced placement scores;
- Collaboration on advanced placement between K–12 and higher education
  systems;
- State support for encouraging access to advanced placement courses; and /or
- State postsecondary institutions required to award credit for minimum
  scores.

In terms of access, many states do not require advanced placement course offerings, and others only require a low minimum at the high school level. In terms
of encouraging access, many states now operate online, virtual schools through
which advanced placement credit may be gained. By contrast, accountability
mechanisms related to advanced placement courses are mixed throughout the
states and might be improved to open doors for African American or other

minority students who are traditionally underrepresented in these courses. Earning advanced placement credit is a promising way to encourage disadvantaged students and their families to consider higher education.

Create and implement equitable disciplinary policies

In conjunction with determining how to allow greater access for African-American students, districts also need to determine how to best operate a system that is not unfairly punitive toward certain student groups. As outlined in Chapter 2 and illustrated throughout the book, black students are more likely to receive discipline and are more likely to receive harsher levels of discipline as compared to their peers. States should create a more uniform policy related to what actions are punishable by expulsion as well as by out-of-school and in-school suspension. Further, zero tolerance policies should be reviewed for effectiveness. The American Psychological Association, in a review of existing literature, found very little evidence that could support the assumptions made through the zero tolerance approach (e.g., that zero tolerance will apply discipline more equitably and will create a climate more conducive for learning) (American Psychological Association Zero Tolerance Task Force 2008). Instead, these policies have been shown to negatively affect adolescent development and may bolster the pipeline to prison for many students.

Once states and local districts review disciplinary procedures, training should be made available to all school administrators and teachers. This is especially important, as research has shown that disproportionate discipline may be due to lack of teacher preparation, cultural competencies, or biased stereotypes (Ferguson 2001; Graham and Lowery 2004; Vavrus and Cole 2002). Corrective actions can also replace punitive actions where feasible. Bear (2010) argues that misbehavior can be used as a way to teach self-discipline and responsibility as well as to illustrate what desired behaviors can replace undesired behaviors. While punitive policies may be needed for more egregious violations, nonviolent behavioral problems can be approached with other types of interventions that do not remove students from school, disrupting chances for educational achievement and increasing chances of the school-to-prison pipeline. Roch, Pitts, and Navarro (2011) show that, in the state of Georgia, schools with balanced racial and ethnic representation are more likely to adopt these corrective, or learning-oriented, policies while unbalanced representation is linked with the use of sanctioned-oriented policies. This again illustrates the importance of representation at all levels of management in schools.

Have stronger national standards for state testing and annual yearly progress

Much conflict continues over whether and to what extent education should be localized or centralized. School districts have traditionally been governed by local communities, and federal involvement has only become more pronounced in more recent years. This study illustrated just one example of the difficulty that exists in trying to compare educational access and outcomes across state lines. Different data are available by state, and national systems generally collect incomplete information from a sample of districts. State exams, further, cannot be compared in a straightforward manner. This difficulty in comparing districts across states and the need to ensure that educational opportunities are being afforded to African-American students suggests that stronger national standards for state testing, accountability, and annual yearly progress are needed. This effort will require a good deal of political work as well as monetary resources to provide for new tools and technology in schools but can also have long-term benefits for securing the country as one recognized for providing quality education for all students. Change in current education norms will be met with resistance including the possibility of teacher and administrator turnover, deviation from implementation at the local level, or disagreements among elected officials, yet it may be required in order to meet goals such as closing the achievement gap and being more competitive on a global level.

This proposal should not be taken as advocating for greater testing. The pendulum has swung too far in that direction. A survey conducted by the Council of Great City Schools (Hart et al. 2015) found that students in sixty-six large districts took an average of 112 tests between pre-K and grade twelve. Only seventeen of these tests are required by federal law. The movement to a national test could provide both a comparable metric for schools and school districts and reduce the overall level of testing for students.

Revitalize the VRA

As related to representation more broadly, the VRA should be revitalized, not invalidated. Issues of segregation and racial tensions are clearly not an issue of the past, and much work remains to be done in order to offer African Americans equal opportunities. Though little empirical research has been conducted to examine the link between specific types of VRA coverage and representation, Shah, Marschall, and Ruhil (2013) find that Section 5 coverage leads to greater black representation on city councils and school boards (see also Marschall and Rutherford 2015 on Latino representation in school districts covered by Sections 203 and 4(f)(4)). This research and many other anecdotal accounts (e.g., Parker 1990) should be used to reinstate the provisions of the VRA nullified by *Shelby County v. Holder*. Policy makers can update qualification standards where needed (many have argued that some of these requirements are out of date because they rely on data from the 1960s and 1970s) and can also define more specific standards for implementation. Subsequently, agencies like the Department of Justice should ensure enforcement through the use of federal observers as well as legal action (both of these mechanisms have been used in the past to varying extents). The hurdles for this recommendation may be quite high, of course. The VRA will need to gain enough political support to be fully reenacted and/or updated. Even if this hurdle is cleared, existing evidence suggests that many instances of the policy showing little change are due to sub-standard implementation and compliance (Jones-Correa and Waismel-Manor 2007; Tucker 2009).

Conclusion

Equal access to quality education is an elusive goal in the United States. Politics is a time-honored way to press political issues and seek to redress inequalities in all areas of life; race and education are no exception to this rule. For African Americans, US education as presented in this analysis has evolved into two distinct systems based on partisanship. African-American students receive more equitable treatment whether the issue is class assignments, discipline, or education performance in school districts with Democratic majorities than they do in Republican majority school districts.

The gains in education by students are matched by gains in political and bureaucratic representation; African Americans are more likely to be represented by other African Americans in Democratic school districts than in Republican school districts. At times, these differences are substantial and these political gains are directly correlated with the educational gains. Partisanship is even further enhanced by the ability of African-American representatives in both legislative and bureaucratic arenas to form coalitions with sympathetic whites in Democratic majority districts. African-American school board members, administrators, and teachers are all more effective if they are in Democratic districts than if they are in Republican ones.

Issues of electoral and system structure (the independent school district) are not irrelevant to this partisan process, but the influence of these structural factors is greatly affected and often transformed by politics. The findings of this study are corroborated by what appears to be the rise of partisan issues on the state and national agendas that relate to federal initiatives, the adoption of Common Core standards, and the long contentious local issues on subject content in terms of teaching science, history, and health. Pretending that education in the United States is a nonpartisan issue is simply no longer feasible. Rather than lament this evolution, if indeed this is a change in direction rather than a change in visibility, scholars and policy makers need to recognize the partisan aspects of education and bring them to the forefront of decision-making processes. The problem of unequal access to quality education have their origins in politics; the solution to this inequity will of necessity also be in politics.

References

Alexander v. Holmes County Board of Education, 396 U.S. 19 (1969).

Allen v. State Bd. of Elections, 393 U.S. 544, 89 S. Ct. 817, 22 L. Ed. 2d 1 (1969).

Almy, Sarah, and Christina Theokas. 2010. *Not Prepared for Class: High-Poverty Schools Continue to Have Fewer In-Field Teachers.* Washington, DC: The Education Trust.

Alston v. School Board of City of Norfolk, 112 F.2d 992 (4th Cir. 1940).

Alvarez v. Board of Trustees of the Lemon Grove School District, Superior Court of the State of California, County of San Diego, Petition for Writ of Mandate, No. 66625 (1931).

American Psychological Association Zero Tolerance Task Force. 2008. "Are Zero Tolerance Policies Effective in the Schools? An Evidentiary Review and Recommendations." *American Psychologist* 63(9): 852–862.

Anderson, James D. 1988. *The Education of Blacks in the South, 1860–1935.* Chapel Hill: University of North Carolina Press.

Andrews, Rhys, Rachel Ashworth, and Kenneth J. Meier. 2014. "Representative Bureaucracy and Fire Service Performance." *International Public Management Journal* 17(1): 1–24.

Anzia, Sarah F. 2011. "Election Timing and the Electoral Influence of Interest Groups." *Journal of Politics* 73(2): 412–427.

Arnwine, Barbara, and Marcia Johnson-Blanco. 2013. *Voting Rights at a Crossroads: The Supreme Court Decision in Shelby Is the Latest Challenge in the "Unfinished March" to Full Black Access to the Ballot.* Washington, DC: Economic Policy Institute.

Arrington, Theodore, and Thomas Gill Watts. 1991. "The Election of Blacks to School Boards in North Carolina." *Western Political Science Quarterly* 44(4): 1099–1105.

Artiles, Alfredo J., and Stanley C. Trent. 1994. "Overrepresentation of Minority Students in Special Education a Continuing Debate." *The Journal of Special Education* 27(4): 410–437.

Atkins, Danielle N., and Vicky M. Wilkins. 2013. "Going Beyond Reading, Writing, and Arithmetic: The Effects of Teacher Representation on Teen Pregnancy Rates." *Journal of Public Administration Research and Theory* 23(4): 771–790.

Aud, Susan, William Hussar, Michael Planty, Thomas Snyder, Kevin Blanco, Mary Ann Fox, Lauren Frohlich, Jana Kemp, and Lauren Drake. 2010. *The Condition of*

Education 2010. NCES 2010–028. Washington, DC: US Department of Education, Institute of Education Sciences.

AVID. 2015. "AVID College Readiness System: An Overview."

Baker v. Carr, 369 U.S. 186, 82 S. Ct. 691, 7 L. Ed. 2d 663 (1962).

Baldez, Lisa. 2006. "The Pros and Cons of Gender Quota Laws: What Happens When You Kick Men Out and Let Women In?" *Politics and Gender* 2(1): 102–109.

Bandeira de Mello, Victor. 2011. *Mapping State Proficiency Standards onto the NAEP Scales: Variation and Change in State Standards for Reading and Mathematics, 2005–2009*. NCES 2011–458. Washington, DC: National Center for Education Statistics, Institute of Education Sciences, US Department of Education.

Banducci, Susan A., Todd Donovan, and Jeffrey A. Karp. 2004. "Minority Representation, Empowerment, and Participation." *Journal of Politics* 66(2): 534–556.

Baretto, Matt A., Mara A. Marks, and Nathan D. Woods. 2007. "Homeownership: Southern California's New Political Fault Line?" *Urban Affairs Review* 42(3): 315–341.

Bascia, Nina. 1994. *Unions in Teachers' Professional Lives*. New York: Teachers College Press.

Bear, George. 2010. "Discipline: Effective School Practices." *National Association of School Psychologists*. Available at http://www.nasponline.org/advocacy/updates/documents/S4H18_Discipline.pdf. Accessed March 10, 2015.

Behr, Joshua G. 2004. *Race, Ethnicity and the Politics of City Redistricting*. Albany: State University of New York Press.

Belton v. Gebhart, 87 A. 2d 862 (1952).

Berkman, Michael, and Eric Plutzer. 2010. *Evolution, Creationism, and the Battle to Control America's Classrooms*. New York: Cambridge University Press.

Berkshire, Jennifer. 2015. "'Reform' Makes Broken New Orleans Schools Worse." *Salon*. Available at http://www.salon.com/2015/08/03/reform_makes_broken_new_orleans_schools_worse_race_charters_testing_and_the_real_story_of_education_after_katrina/. Accessed November 10, 2015.

Berliner, David C., and Bruce J. Biddle. 1995. *The Manufactured Crisis: Myths, Fraud, and the Attack on America's Public Schools*. Reading, MA: Addison-Wesley Publishing.

Berry, Christopher R., and Martin R. West. 2010. "Growing Pains: The School Consolidation Movement and Student Outcomes." *Journal of Law, Economics, and Organization* 26(1): 1–29.

Berube, Maurice R., and Marilyn Gittell. 1969 *Confrontation at Ocean Hill-Brownsville: The New York School Strikes of 1968*. New York: Praeger Publishers.

Bidwell, Allie. 2014. "The Politics of the Common Core." *U.S. News and World Report*. Available at http://www.usnews.com/news/special-reports/a-guide-to-common-core/articles/2014/03/06/the-politics-of-common-core?page=2. Accessed May 23, 2015.

Birnie, W. W. 1927. "Education of the Negro in Charleston, South Carolina, Prior to the Civil War." *Journal of Negro History* 12(1): 13–21.

Blackman, Lee L., and Erich R. Luschei. 1999. "Voting Rights Legislation." In *Local Government Election Practices: A Handbook for Public Officials and Citizens*, R. L. Kemp (ed.). Jefferson, NC: McFarland and Company.

Blad, Evie. 2014. "Discipline Debates Turn to Broad Terms Like 'Defiance.'" *Education Week*. Available at http://www.edweek.org/ew/articles/2014/09/24/05defiance.h34.html#. Accessed May 15, 2015.

Bloom, Molly. 2013. "2012–13 Ohio School District Report Cards." *StateImpact.* Available at http://stateimpact.npr.org/ohio/2013/08/22/2012-13-ohio-school-district-report-cards/. Accessed March 22, 2015.

Board of Ed. of Oklahoma City Public Schools v. Dowell, 498 U.S. 237, 111 S. Ct. 630, 112 L. Ed. 2d 715 (1991).

Bohte, John, and Kenneth J. Meier. 2000. "Goal Displacement: Assessing the Motivation for Organizational Cheating." *Public Administration Review* 60(2): 173–182.

Bolling v. Sharpe, 347 U.S. 497 (1954).

Boreman, Geoffrey D., and Laura T. Rachuna. 2001. *Academic Success among Poor and Minority Students: An Analysis of Competing Models of School Effects.* Washington, DC: ERIC.

Boser, Ulrich, and Robert Hanna. 2014. *In Quest to Improve Schools, Have Teachers Been Stripped of Their Autonomy?* Washington, DC: Center for American Progress.

Bowen, Ezra. 1988. "Education: Getting Tough." *Time.* Available at http://content.time.com/time/magazine/article/0,9171,966577,00.html. Accessed April 12, 2015.

Bratton, Kathleen A., and Kerry L. Haynie. 1999. "Agenda Setting and Legislative Success in State Legislatures: The Effects of Gender and Race." *Journal of Politics* 61(3): 658–679.

Brehm, John, and Scott Gates. 1997. *Working, Shirking, and Sabotage.* Ann Arbor: University of Michigan Press.

Brief for 553 Social Scientists as Amici Curiae Supporting Respondents, *Parents Involved* and *Meredith*, 127 S. Ct. 2738 (2006) (Nos. 05-908, 05-915).

Briggs v. Elliott, 342 U.S. 350 (1952).

Broockman, David E. 2013. "Black Politicians Are More Intrinsically Motivated to Advance Blacks' Interests: A Field Experiment Manipulating Political Incentives." *American Journal of Political Science* 57(3): 521–536.

Brown v. Board of Education of Topeka, 98 F. Supp. 797 (D. Kan. 1951).

Brown v. Board of Education, 347 U.S. 483 (1954).

Brown, Emma. 2015. "Katrina Swept Away New Orleans' School System, Ushering New Era." *Washington Post.* Available at https://www.washingtonpost.com/news/education/wp/2015/09/03/katrina-swept-away-new-orleans-school-system-ushering-in-new-era/. Accessed November 10, 2015.

Brown-Dean, Khalilah, Zoltan Hajnal, Christina Rivers, and Ismail White. 2015. *50 Years of The Voting Rights Act: The State of Race in Politics.* Washington, DC: Joint Center for Political and Economic Studies.

Browning, Rufus P., Dale Rogers Marshall, and David H. Tabb. 1984. *Protest Is Not Enough: The Struggle of Blacks and Hispanics for Equality in Urban Politics.* Berkeley: University of California Press.

Bulah v. Gebhart, 87 A. 2d 862 (1952).

Bullock, Charles S., III, and Charles M. Lamb. 1984. *Implementation of Civil Rights Policy.* Monterey, CA: Brooks/Cole.

Bullock, Charles S., III, and Susan A. MacManus. 1993. "Testing Assumptions of the Totality of the Circumstances Test: An Analysis of the Impact of Structures on Black Descriptive Representation." *American Politics Quarterly* 21(3): 290–306.

Bureau of Labor Statistics. 2008. "Labor Force Statistics from the Current Population Survey." *U.S. Department of Labor.* Available at http://www.bls.gov/cps/race_ethnicity_2008_unemployment.htm. Accessed February 22, 2015.

Bushaw, William J., and Valerie J. Calderon. 2014. "Try It Again, Uncle Sam: The 46th Annual PDK/Gallup Poll of the Public's Attitudes Towards the Public Schools." *PDK International.* Available at http://www.pdkintl.org/noindex/PDK_Poll46_2014.pdf. Accessed September 28, 2015.

California Department of Education. 2014. "A Parent's Guide to the SARC." Available at http://www.cde.ca.gov/TA/ac/sa/parentguide.asp. Accessed April 12, 2015.

2015. "The Public School Accountability Act of 1999—CalEdFacts." Available at http://www.cde.ca.gov/ta/ac/pa/cefpsaa.asp. Accessed April 12, 2015.

Cameron, Charles, David Epstein, and Sharyn O'Halloran. 1996. "Do Majority-Minority Districts Maximize Substantive Black Representation in Congress?" *American Political Science Review* 90(4): 794–812.

Canon, David T. 1999. *Race, Redistricting, and Representation.* Chicago: University of Chicago Press.

Casellas, Jason. 2011. *Latino Representation in State Houses and Congress.* New York: Cambridge University Press.

Center on Education Policy. 2012. *Accountability Issues to Watch under NCLB Waivers.* Washington, DC: George Washington University.

Childress, Sarah. 2013. "After Shelby, Voting-Law Changes Come One Town at a Time." *PBS Frontline.* Available at http://www.pbs.org/wgbh/pages/frontline/. Accessed February 18. 2015.

Christle, Christine A., Kristine Jolivette, and C. Michael Nelson. 2005. "Breaking the School to Prison Pipeline: Identifying School Risk and Protective Factors for Youth Delinquency." *Exceptionality* 13(2): 69–88.

Clewell, Beatriz, and Ana Villegas. 1998. "Diversifying the Teaching Force to Improve Urban Schools: Meeting the Challenge." *Education and Urban Society* 31(1): 3–17.

Clotfelter, Charles. 2004. *After Brown: The Rise and Retreat of School Desegregation.* Princeton, NJ: Princeton University Press.

Clotfelter, Charles T., Helen F. Ladd, and Jacob L. Vigdor. 2007. "Teacher Credentials and Student Achievement: Longitudinal Analysis with Student Fixed Effects." *Economics of Education Review* 26(6): 673–682.

Cochran-Smith, Marilyn. 2000. "Blind vision: Unlearning racism in teacher education." *Harvard Educational Review* 70(2): 157–190.

Cole, Leonard A. 1974. "Electing Blacks to Municipal Office: Structural and Social Determinants." *Urban Affairs Review* 10(1): 17–39.

Coleman v. Franklin Parish School Bd., 702 F.2d 74 (5th Cir. 1983).

Coleman, James S., Ernest Q. Campbell, Carol J. Hobson, James McPartland, Alexander M. Mood, Frederick D. Weinfeld, and Robert L. York. 1966. *Equality of Educational Opportunity.* Washington, DC: National Center for Educational Statistics.

Collins, William J., and Robert A. Margo. 2006. "Historical Perspectives on Racial Differences in Schooling in the United States." In *Handbook of the Economics of Education,* E. A. Hanshek and F. Welch (eds.). Amsterdam, The Netherlands: Elsevier.

Condron, Dennis J., Daniel Tope, Christina R. Steidl, and Kendralin J. Freeman. 2013. "Racial Segregation and the Black/White Achievement Gap, 1992 to 2009." *The Sociological Quarterly* 54(1): 130–157.

Cooper, Lisa A., and Neil R. Powe. 2004. *Disparities in Patient Experiences, Health Care Processes, and Outcomes: The Role of Patient-Provider Racial, Ethnic, and Language Concordance.* New York: Commonwealth Fund.

Cox, Gary. 1997. *Making Votes Count: Strategic Coordination in the World's Electoral Systems*. Cambridge: Cambridge University Press.

Crisp, Brian F., Betul Demirkaya, and Courtney Millian. 2014. "The Informal Paths to Office on Descriptive, Symbolic, and Substantive Representation: Maori in the New Zealand Parliament." Presented at the Annual Meeting of the American Political Science Association, Washington, DC.

Cruse, Keith L., and Jon S. Twing. 2000. "The History of Statewide Achievement Testing in Texas." *Applied Measurement in Education* 13(4): 327–331.

Cumming v. Board of Education of Richmond County, State of Georgia, 175 U.S. 545 (1899).

Darling-Hammond, Linda. 2007. "Race, Inequality and Educational Accountability: The Irony of 'No Child Left Behind.'" *Race Ethnicity and Education* 10(3): 245–260.

Davidson, Chandler. 1979. "At-Large Elections and Minority Representation." *Social Science Quarterly* 60(2): 336–338.

Davidson, Chandler, and Bernard Grofman. 1994. *Quiet Revolution in the South: The Impact of the Voting Rights Act 1965–1990*. Princeton, NJ: Princeton University Press.

Davidson, Chandler, and George Korbel. 1981. "At-Large Elections and Minority-Group Representation: A Re-examination of Historical and Contemporary Evidence." *Journal of Politics* 43(4): 982–1005.

Davis, Belinda Creel, Michelle Livermore, and Younghee Lim. 2011. "The Extended Reach of Minority Political Power: The Interaction of Descriptive Representation, Managerial Networking, and Race." *Journal of Politics* 73(2): 494–507.

Davis v. County School Board, 103 F. Supp. 337 (E.D. Va. 1952).

Davis, Vicki. 2011. "The Greatest Teacher Incentive: The Freedom to Teach." *Washington Post*. Available at https://www.washingtonpost.com/national/on-leadership/the-greatest-teacher-incentive-the-freedom-to-teach/2011/07/19/gIQAd7NYOI_story .html. Accessed October 1, 2015.

Dee, Thomas S. 2001. *Teachers, Race and Student Achievement in a Randomized Experiment*. Cambridge, MA: NBER Working Paper.

2004. "Teachers, Race, and Student Achievement in a Randomized Experiment." *Review of Economics and Statistics* 86(1): 195–210.

2005. "A Teacher Like Me: Does Race, Ethnicity, or Gender Matter?" *American Economic Review* 95(2): 158–165.

Democratic National Convention. 2012. *Moving American Forward: 2012 Democratic National Platform*. Available at https://s3.amazonaws.com/s3.documentcloud.org/documents/422016/2012-democratic-national-platform.pdf. Accessed April 23, 2015.

DeNavas-Walt, Carmen, Bernadette D. Proctor, and Jessica C. Smith. 2013. *Income, Poverty, and Health Insurance Coverage in the United States: 2012*. Washington, DC: US Census Bureau.

Denbo, Sheryl. 2002. "Why Can't We Close the Achievement Gap?" In *Improving Schools for African American Children: A Reader for Educational Leaders*, S. Denbo and L. Beaulieu (eds.). Springfield, IL: Charles C. Thomas Publisher.

DiMaggio, Paul, John Evans, and Bethany Bryson. 1996. "Have American's Social Attitudes Become More Polarized?" *American Journal of Sociology* 102(3):690–755.

Dixon v. Alabama State Board of Education, 294 F.2d 150 (5th Cir., 1961)

Downs, Anthony. 1957. *An Economic Theory of Democracy*. New York: Harper.

Dounay, Jennifer. 2006. "Advanced Placement Policies – All State Profiles." *Education Commission of the States.* Available at http://ecs.force.com/mbdata/mbprofgroupall?Rep=APA. Accessed March 24, 2015.

Druckman, James N., Erik Peterson, and Rune Slothuus. 2013. "How Elite Partisan Polarization Affects Public Opinion Formation." *American Political Science Review* 107(1): 57–79.

Duke, Daniel. 1989. "School Organization, Learning, and Student Behavior." In *Strategies to Reduce Student Misbehavior*, O. C. Moles (ed.). Washington, DC: Office of Educational Research and Improvement.

Durbin, James, and Geoffrey S. Watson. 1951. "Testing for Serial Correlation in Least Squares Regression II." *Biometrika* 28(1–2): 159–177.

Dye, Thomas R. (ed.). 1969. *American Public Policy: Documents and Essays.* Columbus, OH: Merrill.

Edelstein, Fritz. 2006. *Mayoral Leadership and Involvement in Education: An Action Guide for Success.* Washington, DC: US Conference of Mayors.

Editorial Projects in Education. 2008. "Diplomas Count 2008: School to College: Can State P-16 Councils Ease the Transition?" *Education Week*, 27(40).

Editorial Projects in Education Research Center. 2011. "Issues A–Z: Achievement Gap." *Education Week.* Available at http://www.edweek.org/ew/issues/achievement-gap/. Accessed January 14, 2015.

Education Data Partnership. 2014. "Understanding California's Standardized Testing and Reporting (STAR) Program. Available at https://www.ed-data.k12.ca.us/Pages/Understanding-The-STAR.aspx. Accessed March 27, 2015.

Education Trust West. 2010. "Access Denied: 2009 API Rankings Reveal Unequal Access in California's Best Schools." Available at http://west.edtrust.org/wp-content/uploads/sites/3/2015/01/Access-Denied.pdf. Accessed March 27, 2015.

Egalite, Anna J., Brian Kisida, and Marcus A. Winters. 2015. "Representation in the Classroom: The Effect of Own-Race Teachers on Student Achievement." *Economics of Education Review* 45(1): 44–52.

Eisinger, Peter K. 1980. *The Politics of Displacement.* New York: Academic Press.

  1982. "Black Employment in Municipal Jobs: The Impact of Black Political Power." *American Political Science Review* 76(2): 380–392.

Eitle, Tamela McNulty. 2002. "Special Education or Racial Segregation: Understanding Variation in the Representation of Black Students in Educable Mentally Handicapped Programs." *The Sociological Quarterly* 43(4): 575–605.

Engstrom, Richard, and Michael McDonald. 1981. "The Election of Blacks to City Councils: Clarifying the Impact of Electoral Arrangements on the Seats/Population Relationship." *American Political Science Review* 75(2): 344–354.

  1982. "The Underrepresentation of Blacks on City Councils: Comparing the Structural and Socioeconomic Explanations for South/Non-South Differences." *Journal of Politics* 44(4): 1088–1105.

  1986. "The Effect of At-Large Versus District Elections on Racial Representation in U.S. Municipalities." In *Electoral Laws and Their Political Consequences*, B. Grofman and A. Lijphart (eds.). New York: Agathon Press.

  1997. "The Election of Blacks to Southern City Councils: The Dominant Impact of Electoral Arrangements." In *Blacks in Southern Politics*, L. Moreland, R. Steed, and T. Baker (eds.). Santa Barbara, CA: Praeger.

Epps, Edgar G. 1995. "Race, Class, and Educational Opportunity: Trends in the Sociology of Education." *Sociological Forum* 10(4): 593–608.

Epstein, David, and Sharyn O'Halloran. 1999. "Measuring the Electoral and Policy Impact of Majority-Minority Voting Districts." *American Journal of Political Science* 43(2): 367–395.

Eulau, Heinz, and Paul D. Karps. 1977. "The Puzzle of Representation: Specifying Components of Responsiveness." *Legislative Studies Quarterly* 2(3): 233–254.

Evans Jr., Arthur S., and Micheal W. Giles. 1986. "Effects of Percent Black on Blacks' Perceptions of Relative Power and Social Distance." *Journal of Black Studies* 17(1): 3–14.

Evans, Tony. 2012. *Professional Discretion in Welfare Services: Beyond Street-Level Bureaucracy*. London: Ashgate Publishing.

Evans, William N., Shelia E. Murray, and Robert M. Schwab. 1997. "Schoolhouses, Courthouses, and Statehouses after Serrano." *Journal of Policy Analysis and Management* 16(1): 10–31.

Eyler, Janet, Valerie J. Cook, and Leslie E. Ward. 1983. "Resegregation: Segregation within Desegregated Schools." In *The Consequences of School Desegregation*, C. H. Rossell and W. D. Hawley (eds.). Philadelphia: Temple University Press.

Feagin, Joe R., and Clairece Booher Feagin. 1978. *Discrimination American Style: Institutional Racism and Sexism*. Englewood Cliffs, NJ: Prentice Hall.

Ferguson, Ann Arnett. 2001. *Bad Boys: Public Schools in the Making of Black Masculinity*. Ann Arbor: University of Michigan Press.

Ferriss, Susan. 2012. "School Discipline Debate Reignited by New Los Angeles Data." *The Center for Public Integrity*. Available at http://www.publicintegrity.org/2012/04/24/8741/school-discipline-debate-reignited-new-los-angeles-data. Accessed April 5, 2015.

Findley, Warren G., and Miriam M. Bryan. 1971. *Ability Grouping: 1970-Status, Impact, and Alternatives*. Washington, DC: Bureau of Elementary and Secondary Education.

Finn, Chester E. 2003. "Who Needs School Boards?" *Education Gadfly* 3(37). Available at http://edexcellence.net/commentary/education-gadfly-weekly/2003/october-23/who-needs-school-boards-1.html. Accessed February 17, 2015.

Finn, Chester E., and Lisa Graham Keegan. 2004. "Lost at Sea: Time to Jettison One of the Chief Obstacles to Reform: The Local School Board." *Education Next* 4(3): 14.

Flannery, Mary Ellen. 2013. "Local Politics: Why You Should Pay Attention to School Board Races This Fall." *Education Votes*. Available at http://educationvotes.nea.org/2013/09/08/local-politics-why-you-should-pay-attention-to-school-board-races-this-fall/. Accessed February 2, 2015.

Florida Center for Instructional Technology. 2015. "Sunshine State Standards." Available at http://tools.fcit.usf.edu/sss/. Accessed April 3, 2015.

Florida Department of Education. 2015. "K–12 Student Assessment." Available at http://www.fldoe.org/accountability/assessments/k-12-student-assessment/. Accessed April 3, 2015.

Florida Education Association. 2015. "Senate Bill 736: How Will It Affect Me?" Available at https://feaweb.org/senate-bill-736-how-will-it-affect-me. Accessed April 3, 2015.

Foster, Michele. 1997. *Black Teachers on Teaching*. New York: New Press.

Foundation for Florida's Future. 2015. "Florida Formula for Student Achievement: School Grades Q and A." Available at http://www.afloridapromise.org/Pages/Florida_Formula/Facts_on_the_FCAT_and_Floridas_Path_to_Success/School_Grades_Q_and_A.aspx. Accessed April 3, 2015.

Fraga, Luis R. 1988. "Domination through Democratic Means: Nonpartisan Slating Groups in City Electoral Politics." *Urban Affairs Quarterly* 23(4): 528–555.

Fraga, Luis R., and Roy Elis. 2009. "Interests and Representation: Ethnic Advocacy on California School Boards." *Teachers College Record* 111(3): 659–682.

Frankenberg, Erica, Chungmei Lee, and Gary Orfield. 2003. *A Multiracial Society with Segregated Schools: Are We Losing the Dream?* Cambridge, MA: The Civil Rights Project, Harvard University.

Freeman v. Pitts, 503 U.S. 467, 112 S. Ct. 1430, 118 L. Ed. 2d 108 (1992).

Frey, William H. 2013. "Minority Turnout Determined the 2012 Election." Washington, DC: Brookings Institute. Available at http://www.brookings.edu/research/papers/2013/05/10-election-2012-minority-voter-turnout-frey. Accessed March 15, 2015.

Gade, Daniel M., and Vicky M. Wilkins. 2013. "Where Did You Serve? Veteran Identity, Representative Bureaucracy, and Vocational Rehabilitation." *Journal of Public Administration Research and Theory* 23(2): 267–288.

Gaddis, S. Michael, and Douglas Lee Lauen. 2014. "School Accountability and the Black–White Test Score Gap." *Social Science Research* 44 (March): 15–31.

Georgia State Conference of Branches of NAACP v. Georgia, 775 F2d 1403, 1417 (11th Cir., 1985).

Gerber, Elisabeth R., and Daniel J. Hopkins. 2011. "When Mayors Matter: Estimating the Impact of Mayoral Partisanship on City Policy." *American Journal of Political Science* 55(2): 326–339.

Glicksman, Robert L., and Richard E. Levy. 2008. "Collective Action Perspective on Ceiling Preemption by Federal Environmental Regulation: The Case of Global Climate Change." *Northwestern University Law Review* 102(2): 579–648.

Goldstein, Harvey. 2004. "International Comparisons of Student Attainment: Some Issues Arising from the PISA Study." *Assessment in Education: Principles, Policy and Practice* 11(3): 319–330.

Goodnow, Frank J. 1906. *Politics and Administration: A Study in Government.* New York: Russell and Russell.

Gordon, Rebecca, Libero Della Piana, and Terry Keleher. 2000. *Facing the Consequences: An Examination of Racial Discrimination in U.S. Public Schools.* New York: Ford Foundation.

Graham, Sandra, and Brian S. Lowery. 2004. "Priming Unconscious Racial Stereotypes about Adolescent Offenders." *Law and Human Behavior* 28(5): 483–504.

Green v. County School Board of New Kent County, 391 U.S. 390 (1968).

Green, Paul. 2004. "The Paradox of the Promised Unfulfilled: Brown v. Board of Education and the Continued Pursuit of Excellence in Education." *Journal of Negro Education* 73(3): 268–284.

Gregory, Anne, Russell J. Skiba, and Pedro A. Noguera. 2010. "The Achievement Gap and the Discipline Gap Two Sides of the Same Coin?" *Educational Researcher* 39(1): 59–68.

Grissom, Jason A., and Christopher Redding. 2015. "Discretion and Disproportionality: Explaining the Underrepresentation of High-Achieving Students of Color in Gifted Programs." Working paper.

Grissom, Jason A., Emily C. Kern, and Luis A. Rodriguez. 2015. "The 'Representative Bureaucracy' in Education: Educator Workforce Diversity, Policy Outputs, and Outcomes for Disadvantaged Students." *Educational Researcher* 44(3): 185–192.

Grose, Christian R. 2005. "Disentangling Constituency and Legislator Effects in Legislative Representation: Black Legislators or Black Districts?" *Social Science Quarterly* 86(2): 427–443.

2011. *Congress in Black and White.* New York: Cambridge University Press.

Grose, Christian R., Maurice Mangum, and Christopher Martin. 2007. "Race, Political Empowerment, and Constituency Service: Descriptive Representation and the Hiring of African-American Congressional Staff." *Polity* 39(4): 449–478.

Guinier, Lani. 1991. "The Triumph of Tokenism: The Voting Rights Act and the Theory of Black Electoral Success." *Michigan Law Review* 89(5): 1077–1154.

2004. "From Racial Liberalism to Racial Literacy: Brown v. Board of Education and the Interest-Divergence Dilemma." *The Journal of American History* 91(1): 92–118.

Gutmann, Amy, and Sigal Ben-Porath. 1987. *Democratic Education.* New York: John Wiley and Sons.

Hajnal, Zoltan. 2001. "White Residents, Black Incumbents and a Declining Racial Divide." *American Political Science Review* 95(3): 603–617.

Hajnal, Zoltan L., and Taeku Lee. 2011. *Why Americans Don't Join the Party: Race, Immigration, and the Failure (of Political Parties) to Engage the Electorate.* Princeton, NJ: Princeton University Press.

Hansen, Amy, and Mark Urycki. 2013. "Ohio Standardized Testing 101." *StateImpact.* Available at http://stateimpact.npr.org/ohio/tag/testing/. Accessed April 8, 2015.

Hanushek, Eric A. 1996. "School Resources and Student Performance." In *Does Money Matter?* G. Burtless (ed.). Washington, DC: Brookings Institute.

Harry, Beth, and Janette K. Klingner. 2014. *Why Are So Many Minority Students in Special Education? Understanding Race and Disability in Schools.* New York: Teachers College Press.

Hart, Ray, Michael Casserly, Renata Uzzell, Moses Palacios, Amanda Corcoran, and Liz Spurgeon. 2015. *Student Testing in American's Great City Schools: An Inventory and Preliminary Analysis.* Washington, DC: Council of the Great City Schools.

Hawkins v. Coleman, 376 F. Supp. 1330 (N.D. Tex. 1974).

Hays, Samuel P. 1964. "The Politics of Reform in Municipal Government in the Progressive Era." *The Pacific Northwest Quarterly* 55(4): 157–169.

Hedges, Larry V., Richard D. Laine, and Rob Greenwald. 1994. "An Exchange: Part I: Does Money Matter? A Meta-Analysis of Studies of the Effects of Differential School Inputs on Student Outcomes." *Educational Researcher* 23(3): 5–14.

Henig, Jeffrey R., Richard C. Hula, Marion Orr, and Desiree S. Pedescleaux. 1999. *The Color of School Reform: Race, Politics and the Challenge of Urban Education.* Princeton, NJ: Princeton University Press.

Heller, Kirby A., Wayne H. Holtzman, and Samuel Messick. 1982. *Placing Children in Special Education.* Washington, DC: National Academy Press.

Hicklin, Alisa, and Kenneth J. Meier. 2008. "Race, Structure, and State Governments: The Politics of Higher Education Diversity." *Journal of Politics* 70(3): 851–860.

Hindera, John J. 1993. "Representative Bureaucracy: Further Evidence of Active Representation in the EEOC District Offices." *Journal of Public Administration Research and Theory* 3(4): 415–429.

Hobson v. Hansen, 269 F. Supp. 401 (D.C. 1967).

Howell, William (ed.). 2005. *Besieged: School Boards and the Future of Education Politics*. Washington, DC: Brookings Institution Press.

Iannaccone, Laurence. 1975. *Education Policy Systems: A Study Guide for Educational Administrators*. Ft. Lauderdale, FL: Nova University.

Jaschik, Scott. 2015a. "ACT Scores Are Flat." *Inside Higher Ed*. Available at https://www.insidehighered.com/news/2015/08/26/act-scores-year-are-flat-and-racial-gaps-persist. Accessed September 28, 2015.

2015b. "SAT Scores Drop." *Inside Higher Ed*. Available at https://www.insidehighered.com/news/2015/09/03/sat-scores-drop-and-racial-gaps-remain-large. Accessed September 28, 2015.

Jencks, Christopher and Meredith Phillips. 1998. "The Black-White Test Scope Gap: Why It Persists and What Can Be Done." *The Brookings Review* 16(2): 24-27.

(eds.). 2011. *The Black-White Test Score Gap*. Washington, DC: Brookings Institution Press.

Johnson, Keith V., and Elwood Watson. 2004. "The W. E. B. DuBois and Booker T. Washington Debate: Effects upon African American Roles in Engineering and Engineering Technology." *Journal of Technology Studies* 30(4): 65–70.

Jones-Correa, Michael, and Israel Waismel-Manor. 2007. "Verifying Implementation of Language Provisions on the Voting Rights Act." In *Voting Rights Act Reauthorization of 2006: Perspectives on Democracy, Participation, and Power*, A. Henderson (ed.). Berkeley: University of California Press.

Jordan, Reed. 2014. "Millions of Black Students Attend Public Schools That Are Highly Segregated by Race and by Income." *Urban Institute*. Available at http://www.urban.org/urban-wire/millions-black-students-attend-public-schools-are-highly-segregated-race-and-income. Accessed September 28, 2015.

Karnig, Albert K. 1976. "Black Representation on City Councils: The Impact of District Elections and Socioeconomic Factors." *Urban Affairs Review* 12(2): 223–42.

1980. *Black Representation and Urban Policy*. Chicago: University of Chicago Press.

Karnig, Albert K., and Susan Welch. 1982. "Electoral Structure and Black Representation on City Councils." *Social Science Quarterly* 63(1): 99–114.

Katznelson, Ira. 1981. *City Trenches: Urban Politics and the Patterning of Class in the United States*. Chicago: University of Chicago Press.

Keiser, Lael R., Vicky M. Wilkins, Kenneth J. Meier, and Catherine A. Holland. 2002. "Lipstick and Logarithms: Gender, Institutional Context, and Representative Bureaucracy." *American Political Science Review* 96(3): 553–564.

Keller, Edmund J. 1978. "The Impact of Black Mayors on Urban Policy." *Annals of the American Academy of Political and Social Science* 439(1): 40–52.

Kenworthy, Lane, and Melissa Malami. 1999. "Gender Inequality in Political Representation: A Worldwide Comparative Analysis." *Social Forces* 78(1): 235–269.

Kerr, Brinck, and Kenneth R. Mladenka. 1994. "Does Politics Matter? A Time-Series Analysis of Minority Employment Patterns." *American Journal of Political Science* 38(4): 918–943.

Kiefer, Heather Mason. 2003. "Equal-Opportunity Education: Is It Out There?" *Gallup*. Available at http://www.gallup.com/poll/8731/equalopportunity-education-there.aspx. Accessed February 10, 2015.

King, Sabrina H. 1993. "The Limited Presence of African-American Teachers." *Review of Educational Research* 63(2): 115–149.

Kini, Tara. 2005. "Sharing the Vote: Noncitizen Voting Rights in Local School Board Elections." *California Law Review* 93(1): 271–321.

Kluger, Richard. 2011. *Simple Justice: The History of Brown v. Board of Education and Black America's Struggle for Equality.* New York: Vintage Books.

Knight, Jack. 1992. *Institutions and Social Conflict.* New York: Cambridge University Press.

Knott, Jack H., and Gary J. Miller. 2008. "When Ambition Checks Ambition: Bureaucratic Trustees and the Separation of Powers." *The American Review of Public Administration* 38(4): 387–411.

Kozol, Jonathan. 1991. *Savage Inequalities: Children in America's schools.* New York: Crown Publishing.

Krause, George, and Kenneth J. Meier (eds.). 2005. *Politics, Policy, and Organizations: Frontiers in the Scientific Study of Bureaucracy.* Ann Arbor: University of Michigan Press.

Krogstad, Jens Manuel, and Richard Fry. 2014. "Department of Education Projects Public Schools Will Be 'Majority-Minority' This Fall." *Pew Research Center Fact Tank.* Available at http://www.pewresearch.org/fact-tank/2014/08/18/u-s-public-schools-expected-to-be-majority-minority-starting-this-fall/. Accessed January 13, 2015.

Krook, Mona Lena. 2006. "Reforming Representation: The Diffusion of Candidate Gender Quotas Worldwide." *Politics and Gender* 2(3): 303–328.

Kunovich, Sheri, and Pamela Paxton. 2005. "Pathways to Power: The Role of Political Parties in Women's National Political Representation." *American Journal of Sociology* 111(2): 505–552.

Labaree, David F. 1992. *The Making of an American High School: The Credentials Market and the Central High School of Philadelphia, 1838–1939.* New Haven, CT: Yale University Press.

Ladson-Billings, Gloria. 2006. "From the Achievement Gap to the Education Debt: Understanding Achievement in U.S. schools." *Educational Researcher* 35(7): 3–12.

Larkin, Joe. 1979. "School Desegregation and Student Suspension: A Look at One School System." *Education and Urban Society* 11(4):485–495.

Lasswell, Harold D. 1950. *Politics: Who Gets What, When, How.* New York: P. Smith.

Layman, Geoffrey C., Thomas M. Carsey, and Juliana Menasce Horowitz. 2006. "Party Polarization in American Politics: Characteristics, Causes, and Consequences." *Annual Review of Political Science* 9(June): 83–110.

Leal, David, Valerie Martinez-Ebers, and Kenneth J. Meier. 2004. "The Politics of Latino Education: The Biases of At-Large Elections." *Journal of Politics* 66(4): 1224–1244.

Leamon, Eileen J., and Jason Bucelato. 2013. *Federal Elections 2012: Election Results for the U.S. President, the U.S. Senate and the U.S. House of Representatives.* Washington, DC: Federal Election Commission.

Lee, Bill Lann. 2006. "Voting Rights Act: Evidence of Continued Need." Testimony before the House of Representatives Committee on the Judiciary, Subcommittee on the Constitution, March 8.

Levin, Andrew, Chien-Fu Lin, and Chia-Shang James Chu. 2002. "Unit Root Tests in Panel Data: Asymptotic and Finite-Sample Properties." *Journal of Econometrics* 108(1): 1–24.

Lipsky, Michael. 1993. "Street-Level Bureaucracy: An Introduction." In *The Policy Process: A Reader*, M. Hill (ed.). New York: Pearson Education.

2010. *Street-Level Bureaucracy, 30th Anniversary Ed.: Dilemmas of the Individual in Public Service*. New York: Russell Sage Foundation.

Losen, Daniel. 2011. *Discipline Policies, Successful Schools, and Racial Justice*. Los Angeles: UCLA Civil Rights Project.

Losen, Daniel J., and Tia Elena Martinez. 2013. *Out of School and Off Track: The Overuse of Suspensions in American Middle and High Schools*. Los Angeles: UCLA Civil Rights Project.

Losen, Daniel J., Cheri Hodson, Michael A. Keith II, Katrina Morrison, and Shakti Belway. 2015. *Are We Closing the School Discipline Gap?* Los Angeles: UCLA Civil Rights Project.

Lowery, David, and Virginia Gray. 1993. "The Density of State Interest Group Systems." *Journal of Politics* 55(1): 191–206.

Lublin, David. 1997. *The Paradox of Representation: Racial Gerrymandering and Minority Interests in Congress*. Princeton, NJ: Princeton University Press.

1999. "Racial Redistricting and African-American Representation: A Critique of 'Do Majority-Minority Districts Maximize Substantive Black Representation in Congress?'" *American Political Science Review* 93(1): 183–187.

Lublin, David, and D. Stephen Voss. 2000. "Racial Redistricting and Realignment in Southern State Legislatures." *American Journal of Political Science* 44(4): 792–810.

MacManus, Susan A. 1978. "City Council Election Procedures and Minority Representation: Are They Related?" *Social Science Quarterly* 59(1): 153–161.

1979. "'At-Large Elections and Minority Representation': An Adversarial Critique." *Social Science Quarterly* 60(2): 338–340.

Manna, Paul. 2006. *School's In: Federalism and the National Education Agenda*. Washington, DC: Georgetown University Press.

2008. *Federal Aid to Elementary and Secondary Education: Premises, Effects, and Major Lessons Learned*. Washington, DC: Center on Education Policy.

Mansbridge, Jane. 1999. "Should Blacks Represent Blacks and Women Represent Women? A Contingent 'Yes.'" *Journal of Politics* 61(3): 628–657.

Marchbanks, Miner P., III, Jamilia J. Blake, Danielle Smith, Allison Seibert, Dottie Carmichael, Eric A. Booth, and Tony Fabelo. 2014. "More Than a Drop in the Bucket: The Social and Economic Costs of Dropouts and Grade Retentions Associated with Exclusionary Discipline." *Journal of Applied Research on Children* 5(2), Article 17. Available at http://digitalcommons.library.tmc.edu/childrenatrisk/vol5/iss2/17. Accessed March 4, 2015.

Margo, Robert A. 1990. *Race and Schooling in the South, 1880–1950: An Economic History*. Chicago: University of Chicago Press.

Marschall, Melissa J., and Anirudh V. S. Ruhil. 2006. "The Pomp of Power: Black Mayoralties in Urban America." *Social Science Quarterly* 87(4): 828–850.

2007. "Substantive Symbols: The Attitudinal Dimension of Black Political Incorporation in Local Government." *American Journal of Political Science* 51(1): 17–33.

Marschall, Melissa J., and Amanda Rutherford. 2015. "Voting Rights for Whom? Examining the Effects of the Voting Rights Act on Latino Political Incorporation." *American Journal of Political Science* forthcoming.

Marschall, Melissa, Anirudh V. S. Ruhil, and Paru Shah. 2010. "The New Racial Calculus: Electoral Institutions and Black Representation in Local Legislatures." *American Journal of Political Science* 54(1): 107–124.

Marzano, Robert J., Timothy Waters, and Brian A. McNulty. 2005. *School Leadership That Works: From Research to Results*. Washington, DC: ERIC.

May, Peter, and Soren Winter. 2000. "Reconsidering Styles of Regulatory Enforcement: Patterns in Danish Agro-Environmental Inspection." *Law and Policy* 22(2): 143–173.

Mazmanian, Daniel A., and Paul A. Sabatier. 1983. *Implementation and Public Policy*. Glenview, IL: Scott Foresman.

McDaniel, Eric L. 2008. *Politics in the Pews: The Political Mobilization of Black Churches*. Ann Arbor: University of Michigan Press.

McDermott, Kathryn A. 2011. *High-Stakes Reform: The Politics of Educational Accountability*. Washington, DC: Georgetown University Press.

McGuinn, Patrick J. 2006. *No Child Left Behind and the Transformation of Federal Education Policy, 1965–2005*. Lawrence: University Press of Kansas.

2012. "Stimulating Reform: Race to the Top, Competitive Grants and the Obama Education Agenda." *Educational Policy* 26(1): 136–159.

McLaurin v. Oklahoma State Regents, 339 US 637 (1950).

McNeal v. Tate County School District, 508 F.2d 1017 (5th Cir. 1975).

Meier, Kenneth J., and John Bohte. 2006. *Politics and the Bureaucracy: Policymaking in the Fourth Branch of Government*. Belmont, CA: Wadsworth Cengage Learning.

Meier, Kenneth J., and Robert E. England. 1984 "Black Representation and Educational Policy: Are They Related?" *American Political Science Review* 78(2): 392–403.

Meier, Kenneth J., and Angel L. Molina Jr. 2015. "A Substantive Seat at the Table? Election Systems and Policy Responsiveness in Latino Education Policy." Presented at the Annual Meeting of the American Political Science Association, San Francisco, CA.

Meier, Kenneth J., and Jill Nicholson-Crotty. 2006. "Gender, Representative Bureaucracy, and Law Enforcement: The Case of Sexual Assault." *Public Administration Review* 66(6): 850–860.

Meier, Kenneth J., and Laurence J. O'Toole. 2006. "Political Control Versus Bureaucratic Values: Reframing the Debate." *Public Administration Review* 66(2): 177–192.

Meier, Kenneth J., and Amanda Rutherford. 2014. "Partisanship, Structure, and Representation: The Puzzle of African American Education Politics." *American Political Science Review* 108(2): 265–280.

Meier, Kenneth J., and Joseph Stewart Jr. 1991. *The Politics of Hispanic Education*. Albany: State University of New York Press.

1992. "The Impact of Representative Bureaucracies: Educational Systems and Public Policies." *The American Review of Public Administration* 22(3): 157–171.

Meier, Kenneth J., Laurence J. O'Toole, and Sean Nicholson-Crotty. 2004. "Multilevel Governance and Organizational Performance: Investigating the Political-Bureaucratic Labyrinth." *Journal of Policy Analysis and Management* 23(1): 31–47.

Meier, Kenneth J., Joseph Stewart, and Robert E. England. 1989. *Race, Class, and Education: The Politics of Second-Generation Discrimination*. Madison: University of Wisconsin Press.

Meier, Kenneth J., Warren S. Eller, Robert D. Wrinkle, and J. L. Polinard. 2001. "Zen and the Art of Policy Analysis." *Journal of Politics* 63(2): 616–629.

Meier, Kenneth J., Eric Gonzalez Juenke, Robert D. Wrinkle, and J. L. Polinard. 2005. "Structural Choices and Representational Biases: The Post-Election Color of Representation." *American Journal of Political Science* 49(4): 758–769.

Mendez v. Westminster School District, 64 F. Supp. 544 (S.D. Cal. 1946).

Meredith v. Jefferson County Board of Education, 548 U.S. 938 (2006).

Merl, Jean. 2013. "Voting Rights Act Leading California Cities to Dump At-Large Elections." *Los Angeles Times*. Available at http://www.latimes.com/local/la-me-local-elections-20130915,0,295413.story#axzz2iTEfuZ5X. Accessed February 26, 2015.

Middleton, James. 2012. "Spare the Rod." *History Today* 62(11). Available at http://www.historytoday.com/jacob-middleton/spare-rod. Accessed January 21, 2015.

Minta, Michael D. 2011. *Oversight: Representing the Interests of Blacks and Latinos in Congress*. Princeton, NJ: Princeton University Press.

Missouri v. Jenkins, 515 U.S. 70, 115 S. Ct. 2038, 132 L. Ed. 2d 63 (1995).

Missouri ex rel. Gaines v. Canada, 305 U.S. 337 (1938).

Mitchell, Douglas E. 1990. "Education Politics for the New Century: Past Issues and Future Directions." In *Education Politics for the New Century*, D. E. Mitchell and M. E. Goertz (eds.). London: Falmer Press.

Mladenka, Kenneth R. 1989. "Blacks and Hispanics in Urban Politics." *American Political Science Review* 83(1): 165–191.

Mobile v. Bolden, 446 U.S. 55, 100 S. Ct. 1490, 64 L. Ed. 2d 47 (1980).

Moe, Terry M. 1985. "Control and Feedback in Economic Regulation: The Case of the NLRB." *American Political Science Review* 79(4): 1094–1116.

1989. "The Politics of Bureaucratic Structure." In *Can the Government Govern?* J. E. Chubb and P. E. Peterson (eds.). Washington, DC: Brookings.

2009. "Collective Bargaining and the Performance of the Public Schools." *American Journal of Political Science* 53(1): 156–174.

Moncrief, Gary F., and Joel A. Thompson. 1992. "Electoral Structure and State Legislative Representation: A Research Note." *Journal of Politics* 54(1): 246–256.

Montgomery v. Starkville Municipal Separate School Dist., 665 F Supp. 487 (N.D. Miss. 1987).

Morris, Edward W. 2005. "'Tuck in That Shirt!' Race, Class, Gender, and Discipline in an Urban School." *Sociological Perspectives* 48(1): 25–48.

Mossberger, Karen, Caroline J. Tolbert, and Ramona S. McNeal. 2008. *Digital Citizenship: The Internet, Society, and Participation*. Cambridge, MA: MIT Press.

Mosteller, Frederick. 1995. "The Tennessee Study of Class Size in the Early School Grades." *The Future of Children* 5(2): 113–127.

Mulkey, Lynn M., Sophia Catsambia, Lal Carr Steelman, and Robert L. Crain. 2005. "The Long-Term Effect of Ability Grouping in Mathematics: A National Investigation." *Social Psychology of Education* 8(2): 137–177.

Munguia, Hayley. 2015. "Test Scores Don't Tell Us Everything about New Orleans School Reform." *Five Thirty Eight*. Available at http://fivethirtyeight.com/features/research-suggests-education-reforms-after-hurricane-katrina-worked/. Accessed November 10, 2015.

Murray v. Pearson, 169 Md. 478, 182 A. 590 (1936).

NAACP. 2009. "NAACP: 100 Years of History." Available at http://www.naacp.org/pages/naacp-history. Accessed on February 19, 2015.

NAEP. 2014. "State Profiles." *Institute of Education Sciences, National Center for Education Statistics.* Available at https://nces.ed.gov/nationsreportcard/states/. Accessed June 1, 2015.

National Center for Education Statistics. 2011. *Mapping State Proficiency Standards onto the NAEP Scales.* NCES 2011–458. Washington, DC: National Center for Education Statistics.

——— 2014. *Public High School Four-Year On-Time Graduation Rates and Event Dropout Rates: Schools Years 2010–11 and 2011–12.* Available at http://nces.ed.gov/pubs2014/2014391.pdf. Accessed September 27, 2015.

——— 2015. *Education Expenditures by Country.* Available at https://nces.ed.gov/programs/coe/indicator_cmd.asp. Accessed May 31, 2015.

Nettles, Michael T., Linda H. Scatton, Jonathan H. Steinberg, and Linda L. Tyler. 2011. *Performance and Passing Rate Differences of African American and White Prospective Teachers on Praxis Examinations.* Washington, DC: Educational Testing Service.

Nicholson-Crotty, Jill, Jason A. Grissom, and Sean Nicholson-Crotty. 2011. "Bureaucratic Representation, Distributional Equity, and Democratic Values in the Administration of Public Programs." *Journal of Politics* 73(2): 582–596.

Nnazor, Reginald, Jo Sloan, and Patricia Higgins. 2004. "Historically Black Colleges and Universities and the Challenge of Teacher Licensure Tests." *Western Journal of Black Studies* 28(4): 449–452.

Norman, Obed, Charles R. Ault, Bonnie Bentz, and Lloyd Meskimen. 2001. "The Black–White 'Achievement Gap' as a Perennial Challenge of Urban Science Education: A Sociocultural and Historical Overview with Implications for Research and Practice." *Journal of Research in Science Teaching* 38(10): 1101–1114.

Norris, Pippa. 1985. "Women's Legislative Participation in Western Europe." *Western European Politics* 8(4): 90–101.

——— 2004. *Electoral Engineering: Voting Rules and Political Behavior.* New York: Cambridge University Press.

Oakes, Jeannie. 1985. *Keeping Track: How Schools Structure Inequality.* New Haven, CT: Yale University Press.

O'Connor, John. 2014. "Your Essential Guide to the Common Core." *StateImpact.* Available at http://stateimpact.npr.org/florida/tag/common-core/. Accessed March 3, 2015.

Ogbu, John. 1994. "Racial Stratification and Education in the United States: Why Inequality Persists." *Teachers College Record* 96(2): 264–298.

Ohio Department of Education. 1998. "Proficiency Testing in Ohio – A Summary." Available at http://www.chuh.net/school/FAQs/OPTs.background.html. Accessed April 25, 2015.

Oliver, J. Eric, and Tali Mendelberg. 2000. "Reconsidering the Environmental Determinants of White Racial Attitudes." *American Journal of Political Science* 44(3): 574–589.

Opfer, V. Darleen. 2005. "Personalization of Interest Groups and The Resulting Policy Nonsense: The Cobb County School Board's Evolution Debate." In *The Politics of Leadership: Superintendents and School Boards in Changing Times*, G. J. Petersen and L. D. Fusarelli (eds.). Charlotte, NC: Information Age Publishing.

Orfield, Gary, and Chungmei Lee. 2005. *Why Segregation Matters: Poverty and Educational Inequality.* Cambridge, MA: The Civil Rights Project, Harvard University.

Orfield, Gary, and John T. Yun. 1999. *Resegregation in American Schools*. Cambridge, MA: The Civil Rights Project, Harvard University.

Orr, Marion. 1999. *Black Social Capital: The Politics of School Reform in Baltimore, 1986–1998*. Lawrence: University of Kansas Press.

Ouazad, Amine. 2014. "Assessed by a Teacher Like Me: Race and Teacher Assessments." *Education* 9(3): 334–372.

Parenti, Michael. 1967. "Ethnic Politics and the Persistence of Ethnic Identification." *American Political Science Review* 61(3): 717–726.

Parents Involved in Community School. v. Seattle School, 127 S. Ct. 2738, 551 U.S. 701, 168 L. Ed. 2d 508 (2007).

Parker by Parker v. Trinity High School, 823 F. Supp. 511 (N.D. Ill. 1993).

Parker, Frank. 1990. *Black Votes Count*. Chapel Hill: University of North Carolina Press.

Passel, Jeffrey S., Gretchen Livingston, and D'Vera Cohn. 2012. "Explaining Why Minority Births Now Outnumber White Births." *Pew Research Center*. Available at http://www.pewsocialtrends.org/2012/05/17/explaining-why-minority-births-now-outnumber-white-births/. Accessed November 18, 2014.

Paxton, Pamela. 1997. "Women in National Legislatures: A Cross-National Analysis." *Social Science Research* 26(4): 442–464.

Petersen, George J., and Lance Darin Fusarelli (eds.). 2005. *The Politics of Leadership: Superintendents and School Boards in Changing Times*. Charlotte, NC: Information Age Publishing

Peterson, Paul E. 2006. "The A+ Plan." In *Reforming Education in Florida: A Study Prepared by the Koret Task Force on K–12 Education*, P. E. Peterson (ed.). Palo Alto, CA: Hoover Institution, Stanford University.

Pew Research Center. 2012. *Trends in American Values: 1987–2012: Partisan Polarization Surges in Bush, Obama Years*. Washington, DC: Pew Research Center.

2014. *Polarization of the American Public: How Increasing Ideological Uniformity and Partisan Antipathy Affect Politics, Compromise and Everyday Life*. Washington, DC: Pew Research Center.

Pitkin, Hanna. 1967. *The Concept of Representation*. Berkeley: University of California Press.

Pitts, David W. 2005. "Diversity, Representation, and Performance: Evidence about Race and Ethnicity in Public Organizations." *Journal of Public Administration Research and Theory* 15(4): 615–631.

2007. "Representative Bureaucracy, Ethnicity, and Public Schools: Examining the Link between Representation and Performance." *Administration and Society* 39(4): 497–526.

Plessy v. Ferguson, 163 U.S. 537 (1896).

Polinard, J. L., Robert D. Wrinkle, Tomas Longoria, and Norman Binder. 1994. *Electoral Structure and Urban Policy: The Impact on Mexican American Communities*. New York: M. E. Sharpe.

Porter-Magee, Kathleen. 2011. *The Common Core and the Future of Student Assessment in Ohio*. Washington, DC: Thomas B. Fordham Institute.

Portz, John, Lana Stein, and Robin R. Jones. 1999. *City Schools and City Politics*. Lawrence: University Press of Kansas.

Prais, Sig J. 2003. "Cautions on OECD's Recent Educational Survey (PISA)." *Oxford Review of Education* 29(2): 139–163.

Preuhs, Robert R. 2006. "The Conditional Effects of Minority Representation: Black Legislators and Policy Influence in the American States." *Journal of Politics* 68(3): 585–599.

Program for International Student Assessment. 2012. *PISA 2012: What Students Know and Can Do.* Paris: Organisation for Economic Co-operation and Development.

Quarles v. Oxford Municipal Separate School District, 868 F. 2d 750 (5th Cir. 1989).

Reckhow, Sarah, Jeffrey Henig, Rebecca Jacobsen, and Jamie Alter. 2015. "Outsiders with Deep Pockets: The Nationalization of Local School Board Elections." Presented at the Annual Meeting of the Midwest Political Science Association, Chicago, IL.

Redd, Kenneth E. 1998. "Historically Black Colleges and Universities: Making a Comeback." *New Directions for Higher Education* 102(Summer): 33–43.

Redford, Emmette S. 1969. *Democracy in the Administrative State.* New York: Oxford University Press.

Reese, William J. 2002. *Power and the Promise of School Reform: Grassroots Movements during the Progressive Era.* New York: Teachers College Press.

Republican National Convention. 2012. *2012 Republican Platform: We Believe in America.* Available at https://s3.amazonaws.com/s3.documentcloud.org/documents/414158/2012-republican-national-convention-platform.pdf. Accessed May 14, 2015.

Reynolds, Andrew. 1999. "Women in the Legislatures and Executives of the World: Knocking at the Highest Glass Ceiling." *World Politics* 51(4): 547–572.

Reynolds v. Sims, 377 U.S. 533, 84 S. Ct. 1362, 12 L. Ed. 2d 506 (1964).

Riccucci, Norma M., Gregg G. Van Ryzin, and Cecilia F. Lavena. 2014. "Representative Bureaucracy in Policing: Does It Increase Perceived Legitimacy?" *Journal of Public Administration Research and Theory* 24(3): 537–551.

Rich, Wilbur C. 1996. *Black Mayors and School Politics.* New York: Garland Publishing.

Ridley, C. et al., v. State of Georgia et al. (Dublin City School District (2004).

Roberts v. City of Boston, 59 Mass. (5 Cush.) 198 (1850).

Robinson, Theodore P., and Robert E. England. 1981. "Black Representation and Central City School Boards Revised." *Social Science Quarterly* 62(3): 495–502.

Robinson, Theodore P., Robert E. England, and Kenneth J. Meier. 1985. "Black Resources and Black School Board Representation." *Social Science Quarterly* 66(4): 976–982.

Roch, Christine H., and David W. Pitts. 2012. "Differing Effects of Representative Bureaucracy in Charter Schools and Traditional Public Schools." *American Review of Public Administration* 42(3): 282–302.

Roch, Christine H., David W. Pitts, and Ignacio Navarro. 2010. "Representative Bureaucracy and Policy Tools: Ethnicity, Student Discipline, and Representation in Public Schools." *Administration and Society* 42(1): 38–65.

Rocha, Rene R. 2007. "Black-Brown Coalitions in Local School Board Elections." *Political Research Quarterly* 60(2): 315–327.

Rocha, Rene R., and Daniel P. Hawes. 2009. "Racial Diversity, Representative Bureaucracy, and Equity in Multiracial School Districts." *Social Science Quarterly* 90(2): 326–344.

Rosenburg, Gerald N. 2008. *The Hollow Hope: Can Courts Bring about Social Change?* Chicago: University of Chicago Press.

Rourke, Francis E. 1976. *Bureaucracy, Politics, and Public Policy*. 2d ed. Boston: Little Brown.

Rouse, Stella. 2013. *Latinos in the Legislative Process: Interests and Influence.* New York: Cambridge University Press.

Rowan, Brian, Fang-Shen Chiang, and Robert J. Miller. 1997. "Using Research on Employees' Performance to Study the Effects of Teachers on Students' Achievement." *Sociology of Education* 70(4): 256–284.

Rule, Wilma. 1987. "Electoral Systems, Contextual Factors and Women's Opportunity for Election to Parliament in Twenty-Three Democracies." *Western Political Quarterly* 40(3): 477–498.

Rumberger, Russell W. 2001. *Why Students Drop out of School and What Can Be Done.* Los Angeles: UCLA Civil Rights Project.

Rutherford, Amanda. 2014. "Organizational Turnaround and Educational Performance: The Impact of Performance-Based Monitoring Analysis Systems." *American Review of Public Administration* 44(4): 440–458.

Sacerdote, Bruce. 2012. "When the Saints Go Marching Out: Long-Term Outcomes for Student Evacuees from Hurricanes Katrina and Rita." *American Economic Journal: Applied Economics* 4(1): 109–135.

Sacks, Ariel. 2015. "Decoding the Common Core: A Teacher's Perspective." *Education Week.* Available at http://www.edweek.org/ew/articles/2015/03/25/decoding-the-common-core-a-teachers-perspective.html. Accessed October 30, 2015.

Saltzstein, Grace Hall. 1989. "Black Mayors and Police Policies." *Journal of Politics* 51(3): 525–544.

Sanchez, Melissa. 2014. "To Boost Teacher Diversity, State Scraps Limits on Basic Skills Test-Taking." *Catalyst Chicago.* Available at http://catalyst-chicago.org/2014/03/boost-teacher-diversity-state-scraps-limits-basic-skills-test-taking/. Accessed January 18, 2015.

Sass, Tim R., and Stephen L. Mehay. 1995. "The Voting Rights Act, District Elections, and the Success of Black Candidates in Municipal Elections." *Journal of Law and Economics* 38(2): 367–92.

    2003. "Minority Representation, Election Method, and Policy Influence." *Economics and Politics* 15(3): 323–339.

Sass, Tim R., and Bobby J. Pittman Jr. 2000. "The Changing Impact of Electoral Structure on Black Representation in the South, 1970–1996." *Public Choice* 104(3–4): 369–388.

Schneider, Jack. 2008. "Escape from Los Angeles: White Flight from Los Angeles and Its Schools, 1960–1980." *Journal of Urban History* 34(6): 995–1012.

Schwindt-Bayer, Leslie A., and William Mishler. 2005. "An Integrated Model of Women's Representation." *Journal of Politics* 67(2): 407–428.

Scribner, Jay D., and Donald H. Layton. 1995. *The Study of Educational Politics: The 1994 Commemorative Yearbook of the Politics of Education Association 1969–1994.* New York: Routledge.

Selden, Sally Coleman. 1997. *The Promise of Representative Bureaucracy.* Armonk, NY: M. E. Sharpe.

Shah, Paru R., Melissa J. Marschall, and Anirudh V. S. Ruhil. 2013. "Are We There Yet? The Voting Rights Act and Black Representation on City Councils, 1981–2006." *Journal of Politics* 74(4): 993–1008.

Shelby County, Ala. v. Holder, 133 S. Ct. 2612, 570 U.S. 2, 186 L. Ed. 2d 651 (2013).

Shotts, Kenneth. W. 2003a. "Does Racial Redistricting Cause Conservative Policy Outcomes? Policy Preferences of Southern Representatives in the 1980s and 1990s." *Journal of Politics* 65(1): 216–226.

2003b. "Racial Redistricting's Alleged Perverse Effects: Theory, Data and 'Reality.'" *Journal of Politics* 65(1): 237–244.

Sigelman, Carol K., Lee Sigelman, Barbara J. Walkosz, and Michael Nitz. 1995. "Black Candidates, White Voters: Understanding Racial Bias in Political Perceptions." *American Journal of Political Science* 39(1): 243–265.

Sigelman, Lee, and Susan Welch. 1993. "The Contact Hypothesis Revisited: Black-White Interaction and Positive Racial Attitudes." *Social Forces* 17(3): 781–795.

Skiba, Russell J., Reece L. Peterson, and Tara Williams. 1997. "Office Referral and Suspension: Disciplinary Intervention in Middle Schools." *Education and Treatment of Children* 20(3): 295–315.

Skiba, Russell J., Robert S. Michael, Abra Carroll Nardo, and Reece L. Peterson. 2002. "The Color of Discipline: Sources of Racial and Gender Disproportion in School Punishment." *The Urban Review* 34(4): 317–342.

Smith, J. Douglas. 2002. *Managing White Supremacy: Race, Politics, and Citizenship in Jim Crow Virginia*. Chapel Hill: University of North Carolina Press.

Smith, Kevin B. 2003. *The Ideology of Education: The Commonwealth, the Market, and America's Schools*. Albany: State University of New York Press.

Smith, Morgan. 2011. "In Texas' Schools Perry Shuns Federal Influence." *Texas Tribune*. Available at http://www.texastribune.org/tribpedia/race-to-the-top/. Accessed May 1, 2015.

Smith, Stephen Samuel. 2004. *Boom for Whom? Education, Desegregation, and Development in Charlotte*. Albany: State University of New York Press.

Smith, Stephen Samuel, Karen M. Kedrowski, and Joseph M. Ellis. 2004. "Electoral Structures, Venue Selection, and the (New?) Politics of School Desegregation." *Perspectives on Politics* 2(4): 795–801.

Smith-Evans, Leticia, and Russell Skiba. 2014. "Race Debate Should Include School Discipline: Colum." *USA Today*. Available at http://www.usatoday.com/story/opinion/2014/12/20/racism-school-discipline-evans-skiba/20494903/. Accessed January 8, 2015.

Snyder, Thomas D. 1993. *120 Years of American Education: A Statistical Portrait*. Washington, DC: National Center for Education Statistics.

Snyder, Thomas D., and Sally A. Dillow. 2012. *Digest of Education Statistics 2011*. Washington, DC: National Center for Education Statistics.

Sowa, Jessica E., and Sally Coleman Selden. 2003. "Administrative Discretion and Active Representation: An Expansion of the Theory of Representative Bureaucracy." *Public Administration Review* 63(6): 700–710.

Spring, Joel. 1994. *The American School 1642–1993*. New York: McGraw Hill.

Stedman, Lawrence C. 1994. "The Sandia Report and U.S. Achievement: An Assessment." *The Journal of Educational Research* 87(3): 133–146.

Steele, Claude M. 1997. "A Threat in the Air: How Stereotypes Shape Intellectual Identity and Performance." *American Psychologist* 52(6): 613–629.

Stewart, Joseph, Robert England, and Kenneth Meier. 1989. "Black Representation in Urban School Districts: From School Board to Office to Classroom." *Western Political Quarterly* 42(2): 287–305.

Stiglitz, Joseph E. 2013. "Equal Opportunity, Our National Myth." *The New York Times*. Available at http://opinionator.blogs.nytimes.com/2013/02/16/equal-opportunity-our-national-myth/?_r=1. Accessed February 10, 2015.

Stone, Donald H. 1993. "Crime and Punishment in Public Schools: An Empirical Study of Disciplinary Proceedings." *American Journal of Trial Advocacy* 17(2): 351–398.

Stover, Del. 2012. "Politics and School Board Races." *American School Board Journal*. Available at http://www.asbj.com/TopicsArchive/SchoolGovernance/Politics-and-School-Board-Races.html. Accessed January 23, 2015.

Strauss, Valerie. 2013. "Arne Duncan: 'White Suburban Moms' Upset that Common Core Shows Their Kids Aren't 'Brilliant.' " *The Washington Post*. Available at https://www.washingtonpost.com/blogs/answer-sheet/wp/2013/11/16/arne-duncan-white-surburban-moms-upset-that-common-core-shows-their-kids-arent-brilliant/. Accessed March 23, 2015.

Swain, Carol M. 1993. *Black Faces and Black Interests: The Representation of African Americans in Congress*. Cambridge, MA: Harvard University Press.

Sweatt v. Painter, 339 US 629, 634 (1950).

Tasby v. Estes, 572 F.2d 1010 (5th Cir. 1978).

Tate, Katherine. 2014. *Concordance: Black Lawmaking in the U.S. Congress from Carter to Obama*. Ann Arbor: University of Michigan Press.

Taylor, Quintard. 1999. *In Search of the Racial Frontier: African Americans in the American West 1528–1990*. New York: W. W. Norton and Company.

Texas Education Agency. 2012. "Frequently Asked Questions about the Academic Excellent Indicator System." Available at http://ritter.tea.state.tx.us/perfreport/aeis/faq.html. Accessed May 1, 2015.

2015. "STAAR Resources." Available at http://tea.texas.gov/student.assessment/staar/. Accessed May 1, 2015.

Theobald, Nick A. 2007. "Muestreme el Dinero: Assessing the Linkage between Latino School Superintendents and English-Language Learner Program Resources." In *Latino Politics: Identity, Mobilization and Representation*, R. Espino, D. L. Leal and K. J. Meier (eds.). Charlottesville: University of Virginia Press.

Thernstrom, Abigail, and Stephan Thernstrom. 2003. *No Excuses: Closing the Racial Gap in Learning*. New York: Simon and Schuster.

Thornburg v. Gingles, 478 U.S. 30, 106 S. Ct. 2752, 92 L. Ed. 2d 25 (1986).

Thorton, Clarence H., and William T. Trent. 1988. "School Desegregation and Suspension in East Baton Rouge Parish: A Preliminary Report." *The Journal of Negro Education* 57(4):482–501.

Tindall, George Brown. 1952. *South Carolina Negroes, 1877–1900*. Columbia: University of South Carolina Press.

Trounstine, Jessica. 2010. "Representation and Accountability in Cities." *Annual Review of Political Science* 13(June): 407–423.

Trounstine, Jessica, and Melody E. Valdini. 2008. "The Context Matters: The Effects of Single Member versus At-Large Districts on City Council Diversity." *American Journal of Political Science* 52(3): 554–569.

Tucker, James. 2009. *The Battle over Bilingual Voters*. New York: Ashgate.

Tyack, David B. 1974. *The One Best System: A History of American Urban Education*. Cambridge, MA: Harvard University Press.

1991. "Public School Reform: Policy Talk and Institutional Practice." *American Journal of Education* 100(1): 1–19.

Tyson, Karolyn. 2003. "Notes from the Back of the Room: Problems and Paradoxes in the Schooling of Young Black Students." *Sociology of Education* 76(4): 326–343.

United States v. Gadsden County School District, 572 F. 2d 1049 (1978).

United States v. Tunica County School District, 421 F. 2d. 1236 (1970).

United States & Coleman v. Midland Independent School District (W.D. Tex.)

United States v. Yonkers Board of Education, 984 F. Supp 687, 123 Ed. Law Rep 544 (1997) (S.D.N.Y.).

US Census. 2010. "2010 Census Data." Available at http://www.census.gov/2010census/data/. Accessed January 14, 2015.

US Congress. 1956. *Congressional Record*, 84th Cong., 2d sess., 1956, 102, pt. 4: 4515–16.

US Department of Education. 2009. "Race to the Top Program Executive Summary." Available at http://www2.ed.gov/programs/racetothetop/executive-summary.pdf. Accessed April 20, 2015.

 2013. "States Granted Waivers from No Child Left Behind Allowed to Reapply for Renewal for 2014 and 2015 School Years." Available at http://www.ed.gov/news/press-releases/states-granted-waivers-no-child-left-behind-allowed-reapply-renewal-2014-and-2015-school-years. Accessed April 20, 2015.

 2014. "Table 05.20: Enrollment in Educational Institutions, by Level and Control of Institution, Enrollment Level, and Attendance Status and Sex of Student: Selected Years, Fall 1990 through Fall 2023." National Center for Education. Available at http://nces.ed.gov/programs/digest/d13/tables/dt13_105.20.asp. Accessed April 20, 2015.

Valenzuela, Angela. 2002. "High-Stakes Testing and US-Mexican Youth in Texas: The Case for Multiple Compensatory Criteria in Assessment." *Harvard Journal of Hispanic Policy* 14: 97–116.

Valenzuela, Angela (ed.). 2005. *Leaving Children Behind: How "Texas-style" Accountability Fails Latino Youth*. Albany: State University of New York Press.

Vavrus, Frances, and Kim Marie Cole. 2002. "'I Didn't Do Nothin'": The Discursive Construction of School Suspension." *The Urban Review* 34(2): 87–111.

Walker, Vanessa. 2005. "Organized Resistance and Black Educators' Quest for School Equality, 1878–1938." *The Teachers College Record* 107(3): 355–388.

Warshaw, Christopher, and Jonathan Rodden. 2012. "How Should We Measure District-Level Public Opinion on Individual Issues?" *Journal of Politics* 74 (2): 203–219.

Waterman, Richard W., and Kenneth J. Meier. 1998. "Principal-Agent Models: An Expansion?" *Journal of Public Administration Research and Theory* 8(2): 173–202.

Watkins-Hayes, Celeste. 2011. "Race, Respect, and Red Tape: Inside the Black Box of Racially Representative Bureaucracies." *Journal of Public Administration Research and Theory* 21(Suppl. 2): i233–i251.

Weber, Max. 2009. *From Max Weber: Essays in Sociology*. New York: Routledge.

Weinberg, Meyer. 1977. *A Chance to Learn: The History of Race and Education in the United States*. London: Cambridge University Press.

Welch, Susan. 1990. "The Impact of At-Large Elections on the Representation of Blacks and Hispanics." *Journal of Politics* 52(4): 1050–1076.

Wenglinsky, Harold. 1997. "How Money Matters: The Effect of School District Spending on Academic Achievement." *Sociology of Education* 70(3): 221–237.

White v. Regester, 412 U.S. 755, 93 S. Ct. 2332, 37 L. Ed. 2d 314 (1973).

Wiebe, Robert H. 1962. *Businessmen and Reform: A Study of the Progressive Movement.* Cambridge, MA: Harvard University Press.

1967. *The Search for Order, 1877–1920.* New York: Macmillan.

Wiliam, Dylan. 2010. "Standardized Testing and School Accountability." *Educational Psychologist* 45(2): 107–122.

Wilkins, Vicky M., and Lael R. Keiser. 2006. "Linking Passive and Active Representation by Gender: The Case of Child Support Agencies." *Journal of Public Administration Research and Theory* 16(1): 87–102.

Wilkins, Vicky M., and Brian N. Williams. 2008. "Black or Blue: Racial Profiling and Representative Bureaucracy." *Public Administration Review* 68(4): 654–664.

Williams, Simon, and James D. Laurits. 1954. "Scientists and Education." In *Public Education under Criticism*, C. W. Scott and C. M. Hills (eds.). Englewood Cliffs, NJ: Prentice Hall.

Wilson, Franklin D. 1985. "The Impact of School Desegregation Programs on White Public Enrollment, 1968–1976." *Sociology of Education* 58(3): 137–153.

Wilson, Woodrow. 1887. "The Study of Administration." *Political Science Quarterly* 2(2): 197–222.

Wiltz, Teresa. 2012. "Educators Alarmed: Black, Latino High School Students Perform at Level of 30 Years Ago." *America's Wire.* Available at http://americaswire.org/drupal7/?q=content/educators-alarmed-black-latino-high-school-students-perform-levels-30-years-ago. Accessed September 28, 2015.

Wirt, Frederick M., and Michael W. Kirst. 1997. *The Political Dynamics of American Education.* Berkeley, CA: McCutchan Publishing Corporation.

Witte, John. 2000. *The Market Approach to Education: An Analysis of America's First Voucher Program.* Princeton, NJ: Princeton University Press.

Wolfinger, Raymond E. 1965. "The Development and Persistence of Ethnic Voting." *American Political Science Review* 59(4): 896–908.

1980. *Who Votes?* New Haven, CT: Yale University Press.

Wong, Kenneth K. 1999. *Funding Public Schools: Politics and Policies.* Lawrence: University Press of Kansas.

Woods v. Wright, 334 F. 2d 369 (1964).

Wooldridge, Jeffrey M. 2003. "Cluster-Sample Methods in Applied Econometrics." *The American Economic Review* 93(2): 133–138.

Yell, Mitchell L., Antonis Katsiyannas, and James G. Shiner. 2006. "The No Child Left Behind Act, Adequate Yearly Progress, and Students with Disabilities." *Teaching Exceptional Children* 38(4): 32.

Zhu, Ling, and Meredith B.L. Walker. 2013. "'Too Much Too Young': Race, Descriptive Representation, and Heterogeneous Policy Responses in the Case of Teenage Childbearing." *Politics, Groups, and Identities* 1(4): 528–546.

Zimmer v. McKeithen, 485 F.2d 1297 (5th Cir. 1973).

Index